Serving Online Customers

Serving Online Customers

Lessons for Libraries from the Business World

DONALD A. BARCLAY

ROWMAN & LITTLEFIELD
Lanham • Boulder • New York • London

Published by Rowman & Littlefield
A wholly owned subsidiary of The Rowman & Littlefield Publishing Group, Inc.
4501 Forbes Boulevard, Suite 200, Lanham, Maryland 20706
www.rowman.com

16 Carlisle Street, London W1D 3 BT, United Kingdom

British Library Cataloguing in Publication Information Available

Library of Congress Cataloging-in-Publication Data

Barclay, Donald A.
 Serving online customers : lessons for libraries from the business world / Donald A. Barclay.
     pages cm
 Includes bibliographical references and index.
 ISBN 978-0-8108-9317-7 (cloth : alk. paper) — ISBN 978-0-8108-8732-9 (pbk. : alk. paper) — ISBN 978-0-8108-8733-6 (electronic) 1. Libraries and the Internet. 2. Library Web sites. 3. Libraries—Customer services. 4. Electronic reference services (Libraries) 5. Libraries and distance education. 6. Library users—Effect of technological innovations on. I. Title.
 Z674.75.I58B37 2014
 020.285'4678—dc23

2014015462

♾™ The paper used in this publication meets the minimum requirements of American National Standard for Information Sciences—Permanence of Paper for Printed Library Materials, ANSI/NISO Z39.48-1992.

Printed in the United States of America

Contents

Acknowledgments

As activities go, writing a book is about as solitary as a barn raising. Many hands mean many people to thank. I must begin by thanking my patient and brilliant editor Charles Harmon, who has been putting up with my missed deadlines and lapses in authorial judgment for something like twenty years. Also on the list is my former boss, mentor, and all-around cool retired guy Bruce Miller, who dutifully read drafts of chapters and invariably responded with good sense and encouragement. Thanks go to UC Merced Library colleagues who listened to my overwrought descriptions of shifty ideas that had yet to make it to paper and endured my moans about missed deadlines. Finally, I must thank my family for their love and encouragement: Caroline, Tess, Emily, and Alexandra. This book is dedicated to you.

Introduction

Libraries have been facing the challenge of serving online customers since computer users were first granted dial-up access to online library catalogs circa 1980. In the decades since, libraries have seen a continuous increase in the number of customers* who access library information resources and services remotely via computer. At the same time, libraries have seen people who were, or could have been, library customers going online to fill their information needs without so much as setting foot in a library or visiting a library website. Given the convenience and usefulness of information tools like Google and Wikipedia, is it really a surprise that librarians hear politicians, faculty members, students, campus administrators, and ordinary citizens making statements along the lines of, "Why do we need libraries when everything is on the Web?"

Of all the things that are wrong with that question, one of the most troubling is the unspoken implication that libraries and the people who work in them are somehow ignorant of, and possibly opposed to, digital technology. Far from ignoring the digital revolution, librarians and libraries have frequently led the storming of the barricades.

---

* Many librarians balk at the use of the word *customer* to describe the people they serve. While customer is not a perfect word, it is better than either the archaic *patron* or the nebulous *user*, the latter of which has a reputation for hanging out on the same street corner as the adjective *drug*.

1

- Libraries were sharing electronic data via bibliographic utilities when Steve Jobs was still in middle school.
- Libraries provided public-access computers before most people had computers in their home.
- Librarians created some of the earliest websites.
- Libraries spent (and continue to spend) millions every year making databases, journals, and e-books available via the Web.
- Librarians provide online reference services through such media as e-mail, digital chat, and text messaging.
- Librarians have been a driving force behind digitization projects that will preserve and disseminate humanity's collective cultural heritage for decades to come.

So why does it feel like libraries are coming out on the losing side of the digital revolution?

One reason is that, prior to the explosion of the Web in the mid-1990s, libraries had no serious competition when it came to providing information at no cost to the end user. Before the Web existed, the choice was either getting information for free from a library or paying for it from a commercial entity. It was inevitable that the vast amount of free information accessible via the Web would cut into the library's monopoly. After all, if one day millions of free maple bars and crullers rained down like manna from heaven, would anybody be surprised if business at donut shops took a sudden nosedive? (Or if an alarming number of us suddenly packed on ten pounds?)

But there is more to the story than libraries losing their monopoly on information. When the Web exploded into the biggest cultural and economic phenomenon of the last, oh, thousand years, every organization that previously existed in brick-and-mortar form was faced with the following options:

1. Ignore the Web entirely and continue doing business as usual.
2. Divide organizational resources between developing a Web presence and maintaining brick-and-mortar operations.
3. Abandon brick-and-mortar operations and go entirely online.

Aside from small businesses exclusively catering to a local clientele, most who went with option 1 either ceased to exist or changed their strategy once it became clear they were heading down a dead-end road.

Very few chose option 3, though some had this option thrust upon them. Britannica, for example, is an information company that reluctantly abandoned the business of selling printed encyclopedias to devote all of its resources to competing as an online enterprise. The final printing of the *Encyclopedia Britannica* took place in 2010; of the 12,000 sets printed at that time, 3,500 remained unsold by 2012, the year Britannica declared the print version of its product officially dead.[1]

Option 2 was by far the most common choice, though once that choice was made, each entity had to decide how to divide itself between the online and brick-and-mortar worlds. For-profit businesses had an easier time of it because they could let themselves follow the money without a lot of sentimental regard for their corporate past. If a business could make more money selling widgets online than it could selling them in a widget store, nobody was going to stop that business from closing its store. Libraries, of course, had sound reasons for maintaining their brick-and-mortar presences; in addition, libraries were, and still are, occasionally pressured into maintaining the physical status quo even when doing so does not make a lot of sense in the digital age, as when an academic library wishing to weed low-use print materials made superfluous by digital surrogates finds itself thwarted by traditionalist faculty.

Besides being hampered by the need (or mandate) to continue past practices, libraries are finding their financial resources stretched thin as the digital age unfolds. Purchasing hardware and maintaining websites add operating costs that did not exist in the past. Subscriptions to new online databases and publications take a bite out of collection budgets, while the transition of journals from print to electronic formats has not slowed publisher demands for increased subscription rates. Making matters worse, at the same time that libraries have been absorbing new costs related to the digital age, their overall funding has dwindled—in part because the value of libraries has come into question in a world where free digital information is seemingly available everywhere.

It is not the thesis of this book that, in order to survive in the digital environment, libraries must somehow turn themselves into business organizations and charge full tilt into the arena of private-sector competition. Libraries are not businesses, and, like it or not, libraries would not stand a chance in so unbalanced a competition. Instead, the purpose of this book is to examine those practices of digital-age business that are most relevant to the missions and goals of libraries and to illuminate what libraries can learn from the private sector. As an unintended and unforeseen consequence of the onset of the digital age, businesses have invaded what was once strictly library turf, and like many invasive species they have been remarkably successful. To deny their success or ignore it on trumped-up moral grounds is a luxury libraries cannot afford; to learn from their success and apply the lessons wisely will help libraries to survive and maybe even flourish in a digital environment we are only beginning to understand.

NOTE

1. Shalini Ramachandran and Jeffrey A. Trachtenberg, "End of Era for Britannica," *Wall Street Journal—Eastern Edition* 259, no. 60 (March 14, 2012): B1.

Living in the Market

Libraries and Businesses

If elected, I intend to run our _____ like a

(Choose one from column A.)

_____ .

Column A
a. nation
b. state
c. county
d. city
e. school system

There is no need to offer choices for filling in the second blank because the correct answer, the only answer, is as familiar as the lyrics to "Happy Birthday" or the way you are expected to respond when someone says, "Knock, knock." No political candidate would ever be so naive as to suggest that it makes sense to run a state like a state or a city like a city. How absurd. Everyone knows that the best way, the *only* way, to run any organization is like a, well, like a you-know-what.

WHY CAN'T A LIBRARY BE MORE LIKE A BUSINESS?

Management guru Jim Collins authored a slim book entitled *Good to Great and the Social Sectors: Why Business Thinking Is Not the Answer* as an accompaniment to his well-respected, widely read *Good to Great: Why Some Companies Make the Leap . . . and Others Don't*. In fewer than forty pages, *Good to Great and the Social Sectors* posits convincing arguments for why the politician's mantra for fixing all social-sector organizations does not work out so well in the real world:

- Because most businesses are not great, it is a mistake to assume that practices that contribute to mediocrity in the business world will produce greatness in the social sector.
- Unlike the business world, in the social sectors greatness cannot be measured in dollars.
- Compared to business CEOs, social-sector leaders have little power to implement changes in the organizations they manage.
- Unlike the business world, in the social sector resources do not rationally flow in to support the organizations that are doing the best work (e.g., resources may not rationally flow to a great library organization serving a poor community while irrationally flowing to a mediocre library organization serving a wealthy community).[1]

Most librarians will readily agree with Collins's assertion that business thinking is not the solution for libraries; indeed, most librarians' hackles go straight up at any suggestion that libraries be run like businesses. As a species, librarians are loath to see the highly competitive, winners-versus-losers ethos of the business world imposed on the library, an institution dedicated to the betterment of all rather than the elevation of a few. From a more self-interested perspective, librarians often interpret the phrase "run it like a business" as political code for "pay the employees less, reduce their benefits, lay off as many as you can, and force the grateful survivors to take up the slack by working harder than ever." The fact that, as of 2014, a single for-profit company had assumed management of public libraries in seventy-eight U.S. cities and towns has only served to increase librarian wariness of private-sector solutions.[2]

Extending the "run it like a business" proposition to its logical extreme leads to the philosophical question of whether or not libraries are deserving of public financing. A strict objectivist would contend that libraries should get no public funding whatsoever, that they should be subject to the same sink-or-swim economic forces that determine whether or not businesses (as well as private non-profits) survive or fail. Proponents of the objectivist view can point to the fact that some libraries do manage to survive quite well without public funding. Though in the contemporary western world the number of privately funded subscription libraries is small, in other parts of the world privately funded libraries are more common, especially in countries where publicly funded libraries are woefully inadequate. Several of the larger Indian cities, for example, support for-profit book-lending services that operate on a business model very similar to that of Netflix.

Library supporters, on the other hand, argue that libraries are a social good worthy of public financial support because the unique services they provide could not be provided by market-driven enterprises. For example, public libraries provide information for job seekers who, in many cases, could not afford to pay for access to the information they need to enter or reenter the workforce. Similarly, publicly funded academic libraries provide information to college students who could not begin to afford all the information they must access in order to complete their degree programs. Libraries are also often the sole repositories of obscure, or simply outdated, information resources that no market-driven organization would go to the cost of preserving because the economic value of such resources is negligible even though their cultural value may be priceless.

When objectivists argue that free-market competition would improve social-sector organizations by weeding out those that are underperforming, their reasoning might carry more weight with librarians if it were not for the fact that libraries do not fully enjoy the benefits of free-market competition. For better or worse, copyright law mandates that most information resources—the stock-in-trade of libraries large and small—are available exclusively from monopoly suppliers who can set prices without fear of competition. If libraries cannot shop for lower prices in a competitive marketplace, why should anyone expect them to operate like a free-market business? More to the point, librarians can argue that the non-competitive nature of libraries is a strength rather than a weakness. Unlike competitive businesses, libraries do not care which library ends up "making the sale" so long as the customer's need for information is filled. Librarians routinely refer customers to other libraries, and it is the non-competitive nature of libraries that makes possible two of the greatest library innovations of the last century—interlibrary loan and shared catalog records.

Beyond any public-versus-private-support debate, librarians in general believe that their main concern should not be the business's bottom line, but rather the true information needs of those they serve, regardless of whether those needs might involve planting a vegetable garden, laying hands on an enjoyable mystery novel, or successfully completing a Ph.D. dissertation. This emphasis differentiates libraries from the business world where profit rules. If a shopper visits a store in need of a basic cell phone but is instead convinced by an expert salesperson to purchase the most expensive, top-of-the-line smart phone, complete with the most memory and the priciest data plan, that is simply the way business is done. In the library world, on the other hand, it would be entirely unethical for a librarian to convince someone whose true information need is the phone number of a feed store in Pekin, Illinois, to instead check out all seven volumes of Harry Potter, regardless of how badly the circulation count is in need of a boost.

So black-and-white a view of libraries and businesses is, of course, an oversimplification. The business world is not devoid of ethics. An ethical stockbroker would never encourage an octogenarian to invest her entire life savings in high-risk junk bonds. An ethical airline executive would not allow passengers to fly on aircraft known to be unsafe. Conversely, librarians are not so saintly that putting the interests of themselves or their organization ahead of the interests of those whom they serve is entirely unheard of in the profession. Have libraries ever backed away from controversial books, exhibits, or programs in order to protect their publicly funded bottom line? Have librarians ever demanded raises even when it means fewer books on the shelves and shorter opening hours?

WHAT MAKES LIBRARIES AND BUSINESSES ALIKE

Jim Collins makes a strong case for the difference between social-sector organizations and businesses, and while Collins's thinking holds on the high level of organizational vision, the two nonetheless share many similarities when it comes to the day-in, day-out reality of keeping the doors open and the lights on. Such business concepts as marketing, inventory control, accounting, strategic planning, and human resources are quite familiar to anyone who has spent much time working in the social sector. Both business and social-sector organizations have managers, employees, customers, supporters, detractors, boards of directors, suppliers, assets, income, and expenses. Both are subject to vagaries ranging from legislative action to the forces of Mother Nature. Just as legislative spending cuts can put libraries on the ropes, a new environmental regulation can bankrupt a manufacturing concern. Just as hotels, restaurants, and stores may be damaged or destroyed when hurricanes make landfall, homeless shelters, food banks, and libraries may suffer losses as well.

Another similarity is that, with few exceptions, social-sector and business organizations are accountable to outsiders. For-profit businesses must answer to their investors, with their metric for accountability being the straightforward calculus of profit and loss. Social-sector organizations are accountable to those they serve, most typically via such intermediaries as elected officials, appointed boards of directors, or campus committees. Of course the metrics for accountability in the social sector are far more nuanced than the straightforward profit and loss of the business world—so much so that in the social sector a metric one person sees as a sign of success, another may see as a sign of failure or mismanagement. Pity the poor library director who points to extended open hours as a measure of success only to have an elected budget hawk interpret it as justification for cutting what is obviously an overly lavish library budget.

While it is common to conveniently divide the business world from the social sector through the use of the cliché phrases "big business" and "tiny non-profit," this is not always the case. There are many successful one-person businesses, just as there are giant social-sector non-profits. The Online Computer Library Center (OCLC), a non-profit bibliographic utility, reported revenues over $200 million for both FY 2011/12 and 2012/13.[3] As of the last day of 2012, the American Chemical Society, a non-profit scholarly society and publisher, reported annual operating revenues of $518 million along with $1.2 billion in assets.[4] It is hard to imagine that non-profit organizations controlling such huge sums of money could be run in any way other than as businesses. Being not-for-profit does not, after all, mean that an organization is for loss.

Large or small, libraries and businesses are alike in that both are subject to market forces. Whether it is the cost of electricity going up or the price of computer chips coming down, libraries ride the market wave, a wave they have ridden since long before the dawn of the digital age. In the time of the handwritten manuscript, when the cost of a book was comparable to the cost of several acres of arable land, the market assured that libraries were tiny, exclusive, and not very much like the libraries of today. In 1661, about 220 years after the invention of printing from movable type, Isaac Newton was admitted to Cambridge University. At that time, the library of Newton's Trinity College contained some 3,000 to 4,000 volumes, most of them the costly products of printing presses run by well-paid, highly skilled artisans working with expensive handmade paper.[5] By the mid-nineteenth century, when machine-made wood-pulp paper, steam-powered presses, and improved transportation were beginning to significantly drive down the cost of books, the libraries of Princeton, Yale, and Harvard held a *combined* 120,000 volumes, fewer than what you might expect to find in a modest community college library of the early twenty-first century.[6] In 1920, well into the age of the mass-produced, mass-marketed book, the University of Illinois Library held 440,372 volumes, making it at that time the ninth-largest collection of any academic library in the United States.[7] In 2014, when the cost of a book compares more to a few bags of groceries than to a farm, the University of Illinois Library holds 12 million print volumes. Some of Illinois's 12 million volumes were digitized by Google to eventually become part of the HathiTrust online collection, which as of 2014 was providing free access to over 3.5 million public-domain, full-text digital books. What would Sir Isaac, who had a thing or two to say about natural forces, think of the market forces that led to such an outcome?

A disturbing example of the extent to which libraries are at the mercy of the market is the ongoing uncertainty surrounding under what terms, or even if, a number of major publishers will sell their most popular books to libraries in e-book formats.[8] In the extreme case, publishers could decide to simply stop selling some or all of their e-books to libraries, an action that would largely unravel the long-standing market intersection between libraries and the publishing business. Historically, libraries have been a profitable market for printed books as well as an important vehicle for promoting both the sale of books to individual consumers and the culture of reading in general. However, in the eyes of some publishers, these conditions no longer hold true for e-book editions of popular best sellers. While librarians and their supporters may see cutting libraries out of the e-book best-seller market as at worst unethical, or at best as a betrayal of years of mutually beneficial symbiosis, publishers see the situation in an entirely different, market-driven light: if there is more money to be made by not selling to libraries than by selling to them, why sell? That would be bad business. The fact that those who love libraries hate the cold logic of the marketplace holds no more bearing on the case than the fact that book lovers by the tens of thousands hate the marketplace logic that saw independent bookstores all but eradicated by, initially, chain bookstores and, later, their online brethren.

The way books are made and sold is not the only market force at work upon libraries. When the World Wide Web first exploded into the popular consciousness in the mid-1990s, most libraries' experience with public-access hardware started with dumb terminals capable of nothing more sophisticated than accessing the local online public-access catalog (OPAC) and ended with a handful of desktop machines that did nothing more complicated than spin a few CD-ROM bibliographic databases. Quite suddenly, libraries found themselves playing the role of consumers in a dynamic, highly competitive personal-computer market, acquiring full-featured, network-capable desktop machines in numbers unimaginable just a few years before. Though public-access computers had no prior role in the library, the market quickly demanded that libraries provide such machines if they wished to satisfy the changing information needs of their customers. And most libraries did just what the market demanded, in some cases thanks to the generosity of Bill Gates, Mr. Windows himself.

There is an important, albeit subtle, distinction to note here. Although librarians constantly talk about the impacts of technological change, it was not new technologies (**personal computer + World Wide Web = Boffo!**) per se that put libraries in the computer hardware business; rather, it was the market demand for access to these technologies that drove the change. Without market acceptance, technology might as well not exist. E-mail provides an excellent example of this. E-mail technology spent roughly the first twenty years of its existence as the tool/plaything of a relative handful of scientists and assorted technophiles; in, say, 1978, the few people who knew that such a thing as e-mail existed would not have dreamed of going to a library to use it. It was not until a market for the technology of e-mail asserted itself in the mid-1990s that libraries took action to support this new (in fact, by that time, twenty-year-old) technology; by roughly the turn of the twenty-first century, millions of e-mail users fully expected they could, if they wished, drop into a library to check their e-mail. In the second decade of the twenty-first century, the most noteworthy market shift is the ongoing proliferation of mobile computer hardware, primarily in the form of tablets and smart phones.

Today, checking your e-mail (or Facebook or Instagram or Tumblr or . . .) is more about finding a spot where you can get a few bars on your phone rather than finding a library. Mobile computer hardware will not by itself cause libraries to abandon the public-access computer business; however, the seemingly inevitable decrease in market demand for public-access computers will, sooner or later, send the library public-access computer the way of the pay phone.

Acknowledging that libraries are subject to market forces does not always feel good, especially when the market seems to be driving libraries in unfamiliar, dubious, or destructive directions. It is important to remember, though, that acknowledging the power of market forces, and thinking about how to best respond to them, is not the same as condoning them. Clayton Christensen, author of the business classic *The Innovator's Dilemma: When New Technologies Cause Great Firms to Fail*, relates the following anecdote: After dropping his pen on the floor during a class, Stanford professor Robert Burgelman said as he bent over to pick it up, "I hate gravity." Back at the podium, Burgelman continued by observing, "But you know what? Gravity doesn't care. It will always pull things down, and I may as well plan on it."[9]

ARE LIBRARIES IN COMPETITION WITH BUSINESSES?

On one level, it is easy to look at the information landscape of the digital age and conclude that libraries are definitely in competition with businesses. Google for searching. Wikipedia for reference.* Amazon for books. Apple's iTunes for sound recordings. Flickr and Instagram for still images. YouTube for video. As noted in the introduction to this book, the question, "Why do we need libraries when everything is on the Web?" is voiced far too often for the comfort of librarians.

If that question is uncomfortable for librarians, the thought of trying to compete with the above-named companies, plus hundreds of others in the same or similar businesses, should be absolutely painful. Over the span of just a few years, Amazon was able to bring more quality and pleasure to the online experience of identifying and accessing books than all the world's libraries and their online-catalog vendors had been able to achieve in more than two decades of tinkering with OPACs. Of course Amazon achieved its online su-

---

* While Wikipedia is a non-profit organization, considering it a business in the context of competition seems justifiable. Am I right, *Encyclopedia Britannica*?

periority by spending development money in amounts of which libraries can only dream. Similarly, Google not only has vast resources in terms of servers and programmers, but it can afford to employ a full-time Ph.D. researcher who does nothing but study how people search the Web. This researcher's business card describes his position as "Über Tech Lead. Search Quality/User Happiness." How is the average library, which is lucky if it can pull off one modest focus-group study per year, supposed to compete with that?

The bad news is that the answer is, "It can't." But the good news is that it is a mistake to frame the situation in terms of traditional competition.

Here is a provocative thought: Andrew Carnegie, steel baron, and Bill Gates, software executive, will both go down in history as great philanthropic supporters of libraries; however, Gates is the more selfless of the two. The reason is that the Gates Foundation's generous donation of thousands of Windows-based public-access computers to libraries competes directly with Microsoft's sales to individual consumers. Sure, Carnegie built a lot of public libraries, but he was not exactly known for competing with himself by giving away free steel, was he?

The reasoning that underlies the above provocative thought is patently false. Conveniently ignoring the cynical thought that putting Windows-based public-access computers in libraries is a way to build the customer base for Microsoft's premier product, what makes the reasoning of the Gates-versus-Carnegie argument false is the fundamental difference between Information Age intellectual property like software, digital text, and digital images versus tangible Industrial Age products like steel rails, girders, and, yes, printed books.

How are digital and tangible products fundamentally different? While it takes a certain amount of infrastructure to produce the first of any product, whether it be the first production specimen of a new model of automobile or the first production copy of an iPhone app, the game changes drastically at that point. The incremental cost (raw materials, labor, plant maintenance, etc.) of manufacturing one thousand identical automobiles is significant; the incremental cost of making one thousand (or for that matter 1 million) identical copies of an existing iPhone app is pretty close to zero. This is why an automobile manufacturer does not much worry about a customer buying a new car, making unlimited copies of it, and handing them out for free to friends and strangers alike, while the rights holder of an iPhone app, or any other digital product, worries very much about just that possibility. Those who hold the rights to digital products can prevent rampant copying of their property only through constant vigilance, legal action, and/or engaging in endless, costly battles to produce ever-more-secure digital-rights-management technologies, none of which seem to survive very long once they are deployed in the field.

Things were quite different in a pre-digital world where a rights holder's fear of an individual making and distributing multiple copies of printed books, sound recordings, or physical works of art was on about the same level as Chevrolet's fear of rampant Corvette copying. If a time machine were to whisk a crew of hardcore intellectual-property pirates back to 1951 for the purpose of violating the copyright of the then-new best seller *The Catcher in the Rye*, how could they carry out their mission? They could conceivably use a mimeograph to churn out illegal copies of the novel, but the results would be far too feeble in terms of both numbers and quality to have any impact. Even if the time-traveling pirates had at their disposal a printing plant for the production of large numbers of good-quality illegal copies, it would be a simple matter to detect their operation and shut it down via legal action. Copyright law, after all, was always intended to prevent industrial concerns from stealing from each other, and for hundreds of years it served that purpose well. About the only situation in which copyright law significantly failed was in controlling the pirating of foreign works in countries that did not recognize international copyrights. In spite of its successful past, copyright law has proven to be far less effective when the industrial manufacturing process and the concomitant need to recoup costs, if not make a profit, are taken out of the equation. By the time an individual with a scanner has launched a digital copy of the full text of *The Catcher in the Rye* into the networked world, copyright law may be resorted to as a way of punishing the perpetrator (assuming the perpetrator can be identified and located), but no law can effectively undo the damage done, especially if the individual who created the illegal copy has knowledge of various anonymous web-hosting services that have been, so far, quite successful at circumventing copyright protections.

The widespread adoption of digital technology has disrupted more than long-standing notions of copyright. Mash-ups, tributes, fan fiction, and parodies that detractors see as flagrant plagiarism, fans laud as original works of creative art. In the eyes of some, Wikipedia is guilty of undermining the entire concept of authority, while others praise it for democratically unleashing the wisdom of the crowd in a way that was impossible before digital technology. Similarly, the notion of competition has also been disrupted in the digital age.

Under the rules of competition as they were understood in Andrew Carnegie's day, Bill Gates should have sent hired goons to destroy library public-access computers running his company's software instead of doing just the opposite (i.e., providing libraries with free computers and software). If the old rules of competition were based on notions of force and domination, the new rules are perhaps more closely aligned with the concept of the "business ecosystem," a way of looking at competition that takes its metaphors from the biological sciences and which has gained a great deal of acceptance within the world of high-tech business. As originally described by James F. Moore in 1993, in the business ecosystem model a company should

> be viewed not as a member of a single industry but as part of a business ecosystem that crosses a variety of industries. In a business ecosystem, companies coevolve capabilities around a new innovation: they work cooperatively and competitively to support new products, satisfy customer needs, and eventually incorporate the next round of innovations.[10]

If we can begin to see libraries as part of a business ecosystem, it becomes clear that businesses like Google and Amazon—businesses that have developed products that satisfy the needs of library customers—are in a relationship with libraries that is far more symbiotic than, as some seem to believe, predator-prey. As part of an ecosystem, libraries need not compete with businesses for dominance; instead, libraries must, to use Moore's word, *co-evolve* with businesses to find a secure, if perhaps somewhat unfamiliar, niche in a living ecosystem. Co-evolving is not easy, as it takes creative thinking as well as a willingness to let go of the familiar while embracing the new. The task of co-evolving will, however, seem less daunting when you consider that the alternative is to hold ground in a dying ecosystem that, like Professor Burgelman's gravity, does not care that librarians would rather not be brought down to earth with it.

THE POINT

For a book about serving online customers, it may seem odd that the first chapter has so far not touched on that particular subject. The reason for this long discursion was to establish the simple yet crucial point on which this book is premised. Libraries, while not businesses, are part of a business ecosystem. To survive in such an ecosystem, libraries need not abandon their principles and transform themselves into businesses any more than a herbivore must transform itself into a carnivore just because it happens to share a savanna with a pride of lions. However, understanding how lions operate, and how a herbivore species might survive, and even benefit from, the presence of lions is key to the herbivore's survival. If librarians can accept that it is possible to learn from, and co-evolve with, businesses without actually transforming their libraries into businesses, there is much to be gained, especially in the area of serving online customers, an area in which online businesses have outshone libraries for some time.

NOTES

1. James C. Collins, *Good to Great and the Social Sectors: Why Business Thinking Is Not the Answer; A Monograph to Accompany Good to Great: Why Some Companies Make the Leap—and Others Don't* (Boulder, CO: J. Collins, 2005), 1–20.

2. "About Us," Library Systems & Services LLC, http://www.lssi.com/about (accessed January 28, 2014).

3. *OCLC Annual Report 2012/2013* (Dublin, Ohio: OCLC, 2013), 4, http://www.oclc.org/content/dam/oclc/publications/AnnualReports/2013/2013.pdf (accessed January 28, 2014).

4. "Financial Overview," American Chemical Society, http://www.acs.org/content/acs/en/about/aboutacs/financial/overview.html (accessed January 28, 2014).

5. John Harrison, *The Library of Isaac Newton* (Cambridge: Cambridge University Press, 1978), 1, 6.

6. Eugene R. Hanson, "College Libraries: The Colonial Period to the Twentieth Century," in *Advances in Library Administration and Organization: A Research Annual*, ed. Gerard B. McCabe and Bernard Kreissman, vol. 8 (Greenwich, CT: JAI Press, 1989), 181.

7. Winton U. Solberg, "Edmund Janes James Builds a Library: The University of Illinois Library, 1904–1920," *Libraries & Culture* 39, no. 1 (Winter 2004): 67.

8. "Frequently Asked Questions Regarding e-Books and U.S. Libraries," American Library Association, http://www.ala.org/transforminglibraries/frequently-asked-questions-e-books-us-libraries (accessed February 28, 2014).

9. Clayton M. Christensen, *The Innovator's Dilemma: When New Technologies Cause Great Firms to Fail* (Boston, MA: Harvard Business School Press, 1997), 100.

10. James F. Moore, "Predators and Prey: A New Ecology of Competition," *Harvard Business Review* 71, no. 3 (May 1993): 76, http://blogs.law.harvard.edu/jim/files/2010/04/Predators-and-Prey.pdf (accessed March 11, 2013).

What Librarians Can Learn from the Business Literature

Though it should come as no surprise, the sheer number of words written and said about business greatly exceeds the number written and said about libraries. In broadcasting, twenty-four-hour cable channels such as CNBC, Bloomberg Television, and Fox Business Network devote themselves exclusively to business news, while most general television and radio news broadcasts include business reporting as a regular part of their coverage. Leading business publications like the *Wall Street Journal*, the *Financial Times*, *Barron's*, *The Economist*, and *Forbes* are regularly read by millions around the world, in print and online. While libraries do their best to get their story before the public, the media coverage libraries receive is nowhere near the amount devoted to business. As shown in figure 2.1, the total number of periodical titles devoted to libraries is about one-half the total number of management titles and fourteen times less than the total number of business titles. Limiting to scholarly periodicals, the number of scholarly library periodicals is only about one-third the number of scholarly management titles and about eight times less than the number of scholarly business titles. That the size of the scholarly engine devoted to researching business is far larger than the one devoted to library research is only to be expected considering that, as of 2014, only 57 institutions in the Unites States and Canada offered American Library Association (ALA) accredited degree programs,[1] while at the same time some 517

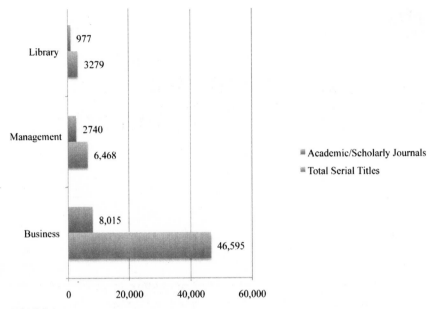

FIGURE 2.1
Search of Ulrichsweb Global Serials Directory, January 2014. Subject (Keyword)
Search Limited to Active Titles.

institutions in the United States and Canada offered degree programs accredited by the Association to Advance Collegiate Schools of Business (AACSB).[2]

Looking at the raw number of articles published on business topics versus library topics reflects a similar disparity. In January 2014 I conducted
searches in the databases *Library Information Science & Technology* and
Library Literature & Information Technology Full Text and compared the
combined results of those two databases with a search in the database *Business Source Complete*, in every search limiting the results to the most recent
thirty years and using fixed-vocabulary terms that (1) are common to all three
databases and (2) touch on subjects of importance to librarians. The results of
these searches are shown in the figure 2.2. While the numbers for the library
literature exceed or are close to those of the business literature for subjects
closely associated with libraries—"database searching," "information searching," "Internet searching"—for most subjects the numbers for the business
literature dwarf those of the library literature.

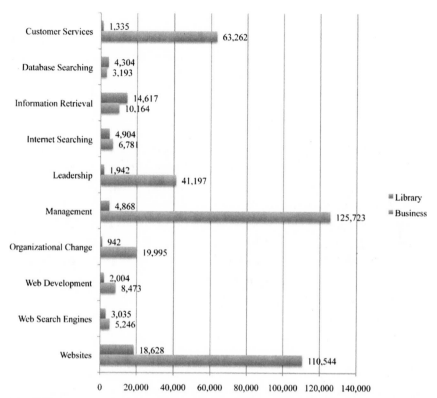

FIGURE 2.2

Hits on Fixed-Vocabulary Search Terms. *Library Information Science & Technology* plus *Library Literature & Information Science Full Text* compared with *Business Source Complete*. Time span: 1984 through 2013.

Given that the business literature is much larger than the library literature, what does it have to offer librarians? Seeing that the business literature includes vast amounts of research and practical guidance in a number of areas of primary importance to librarians—management, customer service, employee training, and marketing, for a few examples—the short answer is that the business literature has much to offer librarians. Because of the money to be made from running a successful business, far greater resources are devoted to the study of business than to the study of libraries. While greater resources do not in themselves make the business literature superior, they do allow the average researcher in a business field to study research questions in far more depth than the average library researcher can. For example, because of the billions to be made in online retail sales, business researchers have been able to study the online behavior of customers more frequently and in far more detail than library researchers have.

The use of the word *customer* just now points to one of the barriers that may prevent librarians from taking full advantage of the business literature. Businesspeople talk about *customers*, while librarians talk about *users* or *patrons*. Businesspeople talk about profits, while librarians talk about *outcomes* or *satisfaction*. Businesspeople talk about *costs* and *efficiency*, while librarians, well, they mostly don't talk about costs and efficiency—even when they should. (Consider the following sporting wager: scouring the library literature, you pay me a dollar for every time a librarian complains about the lack of funding for libraries, while I pay you a dollar for every time a librarian writes about making library operations more cost effective.) No, libraries are not the same as businesses, but in the end there is not a lot of difference between a customer and a patron or between a business success measured in dollars and a library success measured in outcomes (other than the fact that assessing outcomes is much more difficult than counting cash). If librarians can steel themselves not to be put off by the bottom-line terminology and orientation of business, they will see that there is much commonality in what businesses and libraries do, that there is a lot to be learned from the substantial literature of business, and that it is quite possible to learn from the business literature without selling out the core values of libraries.

The intent of this chapter is not to present anything like a comprehensive bibliography of business writing for librarians. The business literature is too vast, varied, and dynamic to cover in a single chapter. Instead, the intent is to suggest some areas of practice and research in which the business literature provides particularly rich offerings for librarians.

BUSINESS-FOCUSED RESEARCH OF INTEREST TO LIBRARIANS

Business researchers are interested in studying the ways in which customers use and navigate the Web because of the straight-line relevance to online marketing and sales. How to attract customers to a website, how to keep their attention, how to help them successfully navigate the website, and how to make the sale are critical concerns for online businesses, and much of what business researchers have learned about online customer behavior holds lessons for libraries. The business literature contains nearly twenty years of research on how customers use the Web, with the first empirical studies appearing in the mid-1990s. For librarians, what may be of most interest are the unexpected directions that business-oriented researchers have taken in their study of online customer behavior. For example, fundamental work on the importance of building trust with online customers has been carried out by such business researchers as D. Harrison McKnight,[3] David Gefen,[4] and the team of Donna L. Hoffman and Thomas P. Novak.[5] Building on psychologist Mihaly Csikszentmihalyi's concept of "flow,"[6] a variety of business scholars have conducted research on how providing visitors with a pleasurable online experience contributes to a successful website. Similarly, business researchers have applied the Technology Acceptance Model (TAM)—first developed by Fred D. Davis[7]—to better understand what factors contribute to an individual's willingness to use a digital technology, such as a website, to carry out a task that could otherwise be conducted in the physical world. In order to study what factors contribute to the success of e-commerce websites, researchers have adapted and updated the well-known Delone and McLean model of Information System Success.[8]

Business researchers have conducted extensive research in the area of customer service in both the physical and online worlds. For example, as self-service has become increasingly common for customers in the online environment, business researchers have enhanced their understanding of self-service technologies,[9] including the recognition of customers' perceived sense of control as a key component of successful self-service technologies.[10] In 1990 Bitner, Booms, and Tetreault[11] rediscovered John C. Flanagan's once-forgotten "Critical Incident Technique,"[12] and since that rediscovery, business scholars have published hundreds of articles on its use as a tool for assessing the quality of customer service in both physical and online environments.

The study of the application of artificial intelligence and the use of avatars as online customer-service tools has been led almost entirely by business-focused researchers. A leader in the study of online avatars is Izak Benbasat of the University of British Columbia's Sauder School of Business, with Benbasat, his colleagues, and his graduate students publishing dozens of articles on their research in this area.

The study of clickstream data by business researchers such as Wendy W. Moe goes far beyond anything libraries have done.[13] Though this disparity

BUSINESS-ORIENTED JOURNALS OF INTEREST TO LIBRARIANS

The following journals routinely publish articles of possible interest to librarians:

BUSINESS TECHNOLOGY
Industrial Management & Data Systems
Information & Management
Information Systems and E-Business Management
Information Systems Journal
Information Systems Research
International Journal of Mobile Communications
Journal of Computer Information Systems
Journal of Management Information Systems
MIS Quarterly

GENERAL BUSINESS
Harvard Business Review
Journal of Applied Business Research
Journal of Business Research

MANAGEMENT
Decision Sciences
Decision Support Systems
European Journal of Economics, Finance & Administrative Sciences
European Journal of Operations Research
International Journal of Business and Management
International Journal of Business Insights and Transformation
International Journal of Management Reviews
International Management Journal
Management Science
Managing Service Quality
MIT Sloan Management Review
Public Management Review

MARKETING

International Journal of Advertising
International Journal of Internet Marketing and Advertising
International Journal of Market Research
International Journal of Nonprofit & Voluntary Sector Marketing
Journal of Advertising
Journal of Consumer Psychology
Journal of Interactive Advertising
Journal of Interactive Marketing
Journal of International Consumer Marketing
Journal of Marketing
Journal of Marketing Research
Journal of Public Policy & Marketing
Journal of Strategic Marketing
Journal of the Academy of Marketing Science
Marketing Research
Marketing Science
Psychology & Marketing
QME—Quantitative Marketing and Economics

SERVING ONLINE CUSTOMERS

Electronic Commerce Research and Applications
International Journal of Electronic Commerce
International Journal of Human-Computer Studies
Internet Research
Journal of Electronic Commerce Research
Journal of Organizational Computing and Electronic Commerce
Journal of Retailing
Journal of Retailing & Consumer Services
Service Industries Journal

is in part attributable to the fact that libraries adhere, in general, to a higher standard of protecting user privacy than do businesses, what business researchers have learned from their studies of clickstream data is of value to librarians hoping to better understand online customer behavior. A similar situation applies to research in the related area of using data mining to better understand and serve online users.

BUSINESS BOOKS FOR LIBRARIANS

Because writing a successful business book is potentially so profitable, the market has been flooded with as many as eleven thousand new business books in a single year.[14] As might be expected, such a high volume of new books makes identifying the best of the bunch difficult. Among the less worthwhile entrants in the business book field are those that take the form of unabashed ego trips embarked upon by captains of industry who made enough money to (1) make themselves believe they have something worth saying and (2) afford a ghostwriter. Donald Trump's *The Art of the Deal* is arguably the poster child of the business-ego-trip subgenre, but it hardly stands alone. Almost as unhelpful are the legions of business books consisting of nothing more than a weak blend of self-help and pop psychology topped with a dollop of unlimited-wealth-can-be-yours cream—any business book marketed via an infomercial very likely falls into this category. Equally unhelpful are those business books that blatantly attempt to cash in on the latest fads catching fire in the worlds of finance, management, economics, and get-rich-quickology. For example, the late 1990s and early 2000s saw an outpouring of books on how to make money on the Internet, most of which were worth less than a share of stock in dotcombubble.com. Then there is the more recent fad of mining the annals of history for management gold, with illustrative titles from this genre including the likes of *Jesus CEO: Using Ancient Wisdom for Visionary Leadership*, *Leadership Secrets of Attila the Hun*, and *Lincoln on Leadership: Executive Strategies for Tough Times*. Which is not to specifically condemn any of the aforementioned books, but rather to suggest that this subgenre has been worked perhaps harder than it should have been.

While it is as easy to smile at an out-of-fashion business fad as it is to smile at oversized *Dynasty*-era hairdos and shoulder pads, the faddishness of business practices is a serious concern for anyone looking to mine the business literature for managerial wisdom and apply it to their own workplace. As Peter M. Senge, author of *The Fifth Discipline*, writes,

> Recognizing that most new ideas in American management get caught up in the dynamics of the fad cycle leads to some sobering questions. What if the time required to understand, apply, and eventually assimilate the new capabilities suggested by a "new idea" is longer than the fad cycle itself? If organizations have an "attention span" of only one or two years (some might say one or two months), is it impossible to learn things that might require five or ten years? How can initial tentative explorations and experiments in developing learning capabilities, which inevitably will meet with a mixture of success and failure, lead to an ongoing learning process that continually increases capability?[15]

Even more practically, how are managers supposed to foster organizational change when it is entirely too easy for the hard-core skeptics among the staff to poison those efforts by dismissing them—possibly with justification—as the latest management flavor of the week?

Complicating the picture for librarians is the fact that even some otherwise excellent business books do not deal with topics of much relevance to the library profession. While books on business leadership, innovation, and technology can speak very directly to the issues librarians face in their workplaces, books about international finance, macro-economics, starting your own business, or earning a million dollars in just six short months are unlikely to have much professional relevance for librarians. The following list, therefore, attempts to serve as a modest "Great Business Books for Librarians." Like any great-books list, this one is subjective. Others might convincingly argue that some books on the list have never been great or that books left off this list should be on it. It is also true that some books on this list may not stand the test of time. At the very least, however, this list can be seen as a kick-starter for any librarian who aspires to learn more about what the world of business can teach the profession of librarianship.

While this list was compiled in part from my own reading, I freely admit I have not read every book on the list, as much as I would like to be able to claim otherwise. Those books on the list that I have not read were chosen because they regularly appear in lists of "Best Business Books" and their reviews and summaries strongly suggest their relevance to the work of librarians. In order from oldest to newest, the books are as follows:

How to Win Friends and Influence People by Dale Carnegie. New York: Simon and Schuster, 1936.

If longevity in business means anything, consider that when Dale Carnegie first walked into a New York City YMCA and started teaching people how to achieve business success and find personal happiness, William Howard Taft occupied the White House; today, people are still taking Dale Carnegie courses—in person and online—and still reading the book that grew out of Carnegie's early courses. Wildly popular from the day it was published, *How to Win Friends* is still regarded as a classic work on the subject of sales, self-improvement, public speaking, corporate training, and getting along with others.

The Practice of Management by Peter Drucker. New York: Harper, 1954.

One of the twentieth century's most influential voices in the field of management, Drucker continues to influence business thinking in the twenty-first century. Ahead of his time, Drucker foresaw the emergence of the information economy, coining the term *knowledge worker* way back in 1959. Although it is a classic, *The Practice of Management* may at times seem obvious, if not clichéd, to a twenty-first-century reader; however, it is important to remember that many of Drucker's central ideas—such as his notion that an organization must "make for willingness and ability to work for the future rather than rest on the achievements of the past, and to strive for growth rather than put on fat"[16]—were positively avant-garde when they first appeared in print. Other highly regarded books by Drucker include *The Effective Executive* (1966), *The Age of Discontinuity* (1969), and *The Essential Drucker* (2001).

In Search of Excellence: Lessons from America's Best-Run Companies by Thomas J. Peters and Robert H. Waterman. New York: Harper and Row, 1982.

In this study of forty-three successful companies, Peters and Waterman lay out eight basic management principles that they believe made these companies successful. A runaway best seller, *In Search of Excellence* routinely appears on lists of the best business books.

The One Minute Manager by Kenneth H. Blanchard and Spencer Johnson. New York: Morrow, 1982.

The management message contained in this slim volume is based on three practical techniques: "One Minute Goals," "One Minute Praisings," and "One

Minute Reprimands." As short and simple as it may be, *The One Minute Manager* has nonetheless sold millions of copies and is still used by managers in organizations large and small.

Influence: The Psychology of Persuasion by Robert B. Cialdini. Melbourne: Business Library, 1984.

Influence is the first, and most influential, of Cialdini's thoroughly researched books on the art and science of getting people to do what you want them to do. Other highly useful books on this topic include Cialdini's *Influence: Science and Practice*, 4th edition (2001) and his *Yes! 50 Scientifically Proven Ways to Be Persuasive* (2008).

Out of the Crisis by W. Edwards Deming. Cambridge: Massachusetts Institute of Technology, Center for Advanced Engineering Study, 1986.

In the decades following the Second World War, Deming worked as a consultant in Japan where his statistically based management theories helped rebuild a shattered economy and turned Japan into a global manufacturing powerhouse. In the early 1980s, Deming used the techniques he had taught in Japan to turn around the sagging fortunes of Ford Motor Company. *Out of the Crisis*, originally published in 1982 under the title *Quality, Productivity, and Competitive Position*, describes a management theory based on Deming's well-known 14 Points for Management. The movement known as Total Quality Management (TQM) has its roots in *Out of the Crisis*, though Deming himself never used the phrase *total quality management*. While Deming's theories are commonly associated with manufacturing processes, his focus on the importance of the manager ensures that his work has relevance in information-based workplaces, libraries included.

The Age of Unreason by Charles B. Handy. Boston: Harvard Business School Press, 1989.

A book about living in a time of great change, *The Age of Unreason* challenges readers to embrace "upside-down thinking." In the opening chapter Charles B. Handy throws down the gauntlet when he writes,

> Circumstances are now once again, I believe, combining in curious ways. Change is not what it used to be. The status quo will no longer be the best way

forward. The best way will be less comfortable and less easy, but no doubt, more interesting—a word we often use to signal an uncertain mix of danger and opportunity. If we wish to enjoy more of the opportunity and less of the risk, we need to understand the changes better. Those who know why changes come waste less effort in protecting themselves or in fighting the inevitable. Those who realize where changes are heading are better able to use those changes to their own advantage. The society which welcomes change can use that change instead of just reacting to it.[17]

Considering that these words were written before most people had heard of the Internet, the word *perceptive* hardly begins to describe Handy's book about the impact of technological and economic change. Though *The Age of Unreason* is more business philosophy than how-to, it nonetheless provides a useful foundation for anyone dealing with change in the workplace and the wider world.

The 7 Habits of Highly Effective People: Powerful Lessons in Personal Change by Stephen R. Covey. New York: Simon and Schuster, 1989.

While *The 7 Habits of Highly Effective People* clearly falls on the self-help/motivational end of the business book continuum, the fact that it is the best-selling business book of all time provides a strong endorsement of its message. Rather than promoting the competitive winners-versus-losers worldview that many associate with the business mentality, *The 7 Habits of Highly Effective People* focuses on building self-confidence, learning to listen to divergent points of view, and finding win-win solutions—approaches to life and organizational management that should feel right at home in library settings.

The Fifth Discipline: Mastering the Five Practices of the Learning Organization by Peter M. Senge. New York: Doubleday/Currency, 1990.

Senge's Zen-influenced thesis is that an organization can adopt the five practices of the book's title to overcome "learning disabilities" and become a "learning organization" capable of continuous adaptation and improvement.

Built to Last: Successful Habits of Visionary Companies by James C. Collins and Jerry I. Porras. New York: HarperBusiness, 1994.

The result of six years of research, *Built to Last* tells the story of eighteen companies the authors defined as visionary. While embracing innovation, the authors do not equate being visionary with heedlessly leaping from bright-shiny opportunity to bright-shiny opportunity, instead recognizing the importance of being in it for the long haul, a sentiment which should resonate with the average librarian:

> What is a visionary company? Visionary companies are premier institutions—the crown jewels—in their industries, widely admired by their peers and having a long track record of making a significant impact on the world around them. The key point is that a visionary company is an *organization*—an institution. All individual leaders, no matter how charismatic or visionary, eventually die; and all visionary products and services—all "great ideas"—eventually become obsolete. Indeed, entire markets can become obsolete and disappear. Yet visionary companies prosper over long periods of time, through multiple product life cycles and multiple generations of active leaders.[18]

The Balanced Scorecard: Translating Strategy into Action by Robert S. Kaplan and David P. Norton. Boston: Harvard Business Review Press, 1996.

The *balance* in *The Balanced Scorecard* comes from balancing measures that show past organizational performance with those that indicate future directions. The appropriateness of *The Balanced Scorecard* for library organizations is reflected in the fact that in 2009 the Association of Research Libraries launched its Balanced Scorecard initiative to help libraries improve their organizational performance.

Leading Change by John P. Kotter. Boston: Harvard Business School Press, 1996.

A central idea of *Leading Change* is that there is a critical difference between managing change and leading change. This highly personal book offers an eight-step process for changing an organization in order to produce a positive outcome.

The Innovator's Dilemma: When New Technologies Cause Great Firms to Fail by Clayton M. Christensen. Boston: Harvard Business School Press, 1997.

In *The Innovator's Dilemma*, Harvard Business School professor Clayton M. Christensen examines technologies as diverse as hydraulic backhoes and hard-disk drives to show that listening to your customers can backfire when new technologies disrupt a seemingly stable marketplace. In short,

Christensen's thesis is that customers cannot tell you what they will need in the future and, more disturbingly, that even when successful organizations identify significant emerging technologies, their ability to adopt them is usually thwarted by ingrained, inflexible organizational structures and cultures. Librarians may also find worthwhile Christensen's later books on the topic of education: *Disrupting Class: How Disruptive Innovation Will Change the Way the World Learns* (2008) and *The Innovative University: Changing the DNA of Higher Education from the Inside Out* (2011).

The Victorian Internet: The Remarkable Story of the Telegraph and the Nineteenth Century's On-line Pioneers by Tom Standage. New York: Walker and Company, 1998.

A fascinating history of nineteenth-century technology and business that will appeal to readers who believe, or strongly suspect, that there really is nothing new under the sun, the Internet included.

Discovering the Soul of Service: The Nine Drivers of Sustainable Business Success by Leonard L. Berry. New York: Free Press, 1999.

Berry studied fourteen companies—ranging from The Container Store to Chick-fil-A to Charles Schwab—to understand the secrets of their success. Rather than finding the answer in the bottom line, Berry proposes that humane leadership is the essential foundation of a great service organization.

Information Rules: A Strategic Guide to the Network Economy by Carl Shapiro and Hal Varian. Boston: Harvard Business School Press, 1999.

Does any book on the topic of online business written during the crazy years of the dot-com bubble still have relevance in the twenty-first century? This one does. Rather than being blinded by the technology-fueled economic optimism of its time, the authors of *Information Rules* use sound economic theory to show what it takes to create a successful business in the digital age. Shapiro, an economist, is a longtime faculty member in the University of California–Berkeley's Hass School of Business and has served in the Antitrust Division of the U.S. Department of Justice. Varian, also an economist, was the founding dean of the University of California–Berkeley's School of Information and later became the chief economist at Google.

Good to Great: Why Some Companies Make the Leap . . . and Others Don't by James C. Collins. New York: HarperBusiness, 2001.

The surprising, sometimes provocative findings of *Good to Great* are based on a five-year study of an elite group of companies that made the transition from being good to being great and sustained their greatness for at least fifteen years. One of the more notable ideas explored in *Good to Great* is the concept of Level 5 leaders, of whom Collins writes,

> Level 5 leaders channel their ego needs away from themselves and into the larger goal of building a great company. It's not that Level 5 leaders have no ego or self-interest. Indeed, they are incredibly ambitious—*but their ambition is first and foremost for the institution, not themselves.*[19]

Equally important for librarians is Collins's 2005 follow-up book *Good to Great and the Social Sectors: Why Business Thinking Is Not the Answer*, a pamphlet-length work that examines the pursuit of greatness from the perspective of non-profit organizations.

Project Management by Gary Heerkens. New York: McGraw-Hill, 2002.

While many librarians routinely manage projects, it is less routine for them to have formal training in project management. Heerkens, an experienced project manager, provides an accessible, highly readable introduction to the art and science of project management.

Strengths Based Leadership: Great Leaders, Teams, and Why People Follow by Tom Rath and Barry Conchie. New York: Gallup Press, 2008.

Based on decades of Gallup research into leadership, the authors of *Strengths Based Leadership* focus on the importance of understanding individual strengths (others' and your own), getting the right people on the team, and understanding the needs of those you lead. With the purchase of this book comes the opportunity to take an online assessment of your management strengths.

The Cluetrain Manifesto: The End of Business as Usual by Rick Levine, Christopher Locke, Doc Searls, and David Weinberger. New York: Basic Books, 2009.

Begun as a website, originally published as a book in 1999, and updated in 2009, *The Cluetrain Manifesto* is perhaps the first born-online book on the topic of doing business online. A manifesto in that it calls for new ways of operating in a new marketplace, the book is structured around a set of ninety-five highly provocative theses, including such eye pokes as "Markets are conversations," "Today, the org chart is hyperlinked, not hierarchical," and "Companies need to realize their markets are often laughing. At them."

Guerrilla Marketing Remix: The Best of Guerrilla Marketing by Jay Conrad Levinson and Jeannie Levinson. Irvine, California: Entrepreneur Press, 2011.

First published in 1983 as *Guerrilla Marketing* and long considered an essential guide for marketing on a shoestring, the updated version is of most interest to librarians because it includes advice on online marketing. At times frenetic in its pacing, *Guerrilla Marketing Remix* is bursting with practical suggestions, often presented in list form. Relentlessly focused on sales and offering maxims such as, "Marketing is the precious connection between you and whoever buys what you sell,"[20] *Guerrilla Marketing Remix* nonetheless has a great deal to teach librarians. But libraries aren't selling anything. Right. Keep telling yourself that until it is true.

OTHER LISTS OF BEST BUSINESS BOOKS

"The 20 Most Influential Business Books." Dan Ackman. *Forbes.* http://www.forbes.com/2002/09/30/0930booksintro.html.

"The 25 Most Influential Business Books." *Time* magazine. http://content.time.com/time/specials/packages/completelist/0,29569,2086680,00.html.

The 100 Best Business Books of All Time: What They Say, Why They Matter, and How They Can Help You by Jack Covert and Todd Sattersten. New York: Portfolio, 2009.

The Best Business Books Ever: The Most Influential Management Books You'll Never Have Time to Read. New York: Basic Books, 2011.

"U.S. News & World Report Best Business Books." *U.S. News & World Report.* http://www.usnews.com/usnews/biztech/bestinbiz/bestbusinessbooks.

Lean In: Women, Work, and the Will to Lead by Sheryl Sandberg. New York: Alfred A. Knopf, 2013.

Sandberg, the CEO of Facebook, examines why women do not hold more leadership positions and offers positive suggestions for what women can do to change the status quo. Sandberg's related 2010 TED Talk, "Why We Have Too Few Women Leaders," is available online and, as of early 2014, has been viewed more than 2 million times.[21]

NOTES

1. "Directory of Institutions Offering Accredited Master's Programs," American Library Association, http://www.ala.org/accreditedprograms/sites/ala.org. accreditedprograms/files/content/directory/pdf/LIS_directory_10-2013.pdf (accessed January 27, 2014).

2. "Schools Accredited in Business—Ordered by Country/Region, State, Name," Association to Advance Collegiate Schools of Business, https://www.aacsb.net/eweb/DynamicPage.aspx?Site=AACSB&WebCode=AccredSchlCountry (accessed January 27, 2014).

3. D. H. McKnight, Vivek Choudhury, and Charles Kacmar, "Developing and Validating Trust Measures for e-Commerce: An Integrative Typology," *Information Systems Research* 13, no. 3 (September 2002): 334–359.

4. D. Gefen, E. Karahanna, and D. W. Straub, "Trust and TAM in Online Shopping: An Integrated Model," *MIS Quarterly* 27, no. 1 (March 2003): 51–90.

5. Donna L. Hoffman, Thomas P. Novak, and Marcos Peralta, "Building Consumer Trust Online," *Communications of the ACM* 42, no. 4 (April 1999): 80–85.

6. Mihaly Csikszentmihalyi, *Beyond Boredom and Anxiety: Experiencing Flow in Work and Play* (San Francisco: Jossey-Bass, 1975).

7. Fred Donald Davis Jr. "A Technology Acceptance Model for Testing New End-User Information Systems: Theory and Results," Ph.D. dissertation, Massachusetts Institute of Technology, 1986, http://dspace.mit.edu/bitstream/handle/1721.1/15192/14927137.pdf?sequence=1 (accessed November 7, 2013).

8. William H. DeLone and Ephraim R. McLean, "The DeLone and McLean Model of Information Systems Success: A Ten-Year Update," *Journal of Management Information Systems* 19, no. 4 (Spring 2003): 9–30.

9. Matthew L. Meuter, Amy L. Ostrom, Robert I. Roundtree, and Mary Jo Bitner, "Self-Service Technologies: Understanding Customer Satisfaction with Technology-Based Service Encounters," *Journal of Marketing* 64, no. 3 (July 2000): 50–64.

10. J. E. G. Bateson, "Self-Service Consumer: An Exploratory Study," *Journal of Retailing* 61, no. 3 (Fall 1985): 73–74.

11. Mary Jo Bitner, Bernard H. Booms, and Mary Stanfield Tetreault, "The Service Encounter: Diagnosing Favorable and Unfavorable Incidents," *Journal of Marketing* 54, no. 1 (January 1990): 71–84.

12. John C. Flanagan, "The Critical Incident Technique," *Psychological Bulletin* 51, no. 4 (1954): 327–358.

13. Wendy W. Moe, "Buying, Searching, or Browsing: Differentiating between Online Shoppers Using In-Store Navigational Clickstream," *Journal of Consumer Psychology* 13, nos. 1–2 (2003): 29–39.

14. Eric Spitznagel, "How to Write a Bestselling Business Book," BusinessWeek.com, July 20, 2012, http://www.businessweek.com/articles/2012-07-19/how-to-write-a-bestselling-business-book (accessed January 10, 2014).

15. Peter M. Senge, *The Fifth Discipline: The Art and Practice of the Learning Organization* (New York: Doubleday/Currency, 1994), x.

16. Peter F. Drucker, *The Practice of Management* (New York: HarperBusiness, 1993), 203.

17. Charles B. Handy, *The Age of Unreason* (Boston: Harvard Business School Press, 1989), 4.

18. James C. Collins and Jerry I. Porras, *Built to Last: Successful Habits of Visionary Companies* (New York: HarperBusiness, 1994), 1–2.

19. James C. Collins, *Good to Great: Why Some Companies Make the Leap—and Others Don't.* New York: HarperBusiness, 2001, 21.

20. Jay Conrad Levinson and Jeannie Levinson, *Guerrilla Marketing Remix: The Best of Guerrilla Marketing* (Irvine, CA: Entrepreneur Press, 2011), 15.

21. Sheryl Sandberg, "Why We Have Too Few Women Leaders," TED, http://www.ted.com/talks/sheryl_sandberg_why_we_have_too_few_women_leaders.html (accessed January 19, 2014).

3

Unlikely Sources

What Librarians Can Learn from the Shady Side of the Web

Most librarians know far more about pornography than anyone outside the profession might expect. On the one hand, librarians routinely deal with library visitors who use public-access computers to access pornography, often in ways that are inappropriate if not actually illegal; on the other hand, librarians must also negotiate with would-be censors who have decided that items in a library's collection are pornographic and so should be restricted if not entirely removed from the collection. Even though many librarians bear scars from their battles in the pornography wars, and even though most librarians wish pornography would simply leave the library to never return, there is actually something to be learned from an aspect of pornography with which most librarians are not familiar—the business of pornography. What is to be learned is a lesson of how an industry firmly rooted in analog technologies transformed itself into one of the most successful industries of the digital age, a lesson that provides some unexpected insights into connecting customers with information in the online environment.

Before going one step further, it is necessary to make clear that even though this chapter examines pornography as an information business, it does not in any way touch on the ethical, moral, legal, or psychosocial aspects of what is a hotly controversial topic. And while this chapter certainly acknowledges the existence of pornography, this acknowledgment is no more an endorsement of pornography than acknowledging the existence of websites like Pirate Bay is an endorsement of copyright infringement or acknowledging the existence of skinhead websites is an endorsement of racial intolerance.

Separated from its exceedingly large quantity of social, psychological, and moral baggage, the pornography business can be seen as nothing more than an information business, one not that different from any other information business, libraries included. Like libraries, the pornography business is, and always has been, closely tied to advances in information technology. Both libraries and the pornography business have undergone rapid transformation during the digital age, though of course both existed long before the emergence of digital technology. In fact pornography pre-dates libraries, as sexual images appear on prehistoric cave walls, Greek amphorae, Pompeian ruins, ninth-century Japanese woodblock prints, and European playing cards that pre-date Gutenberg. Capitalizing on the emerging technology of printing from movable type, Pietro Aretino (1492–1556) was among the first, but certainly not the last, to earn a living from the mass production of printed pornographic texts and images.[1] In the nineteenth century the invention of photography led almost immediately to pornographic photographs. In 1874 British police arrested London pornographer Henry Haylor for the possession of over 130,000 pornographic photographs and slides.[2] The first public showing of a motion picture in 1894 was followed within two years by the premier of what is considered the first pornographic film, *Le Coucher de la Mariée*.[3] During the heyday of the telegraph, amorous couples enlisted the aid of telegraph operators to carry on love affairs and exchange messages "too sexually provocative to merit public airing."[4] The immediacy and privacy of the telephone proved to be even better suited for fulfilling sexual desires than did the telegraph, as is evidenced by such examples as the euphemism *call girl* (which dates back to the first decade of the twentieth century), the existence of a robust telephone sex industry, and the twenty-first-century phenomenon of sexting—the sending of salacious text messages (hello again, telegraph) and images via cell phone. Pornography contributed to the widespread postwar adoption of 8 mm movie gear, as even during the legendarily straitlaced Eisenhower era, local camera stores quietly rented 8 mm pornographic films for showing at home or at such typically all-male events as bachelor parties and lodge meetings.[5] Pornography also contributed to the late 1970s/early 1980s boom in sales of home videotape machines. Commercially produced pornographic videotapes were on the market by 1977, a year before the first mainstream movies debuted in that format, and X-rated tapes held the lion's share of the home video market for several years.[6]

Regardless of pornography's long history of embracing analog technologies, it is digital technology that has proven to be the match made in pornographic heaven. Years before there was a Web, digital pornography was available via dial-up bulletin-board services (BBS) as well as such pre-Web Internet applications as Usenet and Gopher. In 1980s France, the scandalous *"messageries roses"* comprised a significant segment of the early traffic on the pioneering Minitel system. Foreshadowing things to come, in 1993 the U.S. Customs Service raided over forty locations suspected of being part of a BBS-based international child-pornography ring. At the time, a Customs Service official identified the raid as the first such operation ever conducted in the United States, though of course it would not be the last.[7] While pornographers may not have been, as Internet legend has it, the driving force behind every digital innovation from online credit-card transactions to IP-based videoconferencing, modern-day pornographers have tended to be early adopters and exploiters of emerging digital technologies just as their forerunners were early adopters and exploiters of the emerging analog technologies of their day. As one Sun Microsystems executive put it, "The way you know if your technology is good and solid is if it's doing well in the porn world."[8]

Given the present-day recognition that, regardless of how one feels about it, online pornography pervades cyberspace, there is an almost quaint breathlessness to be found in the earliest newspaper and magazine articles alerting the masses to the fact that pornography had somehow found its way onto this computer thing called the Internet. One of the first of these articles to reach a large audience was *Time* magazine's cover story for July 3, 1995, "Online Erotica: On a Screen Near You." The cover image greeting unsuspecting *Time* subscribers and newsstand browsers depicts a stunned, open-mouthed child with his fingers on a keyboard, the glow of an out-of-frame computer monitor uplighting his face in the style of a classic horror-movie poster. The authors of the article write that the idea of combining pornography and computers "seems to make otherwise worldly-wise adults a little crazy" and report on the uproar resulting from a U.S. senator's discovery that anyone with a home computer can download pornographic images from the Internet.[9] In the twenty-first century, a politician's "discovery" that there is pornography on the Internet would no doubt strike a similar chord to the scene in

Casablanca in which Captain Renault strides into Rick's Café Américain to proclaim, "I'm shocked, shocked to find there is gambling going on in here." It was not that long ago, however, that the existence of Internet pornography was far from common knowledge. The following excerpt from a 1995 *Wall Street Journal* article, "Electronic Erotica: Too Much Traffic," illustrates how much both technology and society have changed since the integration of the Web into daily life:

> [There exists] an increasingly abundant trove of explicitly sexual material on the Internet. "Chat" sessions let users talk about every sexual inclination imaginable. Multimedia databases serve up everything anybody might want to know about any kind of sex, and electronic storefronts peddle sexually related products. . . . The feverish development of the World Wide Web, a subset of Internet computers that can deliver graphics and sound, has made viewing images—pornographic and otherwise—on-line easier than before.[10]

The author of the article goes on to point out some of the downsides of accessing pornography on the Internet, noting that it can take up to half an hour to download a single image and that saving images eats up vast amounts of valuable computer storage space. It has been a long, perverse journey from the days of dial-up access, 3.5-inch floppies, and the Web as a "subset of Internet computers" to the present-day reality of high-speed Internet, $100 hard drives measured in terabytes, and Rule 34—a not entirely implausible Internet adage that holds, "If it exists, there is porn of it. No exceptions."

All snickering about the stereotypical computer nerd's legendarily insatiable appetite for online pornography aside, how extensive is the online pornography industry? Pinning down accurate numbers is extraordinarily difficult, in part because so much of the industry operates in the shadowlands of black and gray economies, and in part because both those in the pornography business and those who oppose it as a social evil tend to overstate its economic impact. Stuart Lawley, one of the richest men in Britain and the founder of the entirely pornographic .xxx domain, estimated in 2010 that his ICM registry will make $200 million per year selling .xxx domains (at a cost of $60 per year each) and that his proposed pornographic version of the popular PayPal service will process $3 billion to $4 billion per year in transactions.[11] On the opposite side of the pornography divide, a website

BOOGIE NIGHTS: A TALE OF TECHNOLOGICAL CHANGE

For all its raw treatment of the pornographic film industry circa 1980, the critically acclaimed film *Boogie Nights* is in part about the economic and human impact of technological change. Set in Southern California's San Fernando Valley—the Hollywood of pornographic movies—*Boogie Nights* incorporates a subplot that focuses on the struggles of pornographic movie director Jack Horner (Burt Reynolds) as he is forced to switch from shooting on film stock to shooting on videotape, an emerging technology he disparages as cheap and inferior.

Horner dismisses use of the new technology as disrespectful of long-standing traditions and detrimental to the quality of the work to which he has, for better or worse, devoted his life and talent. Caught up in a tide of technological change he is powerless to resist, Horner suffers the indignity of watching the new technology he despises become wildly successful. Horner's feelings of helpless despair are not far different from those of a staunch defender of print watching sales of e-books climb steadily upward. During the historical time frame in which *Boogie Nights* is set, videotape was creating a huge new audience for pornography by making customers of people who, while never dreaming of venturing into a disreputable adult bookstore or sleazy XXX theater, were willing to view pornographic films in the privacy of their homes. The new demand for pornographic films becomes so great that Horner's financial backers strong-arm him into adopting techniques of mass production, forcing him to ignore the storytelling and character development that Horner considers necessary elements of all films, pornographic or not.

Besides running roughshod over the director's artistic sensibilities, the technological shift from film stock to videotape is shown disrupting traditional business practices within the pornography industry. Rather than being exclusively distributed to adult theaters and bookstores, pornographic videotapes are sold to private individuals via mail order or made available as rentals from the same neighborhood video stores that also rent family films and popular mainstream hits. The adoption of videotape impacts the pornography industry's labor force by taking away the need for film-processing services and reducing the number of skilled employees required for on-set technical crews. Like so many resisters of new technology, Horner can see the new technology's potential to disrupt the world he knows, yet he lacks the vision to see the new possibilities this disruption will create. As with all new technologies, the adoption of videotape brings with it both gains and losses, the latter of which inflict genuine economic and emotional harm on those who cannot adapt.

Boogie Nights was, by coincidence, released in 1997, the same year that DVD video first went on sale in the United States. In less than a decade, videotape would be all but dead as a format for both pornographic and mainstream home video. But DVD was only the digital beginning. In much less than twenty years, the sale of pornographic DVDs would be reduced to a mere sideshow in comparison to the vast amounts of online pornography available via download, streaming, and live videoconferencing. Considering how thoroughly the rise of the Web altered, and continues to alter, the landscape of the pornography business, the videotape revolution seems, in retrospect, no more than a minor disturbance.

promoting Internet-filtering software claims that a study (not cited) found that U.S. pornography revenues totaled $13.3 billion in 2006.[12] By way of a ballpark comparison, the Institute of Museum and Library Studies reported that for FY 2006 the total operating revenues of public libraries in the United States was just under $10.3 billion dollars.[13] So is it fair to conclude that, in the United States, the pornography industry is a bigger economic force (to the tune of $3 billion per year) than public libraries? The answer is that nobody knows for sure, though it is safe to say that the amount of revenue generated by online pornography is big.

SIMILARLY DISRUPTED

Libraries and the pornography industry have been disrupted in remarkably similar ways. This is well illustrated by the way the two have been impacted by black-boxing and commodification.

Black-Boxing

Black-boxing, a concept that comes from the work of sociologist Bruno Latour, describes the situation that occurs when a technology (the metaphorical black box) performs complex functions that were once the work of trained specialists and does so in a way that is invisible to an untrained, non-specialist end user.[14] Black-boxing is not a new phenomenon. Even though it has become common to associate the term *Luddite* with anyone who opposes digital technology, the term originated with early nineteenth-century textile artisans who saw their skills black-boxed by such analog technologies as mechanical spinning machines and power looms. A prime example of a digital-age black box is the word-processing program—a tool that allows the average person to carry out a level of typesetting and document formatting that, at one time, could have been achieved only by highly skilled typesetters and layout artists. Similarly, the camcorder is a black box that allows those with no formal training in cinematography to shoot videos of remarkably high quality. At roughly the same time that both the camcorder and video-editing software (yet another black box) were dropping in price and becoming increasingly easy to use, the Web made it simple for anyone to make their homemade videos (as well as still images) available to the entire online world, whether for free or for a price. By the dawn of the twenty-first century, what once required an entire film crew, a film lab, post-production facilities, and a complex distribution system could be accomplished by just about anyone with a camcorder or, within a few years, anyone with a webcam or a smart phone. Once the making and distribution of videos was opened to the masses, the online world was flooded with pornographic videos, many of them viewable at no cost to the consumer. As might be expected, this abundance had a dampening effect on the established commercial pornographic film industry, reducing the number of commercial films released and driving down salaries for those in the industry.[15]

In ways that are perhaps predictably, perhaps disturbingly, similar to what happened in the pornography industry, those in the library profession have seen some of their professional skills black-boxed by digital technologies. In the year 1990, using the print-format *Science Citation Index* to track citations of a scholarly article was, for the average person, all but impossible without the assistance of a reference librarian; in the present day, using the digital *Web of Knowledge* to carry out the same task is hardly more difficult than doing a Google search. In the United States of 1990, obtaining the addresses and phone numbers of, say, dry-cleaning shops in Marseille, France, very likely required visiting a substantial research library and enlisting the aid of a professional librarian; in 2013, Googling "dry cleaners marsille [*sic*]" retrieves (in spite of the spelling mistake) a Yelp page giving phone numbers, addresses, and customer reviews of dozens of Marseille dry cleaners. Of course Yelp itself is just one example of thousands of crowd-sourced reference tools that rely on amateurs to supply and update the bulk of the content. Want to learn how to install a wood floor? Visit the crowd-sourced Wikihow.com. Trying to settle an argument about who played Lara Antipova in David Lean's *Doctor Zhivago*? Visit the crowd-sourced *Internet Movie Database*. Looking for a recipe for mango chutney? Visit the crowd-sourced Cooks.com.

It is not just the library's reference professionals who find themselves black-boxed. If in the digital age you should wish to build a personal collection of older or esoteric printed books, you are unlikely to need the services of a professional bibliographer. Websites like Amazon, Alibris, and a host of highly specialized online booksellers allow anyone with Internet access and a credit card to track down and purchase all but the most elusive of books. Indeed, some bibliophiles complain that the Web has taken all the fun out of the hunt for rare and out-of-print books. Of course once you amass a nice collection of books you will want to catalog them. How? Why not do it yourself with LibraryThing, a free, Web-based cataloging tool that black-boxes many skills of a library cataloger and introduces the value of crowd-sourced metadata into the mix?

No, the various digital black boxes have not entirely eliminated the need for librarians any more than crowd-sourcing has eliminated professionally produced reference resources, but digital technologies have made those in need of information less dependent on the assistance of librarians as well as less dependent on the standard works of the library reference-collection canon. This change is, in many ways, similar to the way that the flood of free video has made those who seek out pornography less dependent on the professionally produced version of that commodity. Whether you are a weaver, a director of pornographic films, or a librarian, the black-boxing of skills you may have spent years honing is a disturbing prospect.

Commodification

A veteran pornographic film star, bemoaning the downturn in her industry, was quoted as saying that pornography in the digital age has become "like potato chips, everywhere and cheap, to be consumed and tossed."[16] In economic terms, information (including the form of information known as pornography) is being treated, increasingly, as a commodity—a product for which there is a demand but for which there is no qualitative difference among suppliers. Consider a bag of ice of the type that is commonly sold in grocery and convenience stores. For most customers it does not matter if the brand of ice is Penguin's Pride or Sparkle Lake—a bag of ice is a bag of ice and for this reason is treated as a commodity. To use another economic term, a bag of ice has full *fungibility*—the market values each bag of ice equally regardless of who produced it. For commodity products, the main factor that enters into a purchasing decision is price (which includes the labor expended in making a purchase). Similarly, in a world of commodified online information, consumers care more about the price (including the labor required) of accessing information than they do about brand. To state the patently obvious, two big attractions of online information are that much of it is free (at least to the end user), and the labor required to access it is minimal compared to accessing information in physical formats. So long as the information that consumers access meets their needs, they will tend to treat it as a commodity.

But is information truly a commodity? Not in the strictest sense. Commodities like a bag of ice, an ounce of platinum, or a barrel of corn syrup have full fungibility. A product such as a bag of potato chips is less fungible due to such factors as consumer brand and flavor preferences; even so, a bag of chips is still much more a commodity than, say, an original oil painting or a three-bedroom house. Like potato chips, information is not fully fungible—some information is more complete, more authoritative, more up to date, or better formatted than other information—yet information has enough fungibility that, for a consumer of information who is willing to settle for good enough, information seems more like a commodity than not. If you are trying to determine the name of the author of *Robinson Crusoe*, the Wikipedia entry is certainly good enough. If, on the other hand, you are trying to develop a thesis about Daniel Defoe's contemporary impact as a pamphleteer versus his impact as a novelist, you would be well-advised to consult a broader array of sources.

In a world of commodified information—or at least a world in which the sheer volume of available information causes consumers to see it as a commodity—the worst-case scenario is the information-literacy nightmare in which zombified hordes accept as credible whatever piece of information rises to the top of their Web search results, giving no more thought to the reliability of the information they encounter than they give to the type of oil (West Texas Intermediate? Brent Blend? Dubai-Oman? Tapis? Midway Sunset?) used to manufacture the gasoline that powers their automobile. Conversely, it may be that the abundance of online information has led to a growing recognition that not all information can be trusted. The ironic phrase, "I read it on the Internet, so it must be true," has become a popular meme that can be found on web pages, greeting cards, posters, and T-shirts. Everyone gets the joke except, perhaps, for the clueless grandpa who continually forwards chain e-mails about the sick child trying to set a world record for the most get-well cards—assuming, of course, that Clueless Grandpa still exists as anything more than an ongoing Internet meme. The idea that you cannot trust everything you find on the Internet has entered the popular consciousness to the extent that it is now a topic for popular films and television programs, stand-up comedy routines, scholarly and popular articles, blogs, Tweets, and watercooler conversations. People in the information-abundant digital age may well be more skeptical than ever about the credibility of the information they encounter in their daily lives, including information that comes from professionally produced sources, the authority of which was, at one time, accepted almost without question.

Lessons Learned

Of course librarians are not pornographers. (In spite of what some of their opponents in censorship debates might believe.) And of course libraries are not in the business of profiting from the information they make available to their customers. Even so, the business strategies employed by the pornography industry provide librarians with clues for how to survive, and perhaps thrive, in the digital age. One key to unlocking these clues is to consider how the pornography industry has put its spin on the four most common ways of making money (which is to say, surviving) in the online environment:

1. Selling physical products that are subsequently delivered to customers.
2. Selling digital products that customers can access immediately.

3. Selling advertising space on high-traffic websites.
4. Engaging in illegal activities.

Prior to the digital age, pornographic businesses made most of their money by creating and selling physical products, chiefly films and printed publications. Like thousands of other online retailers, pornographers have used the Web as a digital catalog to market their stock-in-trade physical-format products. While this traditional business model still has a role in the pornography industry, it is on the decline. Formerly an industry-leading company, Playboy lost millions by continuing to pour the bulk of its resources into traditional business models centered on the sale of physical-format products while failing to reinvent its brand for the digital marketplace.[17]

Selling information in physical formats is rapidly ceding the field to charging for immediate access to online digital pornography, a business model that dates back to the pre-Web pornographic bulletin-board services and continues today in the form of pornographic websites that charge access fees. As perhaps the first industry to sell digital products directly over a computer network, pornographers blazed a retail trail followed (in all cases belatedly; in some, reluctantly) by the mainstream music, film, video-game, software, and publishing industries. The pornography industry discovered early on that "uninhibited by previous barriers of time and space, cybersex—electronic pornography—is an economist's ideal free good: pornography is easily accessible, incurs minimum transaction costs and enjoys seemingly unlimited demand."[18] Another thing the pornography industry discovered early on was that their "ideal free good" lent itself to the exploitation of niche markets. While the pornography industry had always produced films and publications that cater to highly specific interests, the online environment allowed for specialization to an extent unimaginable under the limitations of physical formats. Thus the not entirely implausible Rule 34.

The pornography industry was also an innovator in making a profit from user-generated content. When services like Flickr (launched February 2004), YouTube (launched May 2005), and Twitter (launched July 2006) debuted as tools for accessing, respectively, user-generated images, videos, and tweets (hello again, telegraph), they were only doing what pornographic websites had been doing for years. Among the most popular of all sites on the Web are pornographic "tube sites" offering vast amounts of free streaming media, much of it user generated.[19] While mainstream sites that feature user-generated content rely on advertising as a major source of income, the advertising opportunities for pornographic websites are more limited because mainstream businesses are unwilling to risk the consumer backlash that comes from being associated with pornography. For this reason, display advertising on pornographic websites is generally limited to ads for pornography; however, many pornographic websites earn income by redirecting their visitors to other pornographic websites, a service for which they are paid a small bounty. Typically, websites that redirect visitors offer free access to user-supplied pornography and produce no content of their own, while the websites that pay bounties for redirects are those that charge fees to access their content.[20] These site-to-site referral systems are extensive, sophisticated, and demonstrate a level of inter-business cooperation that seems improbable for an industry with a reputation for mercenary pursuit of profits. A study conducted in 2010 found some pornographic websites participating in more than one hundred different programs that provide rewards for redirects.[21] Another way in which pornographic websites profit from user-supplied content is by offering soft-core pornography for free while charging for more explicit "premium" content; in these scenarios, the free content serves as a loss leader for premium content. One site that uses such a business model is reported to have 1 million subscribers who pay $25 per year for premium access to user-generated content—content for which the website itself pays nothing.[22]

A factor working against the success of online pornography is customer fear that those involved in the shady, if not outright illegal, business of pornography might not scruple at engaging in business practices ranging from the questionable to the criminal. One of the attractions of online pornography is the (apparent) anonymity it provides, so the idea of being exposed as a consumer of online pornography as a result of identity theft, credit-card fraud, or even blackmail is nearly as strong a deterrent as is the fear of being ripped off. The risk of encountering malicious code on a pornographic website is yet another deterrent to potential customers. A team of academic researchers reports that of 269,566 pornographic web pages in their data set, "3.23% were found to trigger malicious behavior such as code execution, registry changes, or executable downloads," a significantly higher rate than for the Web at large.[23] To put it mildly, the online pornography industry has some serious trust issues to overcome.

If those are the clues, what are the lessons to be learned from this peculiar information industry with its long history of being ahead of the technological curve?

Vanishing Physical Formats

If the pornography industry is truly a harbinger of technological change, then its rapid abandonment of physical formats, principally magazines and DVD/Blu-ray discs, strongly suggests that mainstream information in physical formats is heading toward irrelevance more rapidly than most are willing to believe. That said, one factor that may be accelerating pornography's rush toward an all-digital environment is a strong customer preference for the perceived anonymity of online information. Anonymity is, in general, far more important to consumers of pornography than to consumers of mainstream information.

User-Generated Content

As it has been for the pornography industry, user-generated content will become increasingly important to libraries. For academic and special libraries, this will mean devoting increasingly larger percentages of their resources to the curation of text and data resulting from the work of students, faculty, and researchers. To varying degrees academic and special libraries are already embracing their role as data curators and finding that, in spite of the many technological challenges, this role is not that much of a departure from their traditional function as institutional archives. For public libraries, leveraging user-generated content will mean serving as "community publishing portals" to aid local content creators in producing and disseminating quality self-published digital works.[24] In the words of public-library director Jamie LaRue, "Libraries are producing not just books, but exhibits of scanned photographs, correspondence, and newspapers, not to mention music and video. We're not just the end of distribution line, we are, increasingly, partners and content co-creators ourselves."[25] From a service perspective, ever increasing amounts of user-generated/library-curated information will require librarians to take on the challenge of helping library customers discover and access all that information.

Premium Content

For all libraries, digitizing and making freely available their own versions of premium content—the unique items from their archives and special collections—will ensure that libraries remain relevant in spite of the commodification of information and the twilight of the physical information object. Standing in the way of this opportunity are outmoded notions of special-collections and archival materials as quasi-private property to be selectively doled out to the worthy few while remaining invisible—and inaccessible—to the great unwashed. In some cases aggressive proprietorship of unique library collections is made worse by highly restrictive donor agreements or by a library's desire to generate revenue by charging for derivative uses of unique library materials. While it may be true that a library can legally extract a permission fee from a creator who wants to use an item from its special collections in a derivative work, is the long-term value of those dollars greater than the value of having library materials featured in works that explicitly demonstrate the value of a library as a public good? In light of the growing importance of user-generated content, is it really a good thing when library permission fees frustrate amateur content creators who wish to incorporate images held in a special collection into, say, a local history or guidebook? How do the dollars that come from charging for the use of library archival sound recordings compare to the value of having one of those recordings used in a documentary video that could end up being seen by thousands? By millions?

Niche Markets

The pornography industry has demonstrated that niche markets have a place in the online world, and this holds true for libraries as well. Say, for example, that a public library plays a part in creating, disseminating, and preserving a solidly written and assembled local history comprised of digital text, still images, video, and oral-history interviews. Even if this work is accessed only a handful of times over the course of many years, it should still be considered a success if its availability means that information needs that would otherwise go unmet are, in fact, met. Unlike works in physical formats, user-created digital works do not require large audiences to validate their existence. On principle alone, libraries should be willing to serve as community publishing portals for user-created digital works even if they may attract only niche audiences. Besides, gambling on long shots can sometimes pay off. In the online world there is no telling what seemingly niche creation will suddenly go viral and run up millions of hits.

Cooperation

If websites in the for-profit world of pornography can flourish by operating "on a model of mutual support that would make an Amish community proud,"[26] libraries can certainly do the same. This is not to say that libraries do not cooperate, as they most certainly do. Libraries deserve credit for their pursuit of shared collection-development policies; for developing shared print and digital repositories (e.g., Western Regional Storage Trust and HathiTrust, respectively); and for their emerging efforts to share subject expertise and meta-data services. But libraries can always improve their cooperation. In the area of physical information objects, libraries could be much more liberal about what they will lend via interlibrary loan (ILL). Practices like unilaterally declaring large swaths of a collection ineligible for ILL are antithetical to cooperation, especially when much of what is declared ineligible is not heavily used, unique, irreplaceable, or even especially valuable (in the antiques or collectibles sense). Considering the importance of leveraging premium content, libraries should be far more willing to lend special-collections materials than they have been in the past, especially since there are well-established guidelines for doing so.[27] There is undeniably something wrong when a scholar is forced to travel across the country because a library's special-collections unit will not lend a *microfilm* copy of manuscript letters in its collection.* In addition, ILL cooperation would be enhanced by practices as simple as increasing the length of ILL loan periods or as innovative as allowing an ILL item to remain (once the customer is done with it) at the borrowing library rather than automatically, and perhaps unnecessarily, shipping it back to the lending library. Similarly, as libraries take on larger roles in the creation, dissemination, and preservation of unique digital content, they must rigorously avoid siloing or restricting access to the point that digital content is impossible to discover or use.

---

* This actually happened to a scholar of the author's acquaintance. To put the worst possible face on it, (1) the microfilm the library would not lend was a second copy, not the master; (2) the library owned both the master microfilm and the original manuscript copies of the letters, so *if* the second-copy microfilm never returned, it would not have been an irredeemable loss; (3) because the letters were the public correspondence of a university president and over one hundred years old, there were no donor or privacy restrictions preventing the lending of the microfilm.

Trust

Libraries are miles ahead of the pornography industry when it comes to maintaining the trust of their customers, but they still must do everything they can to maintain and, ideally, enhance the level of trust they enjoy. (See chapter 7, "Designing Websites: Trust and Flow.")

CONCLUSION

Two contrasting stories have arisen to describe the economics of pornography in the digital age. The first story tells of how the potato-chip abundance of online pornography—much of it created by people with no connection to the commercial pornography establishment—has disrupted the pornography industry's business model. This story of disruption conforms closely to the story of what has happened to every other form of established media since the advent of Napster, wikis, blogs, digital self-publishing, fan fiction, iTunes, YouTube, Pinterest, Twitter, and whatever comes next. Just as the once-dominant magazines and film-production companies of the pornography industry have been left behind by their failure to adjust to the new digital marketplace, the solidly mainstream *Encyclopedia Britannica* nearly went under due to competition from, first, CD-ROM encyclopedias and, later, a host of free online information sources—notably Wikipedia.[28] If the harsh lesson of potato-chip abundance is to be believed, then the information barbarians are at the gates and the information gatekeepers had best go hunt their hiding places.

But librarians should be focusing on a different story, the story of the successes achieved by digital innovators who happen to bear the ignominy of being part of the pornography industry. Rather than being overwhelmed by challenges to old business models and systems of distribution, these innovators find ways to prosper. At the most basic level the key to their success is the ability, even willingness, to accept the realities of information in the digital age rather than struggle against them. It turns out that repeating the phrase, "This can't be happening," is no better a business/survival strategy than is insisting that the *Titanic* is unsinkable while standing knee-deep in icy saltwater. When existing business models prove obsolete, these innovators create new business models that lend themselves to the here-and-now digital reality. When user-generated content flooded the market, they found ways to profit from it. When new technologies emerge, they quickly adapt them to their business needs. As unsavory, in some cases repellent, as the digital pornographer's products may be, their collective business success is impressive. They may be among the cockroaches of the information business, but like cockroaches they survive and flourish where other creatures wither and die. If those who work in libraries wish to see their organizations thrive, they could do worse than to follow the innovative examples of the industry that, at first blush, seems a most unlikely source for inspiration.

NOTES

1. Paul Van Dyke, "Pietro Aretino," in *Renaissance Portraits*, ed. Paul Van Dyke, 33–137, Charles Scribner's Sons, 1905; Rpt. in *Literature Criticism from 1400 to 1800*, ed. James P. Draper and James E. Person Jr., vol. 12 (Detroit: Gale Research, 1990), *Literature Resource Center*, http://go.galegroup.com/ps/i.do?id=GALE%7CH1 420010574&v=2.1&u=ucmerced&it=r&p=LitRG&sw=w&asid=d8cbdf437ed8622741 e98cd2eeb69a4b (accessed February 28, 2014).

2. Jonathan Coopersmith, "Pornography, Technology, and Progress," *Icon* 4 (1998): 99.

3. Simon Brown, "Early Cinema in Britain and the Smoking Concert," *Early Popular Visual Culture* 3, no. 2 (2005): 167.

4. Adam Bresnick, "Wired Victorians," *Forbes* 162, no. 6 (September 21, 1998): 287.

5. Frederick E. Allen, "When Sex Drives Technological Innovation," *American Heritage* 51, no. 5 (September 2000): 19.

6. Allen, "When Sex Drives Technological Innovation," 19.

7. Richard Cole, "Crackdown Launched on Computerized International Child Porn Ring," Associated Press, March 4, 1993.

8. Doug Bedell, "Unlikely Innovators—Many Online Technologies Were First Perfected by the Adult Industry," *Dallas Morning News*, April 26, 2001, 1F.

9. Philip Elmer-DeWitt and Hannah Bloch, "On a Screen Near You: Cyberporn," *Time* 146, no. 1 (July 3, 1995): 38.

10. Jared Sandberg, "Electronic Erotica: Too Much Traffic," *Wall Street Journal— Eastern Edition* 225, no. 27 (February 8, 1995): B1.

11. Joseph Galante, Kristen Schweizer, and Jim Aley, "Meet the King of Dot-XXX," *Bloomberg Businessweek* no. 4186 (July 5, 2010): 38.

12. "Internet Pornography Statistics," Top Ten Reviews, http://internet-filter-review.toptenreviews.com/internet-pornography-statistics.html (accessed May 8, 2013).

13. Institute of Museum and Library Services, *Public Libraries Survey Fiscal Year 2006* (Washington, DC: Institute of Museum and Library Services [IMLS], 2008), 58.

14. Bruno Latour, *Pandora's Hope: Essays on the Reality of Science Studies* (Cambridge, MA: Harvard University Press, 1999), 174–215.

15. James Cowan, "Sex Isn't Selling," *Canadian Business* 83, no. 15 (September 27, 2010): 26–30.

16. "Hard Times," *Economist* 392, no. 8648 (September 12, 2009): 35.

17. Russell Adams, "Playboy, Posting Loss, Says It Would Consider Sale," *Wall Street Journal*, February 19, 2009, B8.

18. Jonathan Coopersmith, "Does Your Mother Know What You Really Do? The Changing Nature and Image of Computer-Based Pornography," *History & Technology* 22, no. 1 (March 2006): 2.

19. Scott Fayner, "Down the Tubes," *Technology Review* 113, no. 5 (September 2010): 103–105.

20. Gilbert Wondracek, Thorsten Holz, Christian Platzer, Engin Kirda, and Christopher Kruegel, "Is the Internet for Porn? An Insight into the Online Adult Industry," *Ninth Workshop on the Economics of Information Security*, Boston, June 7–8, 2010, 6–7.

21. Wondracek, "Is the Internet for Porn?," 6.

22. Fabio D'Orlando, "The Demand for Pornography," *Journal of Happiness Studies* 12, no. 1 (March 2011): 54.

23. Wondracek, "Is the Internet for Porn?," 8.

24. Mark Coker, "Libraries to Become Community Publishing Portals," *Huffington Post*, March 28, 2013, http://www.huffingtonpost.com/mark-coker/library-ebooks_b_2951953.html (February 14, 2014).

25. Jamie LaRue, "All Hat, No Cattle," *Library Journal* 137, no. 13 (June 20, 2012), http://www.thedigitalshift.com/2012/06/ebooks/all-hat-no-cattle-a-call-for-libraries-to-transform-before-its-too-late (accessed February 14, 2014).

26. Coopersmith, "Does Your Mother Know What You Really Do?," 8.

27. Association of College and Research Libraries/Rare Books and Manuscripts Section, "Guidelines for the Interlibrary Loan of Rare and Unique Materials," American Library Association, http://www.ala.org/acrl/standards/rareguidelines (accessed June 5, 2013).

28. Jorge Cauz, "Encyclopædia Britannica's President on Killing Off a 244-Year-Old Product," *Harvard Business Review* 91, no. 3 (March 2013): 39–42.

4

Understanding the Self-Service Experience in the Online Environment

A script followed in most North American fast-food restaurants goes like this:

Customer orders and pays for a soft drink.

Counterperson hands over an empty cup.

Customer prepares a drink using a publicly accessible beverage fountain.

In convenience stores, the script varies slightly: the customer chooses a cup and fills it before paying. Bring your own cup and get a small discount. While the self-service beverage script is now familiar, the practice did not really catch on until the 1980s. For example, nearly half of the Burger King restaurant chain's six thousand restaurants still did not have self-service beverage fountains by the middle of 1989.[1] The business logic behind the move to self-service beverages was simple enough: save on labor costs by having customers do some of the work of preparing their fast-food meals. This self-service model proved to be a huge success, spawning a small revolution in the food-service industry.

It is easy to imagine, though, the howls of protest that must have wailed forth from some corners of the food-service world when the notion of self-service beverages was first put forward:

- Endless, uncontrolled refills will swallow up profits.
- Nobody will buy medium or large-sized drinks if they can refill a small cup as often as they wish.
- Customers will waste soda and ice.
- They won't be able to work the machines.
- They will complain about having to fill their own drinks.
- They will sneak in their own containers and rob us blind.
- Self-service beverages is the first step down a slippery slope that will eventually eliminate food-service jobs.

While all of the above concerns were realistic, and while it is likely that each of them came to pass to some extent, in the end none of the anticipated ills manifested on a scale large enough to stop the march of the self-service beverage juggernaut. Although there is not as yet any published scholarly data on the labor savings the fast-food industry enjoys from self-service beverages, a scholarly study of self-service beverage fountains in buffet restaurants finds that statistically significant benefits accrue when soda service is taken out of the hands of restaurant staff and turned over to customers.[2]

Besides saving labor costs, it turns out that nearly all customers like preparing their own drinks.[3] With self-service, customers get their drinks more quickly than when they have to wait for a server; in addition, customers have a small task to keep themselves occupied while their food is being prepared, thereby making the waiting time seem shorter than it actually is. Self-service eliminates the problem of counterpersons mixing up drink orders and empowers customers to add as much or as little ice to their drinks as they wish. Too little or too much ice, it turns out, is a major source of customer complaints in the food-service industry. Self-service allows children (and probably more than a few adults) to indulge in experiments involving the mixing of various flavors of soda. While self-service beverages may be a far cry from a white-tablecloth, fine-dining experience, by and large the public has taken to the concept and never looked back.

Although it provides a convenient and notable example, beverage service is hardly a pioneer in the world of self-service technology. In 1916 Piggly Wiggly became the first grocery store in which customers freely roamed the aisles to fill their own orders rather than handing a shopping list to a clerk. Other successful self-service technologies (SSTs) from the world of business

HALF MEASURES

At the same time that Burger King was busy converting its restaurants to self-service beverages, the Hardee's hamburger chain was testing (in twenty-five of its more than three thousand stores) an automated beverage-dispensing system. When a counterperson entered a drink order into the cash register, an automatic beverage dispenser selected a cup of the proper size, filling it with ice and the beverage of choice. A conveyor belt then moved the filled cup to the counterperson who capped the drink and gave it to the customer.* While the intended outcome of the conveyor-belt beverage system—reduced labor costs—was identical to that of the self-serve system, it left final control of the beverage in the hands of an employee rather than the customer. In this way the conveyor-belt system was a half measure, and, like many half measures, it never succeeded. The unwillingness to risk giving customers full control was the system's downfall.

When facing the prospect of a truly paradigm-changing innovation, organizations too often stop at half measures—or less—because they think too much about the possible bad effects of change and not enough about the potential benefits. It is perhaps understandable for libraries to give more weight to potentially bad effects than to good because for libraries, unlike commercial businesses, the rewards (additional income/resources) that come with increased efficiency are at best deferred and at worst never materialize, while the pain (resistance from customers and staff) that comes from introducing any change in the status quo is immediate. Just because the library's conservatism is understandable does not mean it is justified, however, and libraries that take risks in the interest of doing more with less will, in the long run, be better off than those that always play it safe.

---

*Ken Frydman, Brian Sill, and Richard Martin, "Equipment Solutions to Combat the Effects of a Shrinking Labor Pool, Operators Are Looking to Efficient, High-Tech Equipment to Minimize Labor While Maximizing Productivity," *Nation's Restaurant News*, May 22, 1989, 20.

include vending machines, self-service gasoline, buffet and cafeteria-style restaurants, automated teller machines, and retail self-checkout systems. Of all
the revolutions in self-service, the most notable has to be that brought about
by the widespread availability of online shopping and services (including library services) made possible via the Web. Self-service pervades the physical
and virtual modern world and is, for the most part, well accepted whenever
the convenience and/or perceived sense of control outweigh any associated
negatives. For example, while the negatives of using online banking services
are real—there is a learning curve, it requires some effort, it exposes one to
the risk of cybercrime—the convenience and sense of control that come from
being able to manage accounts from any Internet-enabled device have made
online services the most popular innovation in consumer banking since the
automated teller machine (ATM), itself a revolutionary self-service technology. For another example, doing your own grocery shopping requires more
effort than handing a list to a clerk, but this effort is offset by the perceived
sense of control that comes with being able to browse the aisles and choose
exactly which bag of cookies or package of cheese goes into your shopping
cart. Incidentally, the technology of the wheeled shopping cart, which was
not introduced until twenty-one years after the first Piggly Wiggly opened its
doors, greatly increased the convenience of self-service grocery stores, relieving shoppers of the burden of carrying purchases in a handbasket as well as allowing (and quite possibly encouraging) shoppers to purchase more items in
a single trip. In the twenty-first century many grocery stores (and a growing
number of libraries) offer the option of self-checkout, a form of self-service
that has yet to gain universal acceptance. Whether self-check eventually re-
places traditional checkout service or remains an adjunct will likely depend
on how convenient it can be made by the technologies that power it.

Every new self-service technology tends to draw its share of criticism
when it is launched. In some cases the criticism dries up over time. Although customers still complain about ATM fees, acceptance of the ATM
itself is close to universal, in large part because ATM technology works
flawlessly very close to 100 percent of the time. In other cases, the criticism never stops. Even after decades of use, automated answering systems
("Press 1 for hours. Press 2 for directions. Press 3 to access your account
. . .") continue to be both a source of complaints and fodder for stand-up
comedians. The aversion to automated answering systems is so great that

some companies with strong customer-service orientations attempt to distinguish themselves from their competition by advertising that callers will be able to "talk to a real person" rather than being shunted into touch-tone purgatory. (The fact that the said real person may be located in a different hemisphere than the customer is an entirely different source of complaints and comedy stylings.)

It should come as no surprise, then, that when a new self-service technology is introduced into a library setting there will be expressions of skepticism, if not outright hostility, on the part of at least some library employees and customers. While it is necessary to be skeptical of any proposed innovation, it is a mistake to assume that self-service is, by its very nature, automatically inferior to a service provided by a human intermediary or that the introduction of a self-service technology somehow cheats customers by denying them a complete library experience. The library online public-access catalog (OPAC) is clearly a self-service tool, yet the search experience it provides blows away any service that could be provided by a human intermediary.

A related argument holds that self-service is antithetical to library traditions of service; however, self-service is hardly a new concept in libraries. Near the end of the nineteenth century, the newly introduced card catalog was a tremendous innovation in library self-service, allowing the average person to independently identify and locate books in even a very large library collection. Although the card catalog came with a learning curve, once mastered it offered the twin self-service virtues of convenience (it was far more efficient that thumbing through bound lists of books owned by a library) and control (individuals could use the card catalog to find books without asking a librarian for help). The self-service technology of the card catalog in turn fostered the spread of browsable open stacks, yet another self-service technology that has served libraries and their customers well for generations. (As iconic as browsable stacks may be, it is likely that few champions of the "traditional library" are aware that closed stacks, in which browsing was unknown, were the norm prior to—and in more than a few libraries, decades into—the twentieth century.) Besides the card catalog and open stacks, the library is or has been home to many other self-service technologies, including such long-standing library staples as copy machines, map cases, micro-format readers, subject guides, and computer commons. Because library customers are the same people who take advantage of all the self-service technologies filling the everyday world, it is hard to argue that employing effective self-service technologies in the library setting is a disservice.

FACTORS OF SELF-SERVICE SUCCESS: THE CUSTOMER'S POINT OF VIEW

As mentioned above, convenience and perceived sense of control are two factors that determine whether or not a self-service technology succeeds with customers. Both *convenience* and perceived *control* are broad concepts that require elaboration.

Convenience

A number of factors influence whether or not a customer finds a self-service technology to be convenient:

Time

Self-service is convenient if doing something yourself is significantly faster than having someone else do it for you. Using a self-check system becomes attractive if doing so will get you on your way more quickly than standing in line to wait for a clerk; on the other hand, when there are no lines, having a clerk check you out could be the more attractive option. Another time-related convenience factor is the immediacy of many self-service technologies. Customers are likely to use self-service technologies when doing so can meet—or is the only way to meet—an immediate need. The classic library example is the night-owl student who accesses online journal articles in order to finish a paper that is due the following morning.

Learning Curve

Self-service technologies that are easy to master and use are more convenient than those with steep learning curves. One reason for the success of Google is that any literate person can pull off a reasonably productive Google search with no training or practice.

Geographical Independence

A self-service technology that requires a customer to go to a specific location is less convenient than one that does not. A trip to an ATM is often more convenient than a trip to the bank, but paying with a check or a card (debit or credit) requires no trip at all.

Asynchronicity

A self-service technology that can be used at any time (for example, twenty-four-hour self-service gas) is more convenient than one that can only be used during limited hours.

Cost

Cost can be, but is not always, a factor in choosing a self-service option. Gas stations offering a choice between self-service and full-service gasoline charge a premium for full service. For some customers, the convenience of having an attendant fill their tank is worth the extra cost; however, the fact that the full-service gas option has largely disappeared suggests that most customers would rather pocket the savings that come with doing it themselves. Conversely, when it is the self-service option that comes with a price tag, as when using an out-of-system ATM, the added cost can become a deterrent to using self-service.

Hurdles

Anything that constitutes a hurdle reduces the convenience of a self-service technology. In the online world, unreliable systems, poor feedback mechanisms, bad user-interface designs, poorly worded instructions, poor website navigability, pop-up boxes, click-through agreements, passwords, requirements to download special software or browser plug-ins, requests to provide personal data, and restrictive conditions of use are all examples of hurdles that discourage the use of online self-service tools.

Perceived Sense of Control

The phenomenon of perceived sense of control has been widely studied by environmental psychologists. The general consensus is, perhaps unsurprisingly, that individuals' perceived control of any situation mediates their response, with greater perceived control resulting in more satisfaction with the situation.[4] An extreme, but somewhat common, example is people who fear flying because they perceive they have no control over the factors that determine their safety in the air: weather, pilots, air-traffic control, airline security, maintenance personnel, and aircraft manufacturers.

Success

For any self-service technology, successful completion of a task or attainment of a goal increases the perception of control. If customers can successfully fill their gas tank, purchase just the right pair of shoes from an online store, or seek out and download a highly relevant journal article, they will feel in control of the situation. Conversely, self-service technologies that produce high rates of failure take away customers' perceived sense of control, often to the point where they give up in frustration.

Privacy

Because self-service technologies give customers the feeling (not always justified by the facts) that whatever they are purchasing, reading, or viewing remains their own business, these technologies can contribute to a perceived sense of control. For example, a library customer who needs to read *Mein Kampf* for reasons having nothing to do with admiration for the author or his belief system might genuinely appreciate a self-check system that does not require presenting a copy of so controversial a book to a human clerk.

Time

While saving time increases the convenience of a self-service technology, it is the possibility of taking as much time as you like that increases the perceived sense of control. When shopping online, for example, customers feel in control because they can take as much time as they wish to read descriptions and reviews, view images, and compare prices with no eager salesperson or exasperated next customer in line pressuring them into a hasty decision.

FACTORS OF SELF-SERVICE SUCCESS: THE BUSINESS CASE

The business case for self-service boils down to two somewhat obvious factors: savings and customer satisfaction.

Savings

From a business perspective, self-service technologies must produce cost savings to be successful. The simple idea is that self-service technology allows customers to perform for free at least some of the labor that employees do for pay. In a 2006 survey, the cost of a Web-based self-service transaction ($0.24) was found to be an order of magnitude less than the cost of a call to a live customer-service representative ($5.50).[5] In addition, self-service technologies substitute unpredictable labor costs (How many hours of public-service staffing do we need on Saturday afternoons in July? On Tuesday mornings in October?) with predictable technology costs.[6] It is important to note that self-service does not automatically ensure that there will be cost savings. If a self-service technology requires constant babysitting by information-technology staff, or if it produces a high number of errors that must be corrected by customer-service staff, the end result could be increased staff time per transaction, which of course means increased costs for the organization.

Customer Satisfaction

With a successful self-service technology, customers find doing it themselves to be so convenient, and perceive so strong a sense of control, that they come to prefer self-service to human-mediated options. In fact, the ease and convenience of a successful online self-service technology may lead to a "volume effect" in which any labor savings are wiped out (or worse) due to increased demand.[7] For example, a study of a health-insurance company's Web-based self-service technology found that allowing customers to access information online led to a 14 percent increase in phone calls to the company, though the study also found that when the self-service technology provides unambiguous information that customers can easily find, it reduces the volume of calls by 29 percent.[8] In the library world the convenience of online self-service interlibrary loan (ILL) requests has increased the volume of ILL requests as compared to older ILL models which, in most cases, require the customer to come to the library during business hours and submit paper-based forms to a staff member.

If the volume effect is an unwelcome fallout from the implementation of a self-service technology, even more unwelcome is the possibility that customers prefer self-service because it allows them to avoid staff whom they perceive as unhelpful or even hostile. To quote the somewhat understated language of Meuter et al., "That some customers perceive frontline employees as a nuisance to be avoided highlights the hiring and training problems that some service organizations may currently be experiencing."[9]

THE IKEA EFFECT

It seems like common sense to assume that a self-service technology that off-loads too much of the labor onto the customer will be more likely to fail than a technology that demands less effort. After all, while salad bars (which require a minimum of customer labor) are common, restaurants in which customers cook their own steaks remain (oh dear) rare. However, the authors of "The IKEA Effect: When Labor Leads to Love" come to a seemingly contradictory conclusion about self-service labor, namely that putting significant labor into a do-it-yourself task increases the customer's love of the final result.[*] The findings of "The IKEA Effect" echo earlier research which finds that for some customers "participating more in the production of the service is intrinsically attractive."[†]

While these findings suggests that compelling customers to work for their reward is not a deal breaker, the authors of "The IKEA Effect" caution that customers do not feel any love when they are unsuccessful at completing a do-it-yourself task. If the conclusions of the authors are correct, the lesson for anyone implementing a self-service technology is that it is fine to require labor from the customers so long as this labor leads to tangible success.

---

[*]Michael I. Norton, Daniel Mochon, and Dan Ariely, "The IKEA Effect: When Labor Leads to Love," *Journal of Consumer Psychology* 22, no. 3 (July 2012): 458–459.

[†]J. E. G. Bateson, "Self-Service Consumer: An Exploratory Study," *Journal of Retailing* 61, no. 3 (Fall 1985): 73–74.

TYPES OF SELF-SERVICE . . . AND TYPES OF SERVICE FAILURES

In their seminal year-2000 article on self-service technologies, Meuter et al. identify three types of self-service.[10] While the authors provide illustrative examples of self-service drawn from the business world, it is easy to think of illustrative examples from the library world (see table 4.1).

To illustrate types of self-service failures, Meuter et al. draw examples from the business world; pertinent examples can also be drawn from the library world (see table 4.2).

Table 4.1.

Type of Self-Service	Library Examples
Customer Service	• Library hours • Account information • Status of a request
Transactions	• Interlibrary loan request • Hold/recall request • Room reservation
Self–Help	• Subject guides • Tutorials • Frequently asked questions (FAQs)

When planning the implementation of any kind of self-service, first identifying the type of service (customer service, transaction, or self-help) goes a long way toward deciding how to develop the service to best meet customer needs. If, for example, the type of self-service is a transaction, it is very likely that the starting point, and bulk of the work, will involve finding or creating the appropriate digital technology to make the transaction run correctly every time. If on the other hand the type of service is self-help, the starting point, and bulk of the work, is more likely to involve developing the content (text, images, videos, tutorials, etc.) that will allow customers to effectively help themselves.

Table 4.2.

Type of Self-Service Failure	Library Examples
Technology Failure	• Library website, catalog, or databases are down.
Process Failure	• Request for item was never processed. • Request was filled with the wrong item. • An item that was returned is shown as still checked out.
Technology Design Problem	• Unclear instructions. • Poor feedback loop. • Website is difficult to navigate.
Service Design Problem	• Seemingly arbitrary limits on things like which types of items can be requested via interlibrary loan or length of borrowing privileges. • Failure to notify a customer that an item they requested is available for pickup.
Customer-Driven Failure	• Customer forgot password. • Customer believed they returned a book when they had not. • Customer gave the library the wrong e-mail contact information.

By the same token, when a self-service technology is not working well, identifying the cause of the failure is key. It makes no more sense to ask the library IT staff for a technological solution when the problem is, in fact, a service-design problem (e.g., poor how-to instructions on a web page) than it does to put the public-services staff through intensive training on how to deal with angry customers when the problem is a technology failure (e.g., the library mail server stopped notifying customers that their ILL items had arrived).

SELF-SERVICE IN THE ONLINE WORLD

In order for any self-service technology, virtual or physical, to be considered 100 percent successful, all customers should be able to use it entirely on their own. Achieving such a level of success, or coming as close to it as humanly possible, presents special challenges in the online world.

For self-service technologies in the physical world—things like photocopiers, vendacard machines, public-access computers, or printed subject guides—customers enjoy the advantage of having the object they wish to use right before their eyes in all its three-dimensional tactility. When using, say, a micro-format reader/copier, customers are in position to read adjacent instructional signage* and be guided by such cues as flashing warning lights (e.g. "Insert Vendacard"). A technologically advanced micro-format machine might guide customers via point-of-use digital help screens or by displaying short video tutorials. As a last resort, someone trying to use a micro-format machine might benefit from watching another customer use the machine or by asking for help from another customer or a staff member. The situation is more difficult in the virtual world where users of self-service technologies are denied many of the tactile cues and help options routinely available in the physical world. When using a virtual self-service technology, there are rarely shoulders to peek over or nearby others to ask; there may be automated online help features, and this online help may be quite sophisticated, but accessing it can be unintuitive or involve clumsy jumping back and forth between help features and the task at hand.

Another advantage enjoyed by customers of real-world self-service technologies is that most people bring with them scripts for how such technolo-

---

* Note that excessive signage is an indicator that a self-service technology is too difficult to use and needs to be redesigned or replaced.

gies work. The fast-food beverage script described at the start of this chapter is one example of such a script, but there are many others. Flash back to the days when pay phones were far more common than they are in the twenty-first century. Now flash further back to the days when pay phones did not accept cards—credit or pre-paid. In those days, most functional adults had in their heads the following mental script for using a pay phone:

1. Lift the receiver.
2. Listen for dial tone.
3. Put in coins.
4. Dial number.
5. Add more coins if directed to do so.

The script worked for almost any coin-operated pay phone and only failed when using a device that varied from the norm. For example, while the script as described worked well for North American pay phones, it did not work well with traditional pay phones in the United Kingdom where the script called for adding the coins only after being connected to the number you were calling, not before. North Americans visiting the United Kingdom had to learn a new script before they could use pay phones effectively, and of course the same was true for Britons visiting North America.

The problem in the virtual world is that self-service scripts are often neither as familiar nor as well established as those of the physical world. The script for using a candy machine is about the same as the script for using a soda machine as the script for using a coin-operated photocopier. In the on-line world the script for putting a hold on a library book via OPAC A may be quite different from the script for doing the same task via OPAC B, while the script for doing a Boolean AND search can vary wildly from OPAC to OPAC and database to database. When the phenomenon of the Web first started to take off in the 1990s, one of the difficulties new users faced was that they came to the Web without any familiar scripts to call upon. Even what few experienced Web users there were suffered from the fact that the early Web was short on scripts upon which one could rely. In his early *Alertbox* columns, pioneer Web-usability guru Jakob Nielsen often takes Web designers to task for such transgressions as using non-standard link colors or disabling browser back-arrow buttons because doing so undermined what few accepted scripts there were. As the Web matured, standard scripts began to emerge for certain activities. For example, most regular Web users in the early twenty-first century understand the script for establishing a customer account with a Web-based retailer or service provider:

1. Enter personal information: name, physical address, e-mail address, etc.
   a. Any fields marked with an asterisk are required.
2. Create a username.
3. Create a password.
4. Retype the password.
5. Uncheck (or not) the boxes that have you agreeing to receive unsolicited e-mails.
6. For some customer accounts:
   a. Establish one or more security questions (What was the name of your first pet?); and/or
   b. Type in a series of psychedelic letters to prove you are an actual human being; and/or
   c. Check your e-mail. Open the message from the site with which you just registered. Click the link that establishes your account.

Any online account-registration process that varies from the above script is likely to create confusion and reduce customer success—not to mention royally irritating current and potential customers. For anyone implementing an online self-service technology, the basic issues are clear:

- Customers using self-service technologies in the virtual world are at a disadvantage compared to customers in the physical world. Tasks that would be easy and obvious in the physical world are not necessarily so in the virtual world.
- The more a self-service technology can be designed to conform to, or at least resemble, existing scripts, the more likely it is to succeed. Familiarity may breed contempt, but it also breeds success.

WHEN SELF-SERVICE IS THE ONLY OPTION

What about situations in which self-service is the only option? A classic example is a company that forces customers to use an automated answering system with either no option of speaking to a live person or offering that option only as a deeply buried last resort. A more extreme example is the website that fails to provide any means of communication, whether that might be a phone number, an e-mail address, or an online form. Being forced to use a well-designed self-service technology need not be a bad customer experience, but being forced to use a poor self-service technology is infuriating, to a large extent because reaching a self-service dead end from which there is no obvious exit is the exact opposite of both convenience and a sense of perceived self-control. As common sense might lead you to expect, an empirical study conducted in 2012 found that "forced use" of self-service technology increased users' technology anxiety while increasing their distrust of technology.[11]

There are really only two scenarios in which organizations can get away with offering a self-service-only option. One scenario, and it is far from desirable, is when an organization is simply not afraid of losing customers, typically because it is a monopoly (e.g., a power company or the dreaded Department of Motor Vehicles) or wields extraordinary leverage over its customers (e.g., the customer is locked into a long-term contract or it is especially burdensome and time consuming to take one's business elsewhere). The other, more desirable scenario is when the self-service technology is so foolproof and performs so flawlessly that it meets the needs of nearly every customer.

While libraries may seem like monopolies in that they are rarely in direct competition with each other, they are usually in competition for support (moral as well as financial) from their various constituencies; few, if any, libraries can afford to alienate even small numbers of their customers. Sadly, if a library, or any other organization, provides services online, it will, sooner or later, find itself on the receiving end of a virulent, often profanity-enhanced, electronic message or online posting blasting the organization, its employees, and quite possibly the mothers and fathers of those employees. While frustrated customers can and do come unglued in the physical world, such explosions are more common in the virtual realm. One reason for such behavior is that the virtual world provides a feeling of anonymity that makes lashing out feel less risky than it does in the physical world. Also, while it requires some level of anger to start typing heated words on a keyboard and hitting "send," for most people it takes a much higher level of anger to get into the face of a human being who can and will visibly respond to angry words, intonations, and gestures. Even the disembodied voice of a living, breathing human being on the other end of a phone line can temper an angry response to an extent that an entirely automated online transaction cannot match.

Setting aside the complicated issue of professional cranks and the mentally imbalanced, the most likely cause of angry online outbursts among normally reasonable customers is frustration, specifically the double frustration of not being able to complete a task coupled with hitting a dead end that offers no guidance, next steps, or even any sympathy.

Say that a physical self-service technology, such as a coin/card-operated photocopier, malfunctions in a library. The customer may be frustrated at the malfunction, but an organization that follows sound customer-service practices is in a good position to recover from the service-delivery failure. When the customer reports the problem (something that should be easy to do), the organization responds immediately. Empty paper trays are filled. Jams are unjammed. An out-of-order sign goes up. A service technician is called. Lost money is refunded. Backs are patted and feathers smoothed.

Recovering from a service failure when a customer hits a dead end with an online self-service technology is far more difficult. The system rejects your password three times and then gives you a message telling you that you are locked out for an hour. The .pdf for the article you need to finish a paper that is due in the morning will not download. Absolutely nothing happens when you click the "submit" icon. It can be frustrating to the point of infuriation when you realize there is nothing you can do nor anyone to acknowledge your frustration. To prevent frustration from morphing into infuriation, organizations that employ online self-service technologies must do all that is reasonable to ensure that those technologies are just about perfect and just about foolproof. Because perfection is an unachievable goal and fools never go out of season, there should also be human-mediated support options for those times when customers hit dead ends.

First, it is important to understand that any human-mediated support adds to the cost of offering a self-service technology—in the worst case, to the extent that the service becomes a budget liability instead of an asset. That said, the human-mediated support options are somewhat obvious: live telephone support, digital-chat-based support, a means of sending or posting a text-based message, or a means of leaving a voice-mail message. The factors that determine the usefulness of human-mediated support include the following:

Response Time

The response time for phone and digital chat support should be instantaneous, though waiting in queue for the next available staff member can stretch the limits of instantaneous beyond the breaking point. Non-instantaneous support services (e-mail, texting services, messages submitted via Web-based forms, voice-mail systems) should come with a time-specific service-level agreement that is made clear to users—for example, "All e-mails and text messages will be replied to in twelve hours or less after the time of receipt."

Hours of Service

As with response time, service hours should be made clear to customers. For instantaneous support services like phone and digital chat, the longer the hours of service, the more useful customers will find them. Blackout periods, such as weekends and holidays, should be kept to a minimum for both instantaneous and non-instantaneous support services. Consortial digital chat services have, thus far, proved to be the most cost-effective option for libraries that wish to provide instantaneous, around-the-clock, human-mediated support for online customers.

Quality

Do the support options consistently provide customers with information that meets their needs? Obviously, providing low-quality support is a waste of resources. Fairly or unfairly, the standard complaint about outsourced technical support is that the quality is low because the service representatives are either undertrained or more interested in rushing the customer through the transaction than in solving the problem at hand.

Accessibility

Human-mediated support options should be easy for customers to find rather than being deeply buried under layers of web pages.

COMMUNICATING WITH SELF-SERVICE CUSTOMERS

Most libraries treat reference, instruction, and online presence (website, social media, etc.) as discrete public-service roles. Discrete or not, in most libraries all three roles fall under the aegis of a single department, and those library staff who are responsible for any one of the three public-service roles often have some greater or lesser responsibility for the other two. The common talent possessed by library staff responsible for the three roles has become a bit of a cliché in advertisements recruiting public-service librarians: "The successful candidate must possess excellent written and oral *communication* skills." When it comes to implementing a self-service technology, communication skills matter a great deal, as the success or failure of self-service hinges on how well an organization can communicate with its customers at the point of use. In an online world where opportunities to back up and re-explain a fumbled communication are rare, all communication must conform with "the key dimensions of information quality . . . *accuracy, completeness, currency, and format.*"[12]

If you think about the triad of reference, instruction, and online presence as ways in which libraries communicate with users instead of in terms of traditional library roles, it becomes possible to think about the triad (and the specific functions that are subordinate to them) in non-traditional ways. For example, consider the result when you classify the subordinate functions that comprise reference, instruction, and online presence in terms of recipients (see table 4.3).

Table 4.3.

Single-Recipient Communications	*Multiple-Recipient Communications*
• In-person meeting (drop in)	• In-person group instruction (class or workshop)
• In-person meeting (appointment)	• Guided tours
• Telephone call	• Web pages
• E-mail (one-off)	• Tutorials
• Postal mail (one-off)	• Form letters/e-mail
• Digital chat	• RSS feeds
• Text messaging	• Blogs
	• Podcasts
	• Broadcasts
	• Print publications
	• Online publications*
	• Signage
	• Video
	• Automated telephone system
	• Library catalog†
	• Wikis
	• Social-networking tools‡

* Subject guides, how-to guides, newsletters, etc.

† Though not often thought of as such, a catalog, whether it be a library catalog or a commercial catalog of items for sale, is simply a tool through which an organization communicates with its customers.

‡ "Social-networking tools" encompasses a whole grab bag of technologies typified by such phenomena as Twitter, Facebook, YouTube, Pinterest, Second Life, etc.

Multiple-recipient communication is desirable because, through each of its various forms, organizations can reap potentially larger payoffs than are possible through single-recipient forms of communication. The economies of multiple-recipient communication are obvious. Just think about how often you encounter product placements, billboards, spam, junk mail, and TV/radio/Web advertisements versus how often a door-to-door salesperson comes to call. In libraries, the traditional single-recipient form of communication—the reference-desk transaction—cannot come close to reaching all of a library's current or potential customers. Only multiple-recipient communication can approach that lofty goal.

A second way of looking at communication with customers is from the viewpoint of synchronicity (see table 4.4).

For synchronous communication to occur, the transmitter and receiver of the communication must connect at the same time. Two-way synchronous communication holds the advantage when it comes to back-and-forth communication—it is far easier to conduct a complicated reference interview in person or on the phone rather than via e-mail. On the other hand, asynchronous communication has the advantage of not being limited by service hours, a feature of obvious benefit to the student trying to finish a term paper at 2:00

Table 4.4.

Synchronous Communications	Asynchronous Communications
• In-person meeting (drop in)	• E-mail (one-off)
• In-person meeting (appointment)	• Form letters/e-mail
• In-person group instruction (class or workshop)	• Text messaging
• Guided tours	• Web pages
• Telephone call	• Tutorials
• Digital chat	• RSS feeds
• Broadcasts*	• Blogs
	• Podcasts
	• Print publications
	• Postal mail (one-off)
	• Online publications
	• Signage
	• Video
	• Automated telephone system
	• Library catalog
	• Wikis
	• Social-networking tools

* Of course it is possible to record broadcasts or view them on demand via outlets like YouTube, in which case the broadcasts are neither synchronous nor transitory.

Table 4.5.

Transitory Communications	Persistent Communications
• In-person meeting (drop in)	• Web pages
• In-person meeting (appointment)	• Tutorials
• In-person group instruction (class or workshop)	• Form letters/e-mail
• Guided tours	• RSS feeds
• Telephone calls	• Blogs
• Digital chat	• Podcasts
• Text messaging	• Print publications
• E-mail (one-off)	• Online publications
• Postal mail (one-off)	• Signage
• Broadcasts	• Video
	• Automated telephone systems
	• Library catalog
	• Wikis
	• Social-networking tools

a.m. or the faculty member working on a grant proposal during a university holiday.

A third way to classify communications is to consider whether they are transitory or persistent.

Transitory communications must be re-created every time they occur, a circumstance that makes them labor-intensive. Persistent communications can be created once and then reused repeatedly. While the initial amount of labor required to create persistent communications is often significant, a long shelf life can result in a very low cost per use. In the case of web pages and blogs, the shelf life of a persistent communication may be on the short side (days, weeks, or months), while in the case of permanent signage, the shelf life may be decades. The original MARC (machine-readable cataloging) record for a popular book, along with the copy-cataloging records derived from it, could theoretically last forever and communicate with millions of library customers over the years.

Fourth, you can consider whether or not the communication demands that the recipient go to the place where the communication occurs rather than the communication going to the recipient (see table 4.6).

When you put all of the above together, you get table 4.7.

The upper right-hand box of this table (persistent, asynchronous, location independent, and multiple recipient) includes the most cost-effective types of communication that could be used in conjunction with online self-

Table 4.6

Location Dependent	Location Independent
• In-person meeting (drop in) • In-person meeting (appointment) • In-person group instruction (class or workshop) • Guided tours • Print publications (unless mailed to the recipient) • Signage	• Digital chat • Text messaging • E-mail (one-off) • Form letters/e-mail • Postal mail (one-off) • Broadcasts • Telephone calls • Web pages • Tutorials • RSS feeds • Blogs • Online publications • Podcasts • Video (online) • Automated telephone systems • Library catalog • Wikis • Social-networking tools

Table 4.7

	Single Recipient	Multiple Recipient
Persistent, asynchronous, location independent		• Web pages • Tutorials (online) • Video (online) • Form letters/e-mail • RSS feeds • Blogs • Online publications • Podcasts • Automated telephone systems • Library catalog • Wikis • Social-networking tools
Persistent, asynchronous, location dependent		• Signage • Print publications
Persistent, synchronous, location dependent or independent		
Transitory, asynchronous, location independent	E-mail (one-off) Postal mail (one-off) Text messaging	
Transitory, asynchronous, location dependent		
Transitory, synchronous, location dependent	In-person meeting (drop in) In-person meeting (appointment)	• In-person group instruction (class or workshop) • Guided tours
Transitory, synchronous, location independent	Telephone calls Digital chat	• Broadcasts

service technologies. Whether or not such communications are effective is of course dependent on the quality of their content as well as the ease with which customers can discover and access them. If a bad online how-to video does customers no good, the same is true for a great online how-to video that is hidden away far from the point of need. In addition to those items in the upper-right-hand box, any of the location-independent forms of communication could be used in conjunction with self-service technologies. For one-off e-mail and text messaging, the time delay plus the high cost of single-recipient communications are negatives; digital-reference and live telephone transactions avoid the time delay but still incur the extra costs incurred by single-recipient communications.

Communicating effectively with every customer, every time via a persistent, asynchronous, location-independent, and multiple-recipient method is a laudable goal, but most likely not a realistic one. What, then, is a realistic goal? That depends on the organization and the customers it serves, but the following example suggests a starting point:

Communication Goals for Online Self-Service Customers:

- 80 percent of the time, customers successfully use the self-service technology without any human intervention, relying on instructions (text, video, tutorials, guides, etc.) that are persistently available online.
- 10 percent of the time, customers successfully use the self-service technology after communicating with a staff member via e-mail or text message.
- 10 percent of the time, customers successfully use the self-service technology after communicating with a staff member via digital chat or by telephone.

Of course the above numbers will need to be adjusted based on local experience, the customer base, the complexity of the self-service transaction, and staff capacity.

ASSESSING ONLINE SELF-SERVICE QUALITY

Assessing the reliability of, and user success with, a physical self-service technology is a fairly straightforward process. A library that keeps a log of customer complaints about photocopiers and a record of service calls is in a good position to determine that the copier on the second floor is either a lemon or that, for whatever reason, customers have problems using it. If the library takes steps to remedy the problem with the photocopier on the second floor, it is equally straightforward to determine if those steps are having the desired effect. In the virtual world, things are not so simple. A customer who hits a dead end with an online self-service technology might make a phone call, send an e-mail, or post a (possibly snarky) comment on Yelp or the library's Facebook page; on the other hand, that same frustrated customer might just give up and go watch a YouTube video of a librarian slipping on a banana peel (6,784,362 views). Nobody relishes hearing customer complaints, but because complaints provide a means by which an organization can restore customer confidence, remedy problems, and generally do a better job of satisfying customer needs, it is better to hear them than not.

So how is an organization supposed to assess an online self-service technology, especially if it is likely to hear only from those customers who run into problems, and then from only a self-selected portion of that population? Studies of customer complaints have found that the percentage of dissatisfied customers who actually complain is often 40 percent or lower.[13] Analyzing the amount of use a self-service technology receives is helpful, but only if you can be sure that the numbers represent real people and are not inflated by Web-crawling bots. Even if you know that every hit represents a real person, raw numbers do not tell you if those customers were successful or if they were satisfied with the technology. Attempting to survey online users is a common approach, though response rates tend to be low.

The wholesale collection and analysis of information about customers' online behaviors, a somewhat controversial technique used by companies like Google, is another option for assessing self-service technologies, though the information-technology and analytical resources required to gather and interpret such data, not to mention privacy issues, keep this option off the table for most libraries. Conducting focus groups is more in line with the resources of the average library, though the work involved in conducting a rigorous focus group is considerable. That said, Jakob Nielsen famously contends that iterative processes make it possible to conduct thorough usability testing with as few as five users.[14]

If libraries struggle with how to assess online self-service technologies, they can at least find comfort in the fact that the business world also struggles. As

CRITICAL INCIDENT TECHNIQUE (CIT)

Critical Incident Technique (CIT) is a methodology used to identify major problems in a system. First developed by John C. Flanagan, a psychologist who held the rank of colonel in the U.S. Army Air Force during the Second World War, CIT was initially used to answer such military-oriented questions as why some flight-school candidates never learn to fly, why certain bombing missions fail, and what makes someone an effective combat leader. For a concrete example of how CIT was used during the war, pilots would be asked to recall critical incidents during which they felt disoriented or experienced vertigo. They were then asked to describe exactly what they saw, heard, or felt that brought on these sensations. The experiences of the pilots surveyed were then used to improve cockpit design.*

CIT in the form that it is used today was described by Flanagan in a 1954 article published in the *Psychological Bulletin*:

> The critical incident technique outlines procedures for collecting observed incidents having special significance and meeting systematically defined criteria. . . . To be critical, an incident must occur in a situation where the purpose or intent of the act seems fairly clear to the observer and where its consequences are sufficiently definite to leave little doubt concerning its effects.†

CIT remained relatively ignored until 1990, at which time the methodology experienced a rebirth following the publication of "The Service Encounter: Diagnosing Favorable and Unfavorable Incidents," a landmark study employing the CIT methodology.‡ Over the intervening twenty-plus years, CIT has been used over two hundred times in the marketing literature. Bitner et al. succinctly define critical incidents as "specific interactions between customers and service firm employees that are especially satisfying or especially dissatisfying" and describe the CIT methodology as "essentially a classification technique employing content analysis of stories or 'critical incidents' as data."§

For customer-service purposes, the power of CIT comes from asking interviewees to focus on describing satisfying/dissatisfying incidents in factual detail—when did the incident happen, what did the employee say or do, what was the result—without speculating on the underlying causes of the situation. It is the researcher who makes the inferences, not the interviewee. While conducting a CIT-based study requires trained researchers and more than a little investment of time and energy, the results of a well-conducted CIT-based study can be quite revealing about where a system of service fails and how those failures might be avoided in the future.

---

* John C. Flanagan, "The Critical Incident Technique," *Psychological Bulletin* 51, no. 4 (1954): 329.

† Ibid., 327.

‡ Mary Jo Bitner, Bernard H. Booms, and Mary Stanfield Tetreault, "The Service Encounter: Diagnosing Favorable and Unfavorable Incidents," *Journal of Marketing* 54, no. 1 (January 1990): 71–84.

§ Bitner et al., "The Service Encounter," 73.

the authors of a 2011 study (which cites nine separate scales for assessing online service) state, "Compared with the abundant research examining the quality of face-to-face services, investigations of online service quality remain in their infancy."[15] Given the impossibility of conducting gold-plated assessment, there are really two key things to remember about assessing online self-service technologies. First, no method of serving customers, online or physical, self-service or human mediated, is flawless. An online self-service technology that falls short of perfection may still be better than status quo ways of engaging with and serving customers. Second, remember "that some hard evaluation data, even if the data may be less than perfect, are better than either no data at all or soft data obtained from anecdotal observation."[16] In other words, do the best assessment you can with the resources at your command.

CONCLUSION

In 2011, three of the ten largest (as measured by sales volume) travel agencies in the world—Expedia, Priceline, and Orbitz—did business exclusively via online self-service technologies, while the remaining seven of the top ten provided online self-service technologies as an option for their customers.[17] It has become entirely possible to travel the globe without ever setting foot in the office of a travel agent or speaking to one on the telephone. Online self-service technologies are prevalent in the digital world. If done well, they have the potential to save costs and increase customer satisfaction by providing convenience and a perceived sense of self-control. If done poorly, they have the potential to produce just the opposite effect. Implementing effective online self-service technology involves communicating effectively so as to both enhance customer success and reduce (but probably never eliminate) the need to provide costly human-mediated support. Finally, assessment of online self-service technologies is necessary to measure their effectiveness and improve their performance.

NOTES

1. Ken Frydman, Brian Sill, and Richard Martin, "Equipment Solutions to Combat the Effects of a Shrinking Labor Pool, Operators Are Looking to Efficient, High-Tech Equipment to Minimize Labor While Maximizing Productivity," *Nation's Restaurant News*, May 22, 1989, 20.

2. Arthur Field, Mark McKnew, and Peter Kiessler, "A Simulation Comparison of Buffet Restaurants: Applying Monte Carlo Modeling," *Cornell Hotel and Restaurant Administration Quarterly* 38, no. 6 (December 1997): 79, http://dx.doi.org/10.1016/ S0010-8804(97)85372-4 (accessed February 28, 2014).

3. Rob Townsend, "Self-Serve Soft Drinks Pour on Customer Satisfaction (Use of Self-Serve Equipment in Institutions and Fast Food Restaurants)," *Restaurants & Institutions* 100, no. 31 (December 12, 1990): 90.

4. J. E. G. Bateson, "Self-Service Consumer: An Exploratory Study," *Journal of Retailing* 61, no. 3 (Fall 1985): 73–74.

5. Anuj Kumar and Rahul Telang, "Does the Web Reduce Customer Service Cost? Empirical Evidence from a Call Center," *Information Systems Research* 23, no. 3 (September 2012): 721.

6. Dennis Campbell and Frances Frei, "Cost Structure, Customer Profitability, and Retention Implications of Self-Service Distribution Channels: Evidence from Customer Behavior in an Online Banking Channel," *Management Science* 56, no. 1 (January 2010): 6.

7. Ibid., 6.

8. Kumar and Telang, "Does the Web Reduce Customer Service Cost?," 734.

9. Matthew L. Meuter, Amy L. Ostrom, Robert I. Roundtree, and Mary Jo Bitner, "Self-Service Technologies: Understanding Customer Satisfaction with Technology-Based Service Encounters," *Journal of Marketing* 64, no. 3 (July 2000): 59.

10. Meuter et al., "Self-Service Technologies," 52.

11. Shunzhong Liu, "The Impact of Forced Use on Customer Adoption of Self-Service Technologies," *Computers in Human Behavior* 28, no. 4 (July 2012): 1199.

12. R. R. Nelson, Peter A. Todd, and Barbara H. Wixom, "Antecedents of Information and System Quality: An Empirical Examination within the Context of Data Warehousing," *Journal of Management Information Systems* 21, no. 4 (Spring 2005): 207.

13. Meuter et al., "Self-Service Technologies," 59.

14. Jakob Nielsen, "Why You Only Need to Test with 5 Users," *Alertbox*, 2000, http://www.nngroup.com/articles/why-you-only-need-to-test-with-5-users (accessed March 20, 2013).

15. David Xin Ding, Paul Jen-Hwa Hu, and Olivia R. Liu Sheng, "E-SELFQUAL: A Scale for Measuring Online Self-Service Quality," *Journal of Business Research* 64, no. 5 (May 2011): 509.

16. Donald A. Barclay, "Evaluating Library Instruction: Doing the Best You Can with What You Have," *RQ* 33 (Winter 1993): 196.

17. "Chapter 89: Travel Agents," *Travel & Tourism Market Research Handbook* (Norcross, GA: Richard K. Miller & Associates, 2013): 538–540.

5

Services for Remote Users
Librarians in Search of a Niche

Though thoroughly rooted in fantasy, J. K. Rowling's blockbuster Harry Potter series is atypical of most fantasy fiction in that its principal setting is a real place (the contemporary United Kingdom), and the main events of the story unfold according to a specific real-world timeline (June 1991 to May 1998). Readers of the books know that, rather than being born either "long, long ago" or "many, many years from now," Harry Potter was born precisely on July 31, 1980, a birth date that qualifies him as a member of Generation X, though not by much, as 1982 is the generally agreed upon date for the end of Generation X and the beginning of Generation Y (aka the Millennials). As might be expected from a series of books about a Generation X protagonist, written by a Generation X author (Rowling was born July 31, 1965), and originally intended for a Generation Y audience, Harry Potter has quite a bit to say about how these so-called Echo-Boomer generations perceive the people and institutions—including librarians and libraries—that make up their world.

Harry Potter and his wizarding friends encounter librarians and libraries a number of times over the course of the seven volumes that comprise the series, and it is established right from the start that libraries are not warm and welcoming places in their fictional universe. Early in the opening book of the series, an astounded Harry's initial thought upon receiving a piece of mail for the first time in his young life is that he "didn't belong to the library, so he'd never even gotten rude notes asking for books back." A few chapters later Harry equates setting foot in Olivander's wand shop for the first time with having "entered a very strict library."

When Harry finally arrives at Hogwarts School of Witchcraft and Wizardry, he finds, as foreshadowed, a forbidding library ruled by a forbidding librarian, the stern Madam Pince. Pince (so close to *pinch* it almost hurts) is initially described as "a thin, irritable woman who looked like an underfed vulture," then as the "irritable, vulture-like librarian," and finally as having a "vulture-like countenance." While not necessarily evil, Pince is presented as an antagonist who exhibits all the stereotypical behaviors of the perpetually frowning, rule-bound librarian, constantly shushing whisperers and fretting about the "desecration of books." In her role as Hogwarts's chief information gatekeeper, Madam Librarian locks away any number of volumes in the library's closely guarded Restricted Section, putting jinxes on banned books to prevent them from being read by those she deems unworthy, a group that includes the entire student body of Hogwarts. Pince is so frequently in the company of Argus Filch, Hogwarts's chronically irritated, student-despising caretaker, that Harry and his friends speculate on the possibility of a romance between the two. The coupling of Pince with Filch implies not only that the two are soul mates in their animosity toward students, but also that a librarian and a janitor are somehow professional and social equals. While adept at giving the books a furious going-over with her ever-present feather duster, Pince entirely lacks the information-seeking skills expected from anyone with a decent library education. In the fourth book in the series, Harry becomes so desperate for information needed to survive the Triwizard Tournament that he stoops to asking the "vulture-like" librarian for assistance; true to form, she proves useless at helping Harry fulfill his life-or-death information need.

Even Harry's close friend Hermione Granger, a brilliant young witch who makes Hogwarts Library a second home and whose formidable brain is packed with information gleaned from constant reading, never bothers to consult with Pince. More shocking than her avoidance of the school librarian is the fact that, in spite of being a hard-core book lover and inveterate library habitué, Hermione on two separate occasions rips pages from library books in order to possess the information they contain, while in the final volume of the series she steals several important books from the library's collection. Given the presumed age and rarity of the books in Hogwarts Library, Hermione might as well be rampaging through the Bodleian, ripping pages from medieval manuscripts and making off with priceless first editions. Harry, too, shows no regard for any library rules unlucky enough to get in his way, on one occasion using his magical invisibility cloak to break into Hogwarts Library in order to rummage through the Restricted Section.

While on the one hand Rowling's protagonists have low opinions of librarians and libraries, on the other hand they clearly value information. Every book in the series includes plot elements that involve the pursuit of information crucial to the protagonists' success and, often, survival, and Harry and his friends will stop at nothing in order to get their hands on information to which they feel entitled, an ends-justify-the-means ethos with which anyone who BitTorrents copyrighted books, music, movies, or games would certainly sympathize. A sense of entitlement to information coupled with a general indifference, if not disdain, for librarians and libraries is an attitude Rowling's protagonists share with a considerable segment of the post-Baby-Boom population. Particularly for the born-digital, Web-infused Millennial demographic that grew up reading Harry Potter, going to a library to find information is about as natural as hunting down a pay phone to call a BFF, which is to say, not at all. Information is valuable. Librarians and libraries are, at best, incidental; at worst, in the way.

As convenient as it is to assign generational tags like Generation X or Millennial, the problem with doing so is that such tags are based on the specious argument that a narrow set of beliefs or behavioral traits applies to a significant majority of people born within a given ten-to-twenty-year span. For example, while it is commonly stated that members of Generation X are especially tolerant of racial and cultural differences, this remains as unproven as the proposition that everyone born from July 23 through August 22 is creative, fun loving, noble, and generous. Similarly, if Millennials are, as is routinely claimed, upbeat and positive, how does this account for the thousands of Millennials who identify with the notoriously angsty and depressive Emo subculture? Were such broad stereotypes applied to an ethnic group, it would be dismissed as crass racism, yet the stereotyping of entire generations is somehow tolerated.

Even though every member of any given generation cannot possibly be lumped into lockstep behavioral categories, it is self-evident that the incorporation of digital technology into everyday life has profoundly shaped the behaviors and attitudes of both Generations X and Y (at least within the

UNDERSTANDING INFO BINGERS

Whether you categorize them as "digital natives," "Gen X/Y," "Net-Gens," or "the Facebook Generation," one way to get a sense of how this heavily online demographic thinks is to visit websites that cater to its members. Youth-friendly sites devoted to such topics as entertainment, celebrity gossip, college life, humor, or online gaming can be valuable sources of insight into unfamiliar digitally driven cultures. A perhaps unlikely example of such sources is the humor site Cracked.com, the online stepchild of the now-defunct *Cracked* magazine (1958–2007) itself, the perennial also-ran to its main competitor and inspiration, *MAD* magazine. Aimed at a twentysomething/thirtysomething demographic and resolutely sophomoric in its pursuit of a laugh, Cracked.com nonetheless provides useful cultural insights into, among other youth-oriented topics, online gaming, Internet culture, intellectual property, computing, and the use and misuse of information.

Cracked.com maintains quality control via a team of salaried editors who are also frequent contributors, and its editorial policy requires all contributors to cite sources in their articles (though the bona fides of the sources cited are not always ironclad). Freelancers may submit to Cracked.com, and if their work is accepted for publication they are paid in actual dollars—not always the rule in the digital world. Cracked.com also features a comments section to which anyone can post, and like most website comments sections, this one contains its fair share of trolls, haters, and assorted Internet flotsam and jetsam.

Although far from a routine occurrence, Cracked.com touches on the subject of libraries from time to time. In October 2011 Cracked.com published "6 Reasons We're in Another 'Book-Burning' Period in History," an overwrought article about libraries weeding their print collections in favor of digital surrogates.* Overwrought or not, by July of 2013, "6 Reasons" had recorded nearly 795,000 views. How many articles published in traditional library journals or magazines can make similar readership claims?

In July 2013, one of the Cracked.com editors, Robert Brockway, published an article entitled "5 Creeping Forms of Madness the Internet Is

Spreading." Brockway identifies one of these forms of madness as "Info Binging" and writes of it,

> This is the age of access. Between Wi-Fi, mobile computing, and the sheer, boggling size of the Internet, all of the information in the world bends to our every curious whim. Every question we can think of can be answered within nanoseconds, no matter where we are. . . .
>
> Now we intake info-bits in a constant stream. Broad knowledge with no specialty. That's the opposite of the problem we used to have: It used to be that if you had a question back in ye olden times and nobody within earshot knew the answer—tough shit. Maybe if it really bothered you, you'd go to the library. Sort through a microfiche roll, order a set of specialty books from another library, wait six weeks for them to arrive, and then sit down for a month of afternoon studies. And then, when somebody else asked that question—that first question that started your journey of discovery—you would know the answer. You would know all of the answers.
>
> And they would call you a geek and beat you up for it.†

While it may be too much to proclaim Brockway the Voice of His Generation, he certainly speaks for some of his generation. Maybe even the majority. In any case, the point is that spending a bit of time with Cracked.com—or with any of the other sites catering to the "info binging" demographic that libraries must reach and learn to serve if they are to survive—provides a level of cultural insight that cannot be picked up at a library conference or while lamenting the state of "kids today" with a group of professional peers.

---

* S. P. Davis, "6 Reasons We're in Another 'Book-Burning' Period in History," Cracked. com, http://www.cracked.com/article_19453_6-reasons-were-in-another-book-burning-peri-od-in-history.html (accessed July 10, 2013).

† Robert Brockway, "5 Creeping Forms of Madness the Internet Is Spreading," Cracked. com, http://www.cracked.com/blog/5-creeping-forms-madness-internet-spreading (accessed July 10, 2013).

developed world) as well as the behaviors and attitudes of a significant segment of the older Baby-Boom Generation. Self-evidence aside, the data con-
firm that the way in which Rowling's information-seeking protagonists have
cut librarians out of their research process is more non-fiction than fantasy.
From 2000 to 2008, total reference transactions in U.S. academic libraries
declined from 78,440,492 to 56,148,040, a drop of 28.4 percent.[1] This decline
can be attributed to changing information-seeking behaviors of students and
(increasingly) faculty who are members of Generations X or Y. In U.S. public
libraries the number of per capita reference transactions has been on the decline for more than ten years (see figure 5.1).

If the declining numbers do not cast enough gloom on their own, a recent
review of library reference service concludes, "Not only has the overall number of reference transactions decreased but among the remaining transactions, it appears that the percentage of substantive questions has declined."[2]
The library's highest-priced employees, it seems, are spending a lot of their
time unjamming printers and pointing the way to the restroom. It is not
surprising, then, that librarians have been, for some time now, calling into
question traditional notions of reference service—especially the idea that the
reference desk is as inseparable from reference service as the metaphor from
poetry.

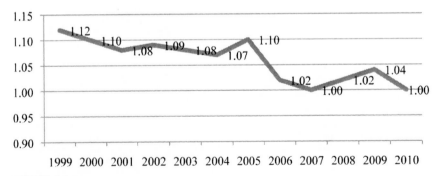

FIGURE 5.1
U.S. Public Library Reference Transactions Per Capita. Chart data compiled from
Institute of Museum and Library Services Research Data Sets: http://www.imls.gov/
research/pls_publications.aspx.

Thelma Freides, 1983:

Reference librarians have never defined their goals or the scope of their work beyond a general intention to assist readers with whatever they might need to facilitate their use of the library. Equally unarticulated and unexamined is the assumption that the hub of this assistance is the reference desk, where a reference librarian, or surrogate, is available to the reader at all times. The arrangement conveys an implicit promise never to let the reader go unserved, but it also pegs the service at a low level.[3]

William Miller, 1984:

Objective analyses of reference desk service indicate the cost of pretending that we can continue to do everything for everybody, and do it well. This is an organizational fiction which needs to be discarded. Our success is turning into failure, and we must acknowledge this reality in order to cope with it. Will we have the courage, or will we continue to burn out staff to keep the fiction alive? Let us show the collective wisdom to look again at our situation, and, when warranted, change it.[4]

Barbara Ford, 1986:

While being hesitant to eliminate face-to face personal interaction between librarians and patrons, reference librarians need to begin to think what has heretofore been the unthinkable, exploring alternatives and possibly eliminating the reference desk.[5]

Karen Storin Summerhill, 1994:

Reference librarians, even at current wage levels, are too highly paid to be doing work on a regular basis that easily could be done by a paraprofessional or a clerical assistant. When we do not operate cost-effectively, everyone loses.[6]

Keith Ewing and Robert Hauptman, 1995:

We take the position that traditional academic reference service, until now held to be a key element within higher education, does not need to be rethought or reformed, it needs to be eliminated.[7]

Jerry Dean Campbell, 2000:

Tomorrow's reference services (if they are called reference services) are already being designed and handed to us by others. And this, not to be alarmist, means the end of the reference world as we know it.[8]

Gabriela Sonntag and Felicia Palsson, 2007:

What does this [drop in the number of reference transactions] mean? Some believe that because of the influence of the web, most people now prefer online reference. If this is the case, then the usefulness of the reference desk is in question. Its past success may have been because it was the only option. Now that users have reference options such as email and chat, some may feel they have no need to come into the library.[9]

Sara Davidson and Susan Mikkelsen, 2009:

Quality reference service is most often defined by accuracy, utility, and user satisfaction. None of these variables are dependent on a face-to-face transaction at the reference desk. Good reference service is really just good customer service. . . . Our users expect, and often prefer, to interact with librarians without coming to the library.[10]

Christy R. Stevens, 2013:

It [the reference desk] looms large not only as a dominant symbol of the profession but also as an actual place where librarians "do" reference. This remains the case for many librarians despite:

1. professional definitions of reference work that position reference transactions (regardless of where they occur) as only one facet of reference and
2. evidence indicating that most reference desk transactions do not meet our own professional definitions of reference work.[11]

Faced with disruptive challenges to traditional reference service, the question for librarians cannot be, "How do we get all the young Harrys and Hermiones back into the library, dutifully lined up in front of the reference desk?" That broomstick has flown, and there is no bringing it back to earth. The concept of a reference desk plunked down next to a (some dare call it dusty) reference collection is as much a relic of the print era as is the assignment of volume and issue numbers to e-journal articles. Rather, the question for librarians must be, "How do we most effectively bring our services to our remote customers?" The choice of verbs is intentional. *Bring* services, not store them behind a desk waiting for customers who never come, and *bring* services that encompass far more than some narrow definition of reference, a library-jargon term that has little to no resonance with most people outside of the profession and which the profession itself would do well to abandon. Ideally, and to the greatest extent possible, the services libraries bring to their customers must seamlessly knit together what were once two separate steps: (1) getting advice from an expert (reference service) and (2) acting on that advice to access information. The expectations of remote customers are so high that toleration for any time lag between the act of seeking assistance and the acquisition of the information is as low as expectations are high. Traditionalists might say that such customers are spoiled, but from the customers' point of view their expectations are as normal as expecting to fly over the Pacific in an airliner instead of taking a sailing ship or expecting anesthesia during a medical procedure instead of being handed a bullet to bite. As high as customer expectations may be, recent history suggests that they will only go higher and go there quickly. Many long-serving librarians can remember when customers were delighted to sit down at a library computer, search a CD-ROM bibliographic database, select and print out a list of citations, and then go off to the stacks to track down items one by one. How long will it be before what is today's normal expectation seems as primitive as using a bibliographic database on CD-ROM?

SOME VERSIONS OF REMOTE

Librarians have been serving, and debating how to best serve, remote customers for decades. First through the mail, then over the telephone, and most recently via digital technology. What is different about digital technology is that it has brought into sharper focus the fact that libraries not only support customers who are physically remote from the library, but also cognitively remote in the sense of having little or no awareness of the services and information resources a library is capable of providing. An example would be someone who sees libraries as belonging so entirely to the world of print as to be entirely absent from, or irrelevant to, the digital world. While having cognitive awareness of libraries is clearly part of being information literate, in the digital age it is possible to have a high degree of information literacy while remaining cognitively remote from libraries.

Librarians find cognitively remote customers frustrating because librarians know that their services could be of great benefit to this population. Even more frustrating are those customers who are so cognitively remote that they actually make use of library digital services or information resources without realizing they have done so. In the pre-digital era it was reasonable to expect that customers who walked in the library door or called the library telephone number understood to one extent or another that they were dealing with a library and what that signified. Even today, when customers walk into the Stephen A. Schwarzman Building at Fifth Avenue and Forty-Second Street wanting to look at a 1909 Honus Wagner baseball card, chances are they are fully aware they are dealing with the New York Public Library and have some cognitive understanding of how a library operates and what services it can provide. On the other hand, if a physically and cognitively remote individual Googles the phrase "1909 honus wagner baseball card," that person could easily download a tobacco-card image digitized and made findable by the New York Public Library with no idea that a library was in any way involved. Another example would be a college student who downloads an article from a scholarly journal without understanding that this is possible only because the campus library pays for an online subscription; as far as such a student is concerned, the article is "something I found on Google."

Admittedly, almost nobody fits perfectly into any of the highly stereo-typical categories shown in table 5.1. If Mrs. Greengage does not live online, she may occasionally visit the online world via a home computer, tablet, or smart phone. A real Professor Peach probably has need of a printed book from time to time. A real Jane Apple might browse the occasional magazine or even approach the reference desk when she needs help with a school as-signment. A non-fiction Danielle Damson might visit a library from time to time, especially during any periods of her life when she is attending school. And of course people change their behavior over time. In ten or fifteen years, Jane Apple might be Jane Apple, Ph.D., and use libraries and information resources in entirely different ways than she does today. Keeping all the ca-veats against stereotyping in mind, sorting library customers into the broad categories in table 5.1 is useful for thinking about whom libraries serve and how to best serve them.

Table 5.1.

	Some Library Customer Types		
Customer	Information-Seeking Behavior	Physically	Cognitively
Mrs. Greengage	Visits the local branch library several times a week, is a voracious reader of cookbooks and mysteries, and the circulation staff can recite her library-card number by heart. Understands the role of the library in providing facilities, services, and information (primarily books).	Present	Present
Professor Peach	Routinely uses digital information resources (primarily online journal articles) provided by the campus library while rarely setting foot in the library building. Understands scholarly information and the library's role in providing it.	Remote	Present
Jane Apple	Hangs out in the library after school to use the wireless (no data charges) via her smart phone. Mostly interested in social networking and online entertainment. Sees the library as a place rather than as an information resource.	Present	Remote
Danielle Damson	All over the Web; never in the library. Would say that she does not use libraries even though she may on occasion unknowingly access information resources provided by libraries.	Remote	Remote

Mrs. Greengage (physically present/cognitively present) is the model of the classic library *patron* in the old-school sense of the word. She knows (cognitively) that she can visit the library for in-person assistance and routinely does just that.

Professor Peach (physically remote/cognitively present) is nearly as easy to serve as Mrs. Greengage. All of the professor's information needs can be met digitally, while any other service needs are most likely dealt with via e-mail or a telephone call. The fact that Professor Peach clearly understands how scholarly information is created and disseminated—and what it requires for the library to bring that information to her desktop—goes a long way toward compensating for the fact that nobody in the library recalls ever seeing her in person.

Jane Apple (physically present/cognitively remote) represents a customer category that may be growing based on the evidence of libraries reporting steady or increasing gate counts while simultaneously reporting declining reference and circulation transactions. Because she is physically present in the library, Jane is potentially reachable via traditional methods of library outreach.

Danielle Damson (physically remote/cognitively remote) represents a huge category of potential library customers, but getting the attention of this demographic is no picnic. Unless Danielle somehow stumbles across some small piece of the Web staked out by a library, the fact that many libraries boast knockout websites, punch all the latest social-networking buttons, serve up e-books and e-journals galore, and provide around-the-clock digital-reference services means nothing to her. At the same time, all the "Read" posters, free bookmarks, and library programs in the world have no chance of making an impact on Danielle.

OLDER THAN THE INTERNET

While having to reallocate resources to effectively serve both in-person and remote customers may seem like a uniquely digital-age dilemma, the question has been on the minds of librarians for over a century, as evidenced by the following letter published in the November 1901 issue of *Library Journal*:

TELEPHONES IN LIBRARIES

In the *Electrical World and Engineer* of October 26 is an article "The Telephone as an Information Bureau," which is worth noting. It describes how the Cuyahoga Telephone Company of Cleveland put into operation a public information bureau for its subscribers, with a young woman and a reference library as the basis of its work. If telephone companies in a large city can afford to do such things as a commercial venture, why could they not do quite as well to supply libraries in smaller places with a "phone" in return for the furnishing of such information by the library to their customers? Would not a library thus be enabled

to earn its telephone rental, and at the same time be justified in paying more attention to inquiries than is sometimes felt necessary; or would it not be a solution of the difficulty in cases where we refrain from putting in a telephone at all, because of the "bother" it may give owing to just such inquiries?
Henry J. Carr
Public Library,
Scranton, Pa.*

If it adds any weight to the opinions expressed in the above letter, at the time it was written its author was president of the American Library Association. Regardless of Carr's stature in the profession, it is telling that his letter raises questions about reference services that are still current in libraries today:

- How can libraries simultaneously provide adequate reference services to both remote and in-person customers?
- How do libraries pay the onetime and ongoing costs of technologies needed to serve remote customers?
- How might libraries collaborate with businesses to reduce such costs?
- Why are businesses beating libraries to the punch when it comes to providing services to remote customers?

* Carr, Henry J. "Telephones in Libraries." *Library Journal* 26, no. 11 (November 1901): 790.

CHOOSING TO PUT PHYSICALLY REMOTE CUSTOMERS FIRST

While it is easy enough for a library organization to say that it serves remote customers, devoting tangible resources to this goal is more difficult, especially when doing so means repurposing resources already devoted to serving in-person customers. On a completely understandable, completely human level, for a library to disadvantage in-person customers in favor of largely unseen somebodies out there in the digital void simply feels wrong, like when a store clerk with a line of in-the-flesh customers picks up the phone to answer a seemingly endless string of questions about hours, directions, and whether or not a sale item is still in stock and available in purple. After all, shouldn't those who took the trouble to be present in the flesh have priority over those who have not? And shouldn't libraries continue their long tradition of providing outstanding service at the reference desk? And shouldn't librarians focus on in-person reference transactions because the service provided has more impact than anything provided online?

The problem is that "feels wrong" should not be a deciding factor when it comes to allocating organizational resources. If the majority of a library's customers are physically remote—and this is, in fact, the reality in which libraries have been operating for some time—then the library must devote the greater share of its service resources to meeting the needs of customers who have left, or may have never entered, the building. That such customers may be more challenging to reach and serve than those who are physically present is no more a reason to give them short shrift than is the fact that reaching and serving them may require libraries to find new ways of conducting their business. That remote customers tend to take the path of least resistance in their pursuit of information is human nature, not a character flaw to be quashed. Even if librarians would like to change what they see as a lack of rigor in how the online masses pursue information, changing mass behavior is a slow and costly undertaking. Consider that it took the full weight of government, the medical profession, and health advocates to reduce the percentage of U.S. adults who smoke from 42.4 percent in 1965 to 18.9 percent in 2011.[12] While that is a significant and welcome behavioral change, achieving it required millions of dollars spent on anti-smoking advertisements, dramatically increased taxes on cigarettes, a series of successful civil lawsuits brought against tobacco companies, and the passage of thousands of pieces of local, state, and federal anti-smoking legislation. And all those resources and all that effort went into discouraging people from doing something that everyone knows will ruin your health and shorten your life. Not only do libraries not have anything close to the resources that went into forty-plus years of anti-smoking efforts, but they also lack evidence of a link between lung cancer and, say, posting a question to Ask.com instead of going to a library.

The digital path of least resistance has changed human behavior, at least for the foreseeable future, but it has not changed the human need for information and information-related services. When video-store customers stopped coming in to rent DVDs, it did not mean that they stopped watching movies. When customers of independent bookstores stopped coming in to buy books, it did not mean that they stopped reading. And when customers stopped coming to the library to ask reference questions, it did not mean they stopped thinking, inquiring, or needing the services of library information professionals. Physically remote customers may be contributing to the downward trend in reference statistics, but that does not mean their information needs are any less important than the needs of those who visit the library in person or that they are less deserving of the services librarians provide.

One of the roadblocks that stops libraries from reallocating resources to better serve their remote customers is the frequently, often passionately, argued point that in-person reference represents the highest possible level of service. However, the evidence to support this argument is simply lacking. Even in the pre-Web age of library reference, study after study rated the effectiveness of in-person reference as low. A 1984 review article examining the findings of thirteen earlier studies of reference service concludes that librarians have only a 50 percent success rate for "questions readily answerable from standard reference sources," and that success rates plunge as low as 18 percent for more difficult questions.[13] While just about anyone (myself included) who has worked a reference desk can come up with anecdotes of great service provided, and while virtually everyone (myself included) who has worked a reference desk will swear in court that their own success rate is far above the numbers produced by the various studies, the reality is that if those responsible for funding library staffing levels went strictly by the empirical evidence there would not be any reference librarians left to passionately argue that in-person reference represents the highest possible level of service.

Which is not to say that libraries have totally failed to embrace technologies that allow them to provide reference services to remote users. In addition to the old standby of the telephone, thousands of libraries currently employ one or more of the following technologies in the interest of serving remote customers: e-mail, web pages, online subject guides (e.g., Springshare's LibGuides), text, chat, two-way video (e.g., Skype), and a constantly evolving grab bag of social-networking tools (e.g., Facebook). While libraries have had some success with the above technologies, none stands out as the ultimate game changer.

Consider, for example, the pros and cons of chat reference. Chat-reference service closely resembles traditional in-person reference in that it allows for real-time back-and-forth interaction between the librarian and the customer, an essential component of a true reference interview. While this can be seen as a plus, it also means that chat reference copies the costly one-to-one, real-time communication model of traditional reference. On the other hand, when used as part of a collaborative service, such as the OCLC 24/7 Collaborative, chat reference allows libraries to provide reference service around the clock, every day of the year, a level of service that no library can afford to provide on its own. Library chat-reference services have reported respectable usage numbers. For example, in academic year 2011–2012, students, faculty, and staff affiliated with the ten-campus University of California system initiated over 23,000 sessions via the OCLC 24/7 chat service.[14] While 23,000 chat-reference sessions is significant given the total number of University of California affiliates (approximately 240,000 students, 13,300 academic employees, and 90,000 administrative staff), this number pales next to the online millions who turn to non-library sources for answers to their questions. A 2010 report issued by OCLC, the vendor of the 24/7 chat service, contends that "the popularity of ask-a-librarian sites has not seen the same spike in use as [non-library] ask-an-expert sites. In fact, ask-a-librarian sites have increased only slightly since 2005 (5% to 7%) and remain relatively unused or undiscovered."[15]

What about the cost of chat reference? An unpublished study I conducted found that, during fiscal year 2010–2011, the University of California Libraries spent $8.04 for every question initiated by a University of California affiliate. This figure considers both salary costs and the cost of the system-wide license for 24/7. Is this a good cost per question? Hard to say. There is disappointingly little in the library literature that attaches dollar costs to reference transactions, digital or in person. While several studies have reached conclusions along the lines of "given the generic nature of the vast majority of enquiries received, it is not cost-effective for librarians to provide reference desk services,"[16] studies that provide actual dollar amounts are sorely lacking. A 2009 study of the cost of staffing the reference desk at Stetson University came up with a cost per in-person reference question of $7.09.[17] An article from 2003 reports per-question costs ranging from $12 to $15 when libraries outsourced chat reference through Library Systems and Services.[18] The library literature appears to remain otherwise silent on this subject, important as it is.

QUALITY, QUANTITY, AND TECHNOLOGY:
BANG-FOR-YOUR-BUCK HISTORY LESSONS

Perhaps surprisingly, there is a lot librarians can learn from the lessons of military history. Although in its mass-market, TV-friendly form, military history tends to focus on bigger-than-life generals and gee-whiz feats of individual heroism, the better military histories have a great deal to teach readers about the perils and promise of adopting new technologies and putting them to effective or (as is often the case) ineffective use. The deployment of the still fairly new technology of armor (i.e., tanks) during the Second World War provides an apt example.

When the German army invaded France in 1940, the French army was equipped with tanks that were, by all the standard measures, superior to the tanks fielded by the German army. Why, then, were the Germans able to overpower the French in just six weeks? First, the French tanks were widely dispersed to support infantry troops (making them easy to pick off one by one) rather than being massed into armored columns that allow tanks to support and defend each other—a failure born of poor tactics. Second, while every German tank had a radio and so could respond to rapidly changing battle plans, relatively few French tanks were radio equipped—a failure born of both not taking full advantage of existing technology and false economy. Third, while the German tanks were operated by five-man crews, French tanks required their three-man crews to perform more tasks than anyone could handle under the stress of combat—a failure born of not taking human factors into consideration.

Later in the war, however, it was Germany's turn to suffer from technological blunders. Flush with the success of its armored forces, Germany embarked on a course of building large, technologically advanced, extremely powerful tanks that outclassed anything the Allies could field against them. The problems with this strategy were that these super tanks (1) could not be manufactured in large enough numbers to turn the tide of the war, (2) consumed oceans of increasingly scarce fuel, and (3) required extensive field maintenance. For all their engineering quality, the German tanks were nonetheless overwhelmed by vast numbers of less advanced, yet perfectly adequate, Soviet T-34 and U.S. Sherman M4 tanks swarming onto the battlefields of Europe.

Even though libraries do not deal in tanks, the parallels are there. Like the French, libraries cannot afford to employ flawed tactics, fail to take advantage of existing technologies, hinder themselves through false economies, or fail to consider human factors when adopting a new technology. At the same time, libraries cannot, like the Germans, afford uncompromising pursuit of quality without consideration of costs—especially when the results achieved through the pursuit of uncompromising quality are only marginally better than what could be achieved with less costly, if lower-quality, solutions.

THE HIGH COST OF REFERENCE SERVICE

But suppose that all of the empirical studies of reference service are seriously flawed in one way or another. And suppose that the indisputably best way to serve library customers would call for armies of reference librarians to provide in-person service. Even with these as givens, the pursuit of quality cannot exist in a vacuum that ignores cost. As Karen Storin Summerhill observed of library services, "Planning of services as a rule must include some consideration of costs, or it is not planning at all but merely wishful thinking."[19] No successful customer-service business would fail to assess the full and exact cost of every type of service it provides; indeed, that service businesses are acutely aware of such costs is made manifest by the ease with which customers can access low-cost help services (websites, FAQs, and company-endorsed user communities) versus the difficulty (if not impossibility) of reaching high-cost live customer-service agents.

As mentioned above, librarians have done next to no research on the costs of reference service. One possible explanation for this lack of research is that few librarians are trained in the area of cost analysis, while another is the large number of factors that must be considered. At a minimum, these factors include salaries (plus benefits), training, technology (hardware, software, and

support), and management overhead. The total number of reference questions is another crucial factor, yet getting a handle on such numbers is not
as straightforward as it might seem, mainly because the traditional method
of collecting reference-service statistics—tick marks on a sheet of paper—is
notoriously unreliable. Rather than recording transactions as they occur, busy
reference-desk staff often guess the number of transactions after the fact; also,
the looming specter of job insecurity can influence desk staff to err on the side
of recording too many, rather than too few, questions answered. Obviously,
overestimating the number of questions answered falsely lowers the calcu-
lated cost of providing reference services. Qualitative analysis of reference-
desk statistics is another crucial part of a thorough cost analysis, yet this
process is compromised by fuzzy definitions of what constitutes a substantial
reference transaction versus a merely directional query. Space is yet another
significant cost factor, but accurately factoring in the space costs of a reference desk and reference collection is a complex undertaking. Any analysis of
the costs of reference service should also consider what use a library might
make of any savings achieved from cutting back or curtailing traditional reference service; if such savings cannot be put to some more productive use,
then why bother making them in the first place? Finally, it is necessary to
consider the public-relations and political costs of curtailing or eliminating
traditional reference services. Universities and colleges that subsidize their
sports teams often make the argument that cutting intercollegiate athletics
would create so much ill will among alumni, the general public, the business
community, and elected officials that the indirect losses incurred would be
far greater than any direct savings the cuts achieved. Any library considering
a reduction or elimination of traditional reference services needs to carefully,
and fairly, evaluate the potential political and public-relations fallout before
moving forward, taking neither the cavalier attitude of "nobody will notice/
it'll all blow over" nor the overly fearful stance that mobs will march on the
library with pitchforks and torches. Of course if a library does choose to make
major changes to its reference services, how those changes are presented to
library customers and supporters is key. Clear and honest explanations of
the reasoning behind changes to reference services will go a long way toward
public acceptance.

THE E.R. PROBLEM

One reason the cost of running a reference desk does not make good business sense is that reference desks run on the emergency-room model. In an emergency room, physicians (the medical profession's highest-priced labor) spend most of their time waiting around for serious cases. The bulk of the cases that come to the emergency room could just as well be treated by non-physicians—nurses, physician's assistants, or nurse practitioners—but the doctors have to be there for the relatively rare times when a truly serious case rolls in the door. Doctors are also there to lend their authority to the care provided by the non-physician hospital staff. As witnessed by the growing number of hospitals that have either closed their emergency rooms or are trying to close them—the number of emergency rooms in the United States decreased from 4,114 in 1997 to 3,935 in 2007, a 5 percent cut*—the emergency-room economic model is not a healthy one.

Besides being costly to operate, emergency rooms often require patients to wait an uncomfortably long time before receiving care, do not always provide the best care, and have found themselves forced into the unwelcome role of serving as primary caregivers for millions of uninsured people. A cold-blooded analysis of the situation might well conclude that, given the relatively small numbers of lives actually saved, emergency rooms are not really worth the cost society pays to keep them running. Such an analysis would be rejected as heartless. Because it is. Emergency rooms are in the business of life or death, and few people in the developed world care to live where there is not reasonable access to one.

At the reference desk, librarians (the profession's highest-priced labor) spend a lot of their time waiting for tough questions. The bulk of the questions that come to the reference desk could just as well be handled by non-librarians—paraprofessionals, clerks, or student employees—but the librarians have to be there for the relatively rare times when a truly tough question rolls in the door. Librarians are also there to lend their authority to the assistance provided by the non-librarians at the desk. A cold-blooded analysis of the situation might well conclude that traditional librarian-staffed reference desks are not really worth the cost libraries pay to keep them running. Such an analysis would be rejected by most librarians as wrongheaded. However, is it in fact wrongheaded to say to library customers, "You cannot just walk in the door any time you want and expect to consult with a librarian"? It is not as if reference service is a matter of life or death; if it were, library reference desks would be open seven days a week, twenty-four hours a day.

The presence of librarians waiting at the reference desk may even have the effect of devaluing the profession in the eyes of library customers. Need to talk to a librarian? Just show up. No need to make an appointment or worry about scheduled office hours. No need to be prepared because the librarian will fall all over the place to help you. In this way, reference librarians behave a lot more like store clerks than lawyers, CPAs, professors, or medical doctors. Given the cost of the reference desk and shrinking library budgets, maybe it is time for librarians to start working by appointment instead of by ambush?

---

* Ning Tang, John Stein, Renee Y. Hsia, Judith H. Maselli, and Ralph Gonzales, "Trends and Characteristics of US Emergency Department Visits, 1997–2007," *JAMA—Journal of the American Medical Association* 304, no. 6 (August 11, 2010): 666.

THE SPIN-OFF GAMBIT

In his highly respected *The Innovator's Dilemma: When New Technologies Cause Great Firms to Fail*, Clayton Christensen provides many examples of how established, industry-leading firms failed to adopt disruptive technologies and suffered dire business consequences as a result. Christensen's thesis is that large, established firms are incapable of adopting disruptive technologies because there is no market for such technologies among their traditional customer bases and because, at least initially, disruptive technologies do not offer enough profit to make them interesting to Fortune 500 firms. Consider a hypothetical library example along the same lines: a library public-services department declines to adopt a chat-based reference service (a disruptive technology) because a survey of walk-in clientele (the library's traditional customer base) shows no interest in such a service; on top of this, estimates indicate that the initial use of chat-based reference would be lower than use of the reference desk.

Christensen extends his thesis even further by providing examples of well-established, industry-leading firms that attempted—in spite of their natural corporate inertia—to adopt a disruptive technology yet failed to do so because these companies' tradition-bound ways of managing employees, allocating resources, and marketing their products unwittingly sabotaged otherwise well-intentioned efforts. As Christensen himself puts it, "Rational resource allocation processes in established companies consistently deny disruptive technologies the resources they need to survive, regardless of the commitment senior management may ostensibly have made to the program."[20] Consider a hypothetical library example: a library public-services department attempts to pilot a chat-based reference service, but the staff assigned to the pilot are not given the time, resources, or professional rewards and recognition necessary to make the pilot successful.

On the bright side, Christensen provides examples of well-established, industry-leading firms that succeeded in adopting disruptive technologies by creating autonomous spin-off businesses for exactly that purpose. Freed, on the one hand, from the firm's traditional ways of doing business, yet charged, on the other, with producing tangible results on a fairly short timeline, these spin-off businesses often succeeded in adopting disruptive technologies where the parent firm would have failed. While it is probably too much to expect that an existing library could spin off an entirely separate public-services organization charged with adopting new, disruptive technologies, the idea that a library might adopt some version of the spin-off approach is not out of the question. For example, a library might separate its services for in-person customers from those for remote customers and assign staff to one or the other based on skills and interests. Having different managers and goals for each part of the operation would further separate the two, allowing each unit to pursue its own goals with greater freedom and less internal resistance to change.

REFERENCE SERVICES IN THE BUSINESS ECOSYSTEM
In the present-day reality, information seekers do not make use of traditional library reference services to the extent they once did because online services,

both for-profit and non-profit, are meeting their needs. Besides facing competition from the usual suspects of general-interest search engines and online encyclopedias, libraries are also seeing questions that once went to the reference desk going instead to subject-specific information services. Ancestry. com, a for-profit genealogy website, reported 2,020,000 paid subscribers as of September 30, 2012, up 19 percent from the previous year.[21] The Amazon. com-owned IMDb (Internet Movie Database) rings up 2.5 billion page views per year and boasts over 20 million registered iOS and Android mobile users.[22] Even more to the point, libraries must reckon with online question-and-answer services that do exactly what reference librarians have done for decades: provide individual customers with personalized answers to specific questions. Some of these services, such as Ask.com (formerly Ask Jeeves), Answers.com, and Quora, rely on the wisdom and willingness of the crowd to respond to individual questions (though the websites of all three services also function as traditional search engines). The quality of the answers provided by the crowd can vary wildly, yet such services partly compensate for this by including mechanisms for rating the quality of individual answers as well as for rating members who regularly provide answers. On a slightly different track, question-and-answer services like ChaCha and kgb have made their reputations by relying on paid human agents to provide direct answers to questions submitted via text (though both services also provide automated responses similar to the results produced by traditional Web-based search engines). That online question-and-answer services manage to turn a profit, either through advertising or by charging for answers, shows that there is a demand for the services they provide. As OCLC's *Perceptions of Libraries 2010* reports,

> Ask-an-expert sites (i.e., question & answer sites) have experienced a tremendous increase in use, nearly tripling since 2005. Today, 43% of information consumers report using an ask-an-expert site, up from just 15% in 2005. Young adults showed the largest growth in demand, with use up 350%. Today, 40% of teens are monthly users of online "ask-an-expert" services.[23]

In 2011, Answers.com reported having a database of 9 million crowd-sourced answers and 5 million registered users.[24] More to the business point, in 2011 a social-media holding company paid $172 million to add Answers. com to its portfolio.[25]

THE WISDOM OF THE CROWD?

The wisdom of the crowd was first demonstrated mathematically by British statistician Francis Galton. In 1906 eight hundred attendees of the West of England Fat Stock and Poultry Exhibition in Plymouth, England, paid 6d each to guess the dressed weight of an ox on exhibit, with the prize for the best guess being the carcass of said ox. After discarding 13 illegible entry slips, Galton conducted a statistical analysis of the weights entered on the remaining 787 entry slips and discovered that, as a whole, the crowd was amazingly accurate. In an article published in the journal *Nature*, Galton reports of his findings, "It appears then, in this particular instance, that the *vox populi* is correct within 1 percent of the real value. . . . This result is, I think, more credible to the trustworthiness of democratic judgment than might have been expected."

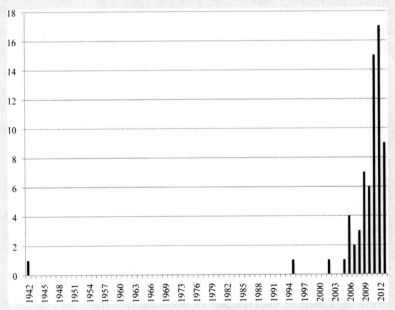

FIGURE 5.2

Citations of Galton's "Vox Populi" article since 1942. Source: Web of Knowledge database, accessed July 9, 2013.

As figure 5.2 shows, there has been a strong resurgence of interest in Galton's article since the emergence of crowd-sourced information resources on the Web. Does this resurgence of interest in Galton verify the wisdom of the crowd? Not necessarily. Asking a crowd to provide a straightforward factual answer (What is the state bird of Idaho?*) is very different from extracting the best answer from a number of volunteered responses to a complex, highly nuanced question (Are electric cars the best solution for reducing greenhouse gases and reliance on fossil fuels?). The crowd's motivation to provide a good answer is another factor to consider. The members of Galton's crowd were motivated to provide their best estimates by both the entry fee (a non-trivial sum at the time) and the prospect of winning a valuable prize. Because the Web allows just about anyone to say just about anything at no cost to themselves, and to do so with some degree of anonymity, the motivation of the crowd to provide quality responses is low at best. In addition, the venue affects the wisdom of the crowd. As Galton himself points out, the venue of a country fair meant that some number of those who guessed at the weight of the carcass were farmers or butchers with considerable knowledge of the subject in question, though there were also many among the crowd who had no relevant expertise whatsoever. Similarly, the Web venue in which one seeks crowd-sourced wisdom matters a great deal. If a would-be car restorer posts a question about rebuilding the transmission on a 1974 Chevrolet Corvette on a Web forum whose members are overwhelmingly owners and aficionados of Corvettes, the chance of getting reliable information is likely to be high. Conversely, imagine the responses if someone were to naïvely post the question, "Who was the greatest figure in the American Civil Rights Movement?" on a skinhead-dominated website.

In 2006 Paul Duguid, a prominent information scientist, published an article in which he used the example of Wikipedia's biographical entry for the author Daniel Defoe to illuminate inherent problems with crowd-sourced information resources.† Duguid points out that some

---

* Mountain bluebird.

of the facts in Wikipedia's Defoe entry were incorrect, that it contained some contradictions, and that the emphasis on different phases of Defoe's career was uneven. Certainly a serious Defoe scholar could find flaws in the Wikipedia entry, though of course a serious Defoe scholar would not use an encyclopedia article—whether from Wikipedia or elsewhere—as a source. For the average reader, however, the virtues of the Defoe entry, of which there are many, more than outweigh its negatives: it is free, convenient to access, and most of its content is accurate and informative. On top of this is the fact that flaws in the Wikipedia entry do not ensure that other sources of information, including commercially produced encyclopedias, are themselves without flaws. In fairness, Wikipedia's Defoe entry can be compared only to what is found in other encyclopedias, not to some abstract standard of perfection. Tellingly, the current (2014) Wikipedia article on Defoe both cites and links to Duguid's 2006 article so that readers can judge the criticisms for themselves. How likely is it that a commercially produced information resource would link to criticisms of its content?

Experiments conducted by sociologists studying group behavior during the middle decades of the twentieth century repeatedly showed that the crowd did better than the experts, even when experts were included as part of the crowd.‡ Additional evidence of the wisdom of the crowd can be found in the success of crowd-sourced projects ranging from the *Oxford English Dictionary* to Amazon Mechanical Turk (a crowd-sourced Internet marketplace) to reCAPTCHA (a crowd-sourced project to digitize text from books printed in antique typefaces that befuddle digital scanners). Of course anyone who lives in a democracy, or simply believes in the democratic process, had better hope that the crowd has the wisdom to make the right choices most of the time.

---

* F. Galton, "Vox Populi," *Nature* 75 (March 1907): 451.

† Paul Duguid, "Limits of Self-Organization: Peer Production and 'Laws of Quality,'" *First Monday* 11, no. 10 (October 2, 2006), http://firstmonday.org/ojs/index.php/fm/article/view/1405/1323 (accessed May 22, 2013).

‡ James Surowiecki, *The Wisdom of Crowds: Why the Many Are Smarter than the Few and How Collective Wisdom Shapes Business, Economies, Societies, and Nations* (New York: Doubleday, 2004), 4–5.

While librarians can certainly snipe at all that is wrong with online question-and-answer services, crowd-sourced encyclopedias, and search-engine algorithms, trying to convince the world that libraries are the better or, more extremely, the only sensible option is futile. Instead, libraries need to find their niche within the business ecosystem of providing reference services (broadly defined) to remote customers. So what might this niche be?

First off, the library profession needs to understand that it is never going to reclaim its former niche at the top of the reference-service ecosystem. To do so would require libraries to somehow overwhelm, outperform, or eliminate the other players in the field. Not only do librarians and libraries lack the necessary resources to pull off any such a coup, but doing so would be a mistake similar to the one that the recording industry made when, in 2001, it used its considerable financial and legal clout to shut down Napster, the file-sharing service that facilitated massive violations of recording-industry copyrights. By effectively wiping Napster off the map of the Internet, the recording industry made room for iTunes and the eventual dominance of the music business by Apple. Just as the recording industry would today be stronger had it found a way to work with Napster—at the time the best-known brand in music downloading—rather than destroying it, libraries will be better off if they can find ways to work with the various online entities that have encroached on what was once reference-librarian turf. Sure, most librarians have gotten past the stage of treating Google as if it were a poisonous snake, and Wikipediaphobia, though still virulent in some library quarters, is not as prevalent as it once was; however, librarians need to do more than wring their hands and watch as their place in the business ecosystem of reference service diminishes.

For example, what if instead of bemoaning the weaknesses of Wikipedia or, worse, trying to create a pathetic hodgepodge of too little, too late Libraripedias, librarians were able to work with the non-profit Wikimedia Foundation to integrate in some formally acknowledged way the work of librarians with the work of Wikipedia? This would need to be more than just editing Wikipedia pages, something a lot of librarians already do. For example (and only as an example), could there be in Wikipedia a way to highlight, distinguish, or otherwise call out bibliographic citations that have been added or endorsed by librarians and other recognized information professionals? What about recognized librarian-authored bibliographic essays that could be attached to appropriate articles in Wikipedia? Or perhaps linking Wikipedia articles to appropriate subject bibliographies of the sort routinely created by librarians? Though none of the above examples is the final answer, it is entirely possible that an initiative along such lines could be an answer. The starting point would be for an official library group, perhaps an ALA division, to approach Wikipedia to explore how both the library profession and Wikipedia might benefit from a formal partnership of one sort or another.

Of course Wikipedia is just one organization that libraries might approach. Could librarians establish formal collaborations with firms like ChaCha, Ask.com, kgb, Answers.com, eHow.com, or other established or emerging question-and-answer sites? For example, as of 2011, Answers.com has a policy of bestowing upon its most trusted participants the status of "volunteer supervisors" endowed with editorial power and tools not available to the community at large. Might a company like Answers.com welcome formal participation from librarians and, in return, offer them special powers, tools, and acknowledgment? Unlike Wikipedia, Answers.com, kgb, and Ask.com are for-profit companies, but it is not as if libraries and librarians have never partnered with for-profit publishers, database vendors, and other information-based businesses.

CONCLUSION: *OGOOGLEBAR*

In 2013 the Language Council of Sweden recommended the addition to the official Swedish dictionary of *ogooglebar*, a word that translates as "ungoogleable." Google, citing trademark concerns, quickly initiated legal action to quash the addition, and as a result the Language Council backed off its recommendation.[26] While news of this legal dustup led to quips along the lines of "Is anything really *ogooglebar*?" it is unlikely that any librarians were cracking wise along such lines. The library profession knows that *everything* cannot be Googled, crowd-sourced, looked up in Wikipedia, or found in the all-knowing magical database that has become a familiar trope of film, fiction, and television. (Yes, Miss Granger, we are looking at you.) More importantly, the profession knows that it has an important, possibly unique, role to play in helping people access and make sense of all the vast amounts of information that cannot be found via quick-and-dirty searches. The problem is that waiting for customers to come to the library's reference desk so that we librarians can prove our worth is a dismal strategy. Almost as problematic is the strategy of waiting for remote customers to find and make use of library websites, ask-a-librarian services, and other library-centric online tools. Sure, when libraries make their services available online they get some use, but this adds up to a fraction of the usage numbers piling up in the wider online world. Rather than sulking in our tents or building it and hoping they will come, the library profession needs to create a new place for itself in the business ecosystem of reference service by integrating its services where the customers—existing and potential—already are. And if we do this in a way that makes people cognitively aware that a librarian or a library is somehow involved, so much the better.

NOTES

1. Denise M. Davis, *The Condition of U.S. Libraries: Academic Library Trends, 1999–2009* (Chicago: American Library Association, Office for Research and Statistics, 2009), 17, http://www.ala.org/research/sites/ala.org.research/files/content/librarystats/librarymediacenter/Condition_of_Libraries_1999.20.pdf (accessed August 19, 2013).

2. Tiffany LeMaistre, Rebecka L. Embry, Lindsey L. Van Zandt, and Diane E. Bailey, "Role Reinvention, Structural Defense, or Resigned Surrender: Institutional Approaches to Technological Change and Reference Librarianship," *Library Quarterly* 82, no. 3 (July 2012): 248.

3. Thelma Freides, "Current Trends in Academic Libraries," *Library Trends* 31 (Winter 1983): 466–467.

4. William Miller, "What's Wrong with Reference: Coping with Success and Failure at the Reference Desk," *American Libraries* 15, no. 39 (May 1984): 322.

5. Barbara J. Ford, "Reference beyond (and without) the Reference Desk," *College and Research Libraries* 47, no. 5 (September 1986): 493.

6. Karen Storin Summerhill, "The High Cost of Reference: The Need to Reassess Services and Service Delivery," *Reference Librarian*, no. 43 (January 2, 1994): 83.

7. Keith Ewing and Robert Hauptman, "Is Traditional Reference Service Obsolete?" *Journal of Academic Librarianship* 21 (January 1995): 3–6.

8. Jerry Dean Campbell, "Clinging to Traditional Reference Services: An Open Invitation to Libref.com," *Reference & User Services Quarterly* 39, no. 3 (Spring 2000): 225.

9. Gabriela Sonntag and Felicia Palsson, "No Longer the Sacred Cow—No Longer a Desk: Transforming Reference Service to Meet 21st Century User Needs," *Library Philosophy and Practice*, paper 111 (February 1, 2007): 3, http://digitalcommons.unl. edu/libphilpract/111 (accessed July 7, 2013).

10. Sara Davidson and Susan Mikkelsen, "Desk Bound No More: Reference Services at a New Research University Library," *Reference Librarian* 50, no. 4 (October 2009): 349.

11. Christy R. Stevens, "Reference Reviewed and Re-Envisioned: Revamping Librarian and Desk-Centric Services with LibStARs and LibAnswers," *Journal of Academic Librarianship* 39, no. 2 (March 2013): 202–214.

12. Centers for Disease Control and Prevention, "Trends in Current Cigarette Smoking among High School Students and Adults, United States, 1965–2011," http://www.cdc.gov/tobacco/data_statistics/tables/trends/cig_smoking (accessed July 10, 2013).

13. Mary Lee Bundy and Amy Bridgman, "A Community Based Approach to Evaluation of Public Library Reference Service," *Reference Librarian* 4, no. 11 (1984): 160.

14. Teal Smith and Donald A. Barclay, "Digital Reference that Supports E-Learning at the University of California," in *E-Learning in Libraries: Best Practices*, ed. Charles Harmon and Michael Messina, 25–38 (Lanham, MD: Scarecrow, 2013), 37.

15. Cathy DeRosa, Joanne Cantrell, Matthew Carlson, Peggy Gallagher, Janet Hawk, and Charlotte Sturtz, *Perceptions of Libraries 2010: Context and Community OCLC* (Dublin, OH: OCLC, 2010), 34, http://www.oclc.org/content/dam/oclc/ reports/2010perceptions/howamericansuse.pdf (accessed August 15, 2013).

16. Anthea Sutton and Maria J. Grant, "Cost-Effective Ways of Delivering Enquiry Services: A Rapid Review," *Health Information and Libraries Journal* 28, no. 4 (December 2011): 253.

17. Susan M. Ryan, "Reference Transactions Analysis: The Cost-Effectiveness of Staffing a Traditional Academic Reference Desk," *Journal of Academic Librarianship* 34, no. 5 (September 2008): 396.

18. R. David Lankes, Melissa Gross, and Charles R. McClure, "Cost, Statistics, Measures, and Standards for Digital Reference Services: A Preliminary View," *Library Trends* 51, no. 3 (Winter 2003): 407.

19. Summerhill, "The High Cost of Reference," 71.

20. Clayton M. Christensen, *The Innovator's Dilemma: When New Technologies Cause Great Firms to Fail* (Boston: Harvard Business School Press, 1997), 217.

21. "Ancestry.com Inc. Reports Q3 2012 Financial Results," Ancestry.com, http://ir.ancestry.com/releasedetail.cfm?ReleaseID=716064 (accessed July 24, 2012).

22. Stephanie Miot, "IMDb Apps Get Makeover after 40 Million Download Milestone," *PC Magazine*, July 2012, http://www.pcmag.com/article2/0,2817,2407038,00.asp (accessed August 20, 2013).

23. DeRosa et al., *Perceptions of Libraries 2010*, 30.

24. Dan Marriott, "Finding the Answers," *Baseline*, no. 109 (March 2011): 28–29.

25. Tamika Cody, "Answers.com Acquired by Summit's AFCV," *Mergers & Acquisitions Report* 24, no. 6 (February 7, 2011): 9.

26. Charles Arthur, "Google and Sweden in War of Words over Ogooglebar," *Guardian*, March 27, 2013, sec. Technology, http://www.guardian.co.uk/technology/2013/mar/27/google-sweden-ogooglebar (accessed August 15, 2013).

Online Education

Will the Twenty-First-Century Library Be on Board?

When Team Gutenberg manufactured its first books using the emerging technology of printing from movable metal type, one of their goals was to produce an object indistinguishable from the manuscript book, a format familiar to, and beloved by, readers of the day.[1] As a result, the first Bibles printed from movable type employ such conventions of the manuscript book as a script-style font, a two-column format, and hand-decorated initial letters while entirely lacking such now-standard book features as punctuation, paragraph breaks, footnotes, tables of contents, page numbers, and title pages located at the front of the volume. In its familiar, fully developed form, the real-time, read-only, full-text, random-access information object that is the modern printed book came to be beloved by readers everywhere and, depending on whom you ask, deserves at least partial credit for some pretty remarkable developments in human history, including the flowering of literacy, education, science, and technology that created, and still sustains, the modern world.

Amazing achievements for a technology that was simply trying to replicate—albeit faster and at reduced cost—a task that humans had been doing by hand for centuries.

As most librarians know, books printed from movable type between 1450 and 1501 are referred to as *incunables* (or, if you prefer, *incunabula*), a word derived from the Latin term for "swaddling clothes" or "cradle." In the early twenty-first century, online education is going through its own cradle period, and just as the invention and spread of printing from movable type was made possible by the convergence of such disparate technologies and market forces as the agricultural screw press, papermaking, oil-based ink, advances in metallurgy, the growth of European universities, and improved transportation, the present-day spread of online education is being propelled by such varied innovations and market forces as the Web; the near ubiquity of high-speed network connectivity; (relatively) cheap, plentiful, and portable computer hardware and software; the information economy's demands for a highly educated workforce; shrinking government support for education; the increasing cost of traditional education; and, lest we forget, the shift from print-based to digital information.

On the other hand, the parallels between early printed books and early ventures into online education are not absolute. Notably, there is remarkably little evidence of controversy surrounding the emergence of printed books. While there are apocryphal tales of producers of manuscript books leveling accusations of witchcraft against early makers and sellers of printed books, the strong similarities between incunables and manuscript books meant that the upstart printed book was generally well accepted and well regarded. Nor did it hurt that such artisans of the manuscript trade as "bookbinders, rubricators, illuminators, and calligraphers would be kept busier than ever after early printers set up shop."[2] Likewise, manufacturers of paper and vellum did not much care whether their products ended up beneath the pen or the press, and most retailers of manuscript books made a seamless transition to selling printed books.

The birth of online education, on the other hand, has witnessed plenty of controversy as reflected in the highly polarized stances taken by proponents and critics of online education:

- Pro: Online education is simply good government and good stewardship of public funds. As the *Wall Street Journal* puts it, "Online education will lead to the substitution of technology (which is cheap) for labor (which is expensive)—as has happened in every other industry—making schools much more productive."[3]
- Con: Online education is a blatant attempt by right-wing interests to dominate what they see as the liberal bastion of education. The title of a 2012 *Wall Street Journal* article makes this agenda plain enough, "The Hidden

Revolution in Online Learning; The Economics of Digital Learning Will Undermine the Liberal Biases Built into the Current Education System."[4]

- Pro: Online education will democratize learning, finally making education available to those who could otherwise never afford it. "The need for educational access and greater effectiveness in teaching and learning is staggering. Today, there are over 30 million people qualified to enter university but denied access due to the restricted seat numbers and restricted finances. . . . A major university would have to be created each week, starting now, to meet this overwhelming demand.[5]

- Con: Online education will harm, or possibly destroy, public education. In May 2013 a group of philosophy professors at San Jose State University formally refused to teach an online course developed for edX (a joint Harvard/MIT non-profit), describing the course as an attempt to "replace professors, dismantle departments, and provide a diminished education for students in public universities."[6]

Most people who care about education find themselves somewhere between the extremes, thoughtfully questioning whether online education will ultimately be a boon or a bane. Princeton sociologist Mitchell Duneier, who started out as an enthusiastic MOOC (massive open online course) practitioner, has since backed off out of concerns that "massive open online courses might lead legislators to cut state-university budgets," but he nonetheless holds out the possibility that he will again teach a MOOC.[7] Just as most people are in the middle, the reality of online education lies somewhere between the extremes. It is quite likely that neither the rosiest predictions of free education for all nor the direst warnings of a digital Dark Ages will come to pass. And it certainly remains to be seen if online education will have as profound a long-term impact on education as printing has had on, well, pretty much everything. Whatever the final outcome, the fact remains that online education is already big, is getting bigger, and shows no sign of being merely the latest in a long line of educational fads. For just a few notable examples, consider the following:

- The Florida Virtual School, an online K–12 public school, offers 120 courses that are free to Florida residents and can be taken for a fee by non-residents.[8]

- Born online in 1993, the American Public University System (APUS) is an entirely online university offering eighty graduate and undergraduate degrees and sixty-nine certificate programs to U.S. military personnel stationed across the globe. A for-profit company that is publicly traded on the NASDAQ exchange, APUS had an enrollment of over 120,000 students in 2012.[9]

- Arizona State University, a non-profit public institution, offers thirty-five undergraduate degrees, thirty-two graduate degrees, and seven certificate programs that can be completed entirely online.[10] In 2009, the Arizona State University Libraries hired a "librarian for online and extended education" and formed a task force to make recommendations for how the library could best serve the growing number of ASU students taking online courses.[11]

- Endeavors such as the for-profit Coursera and Udacity—as well as the non-profit edX—offer MOOCs that can be taken, typically at no charge, by students in numbers that make the traditional 500-seat lecture-hall class seem like an intimate seminar.

- In addition to Coursera and Udacity, commercial businesses such as Apple (with its iTunes U) and Google (with its CourseBuilder software and Oppia tool for creating educational content) are positioning themselves to ride the online education wave.

- Studies conducted on behalf of the Alfred P. Sloan Foundation estimated that during the 2005–2006 school year, 700,000 U.S. K–12 students were enrolled in at least one online or blended course, while during the 2007–2008 school year that estimate rose to 1,030,000 students (2 percent of the entire U.S. K–12 population).[12]

- From 2009 to 2010 the number of higher-education students who took an online course increased from 5.6 million to 6.1 million.[13]

- From 2003 to 2008, the percentage of U.S. undergraduates enrolled in at least one online course rose from 8 percent to 20 percent.[14]

- By 2008, at least one-fourth of the American Library Association–accredited library-school programs offered an online master's degree.[15] As Michael Stephens writes in *Library Journal*, "Frankly, a brick-and-mortar LIS school without a fully online option may become a quaint reminder of days gone by in the next decade."[16]

- Based on a 2013 enrollment of 250,000 domestic and 50,000 international students, the largest academic institution in the United Kingdom is the Open University, a distance-learning institution with a strong online presence.

In general, education has enjoyed extraordinary growth over the last century and a half, a period that has seen, at least in the developed world, the adoption of compulsory primary and secondary education, the establishment of widespread public-library systems, and the founding of thousands of institutions of higher education. In the United States alone, the Morrill Acts of 1862 and 1890 led to the creation of land-grant universities in every state; the Servicemen's Readjustment Act of 1944 (aka "the G.I. Bill") made first-generation college students of millions of Americans; and the Sputnik/Baby-Boom educational investment frenzy resulted in the expansion of colleges and universities on an unprecedented scale. Consider, by way of comparison, that in the twenty-first century the state of Texas alone has thirty-five state-supported universities, about the same as the total number of universities in all of Europe when the first printed Bible came off the presses in Mainz. And that is not even counting Texas's many private institutions of higher education nor its public colleges, law schools, and medical schools. Online education may well prove to be the next major step in the historic growth and spread of education and, as a result, emerge as a force for major change in the way libraries and librarians conduct their business. The library profession must develop both a realistic understanding of online education and effective strategies for accommodating new ways of teaching and learning.

DISTANCE EDUCATION

To understand where online education came from, it helps to know something about the history of distance education, of which online education is the latest incarnation. On one level, writing can be seen as the oldest form of distance education as it allows a teacher/author to instruct learners/readers separated by space, time, or both. Just consider the many millions around the world and across the centuries who have learned from the philosophers of ancient Greece because their ideas are preserved in writing. The first scientific journals, dating from 1665, leveraged the technology of printing to allow geographically dispersed scientists to educate each other on a one-to-many scale that could never have been achieved by in-person meetings or one-to-one handwritten letters. In the nineteenth century the correspondence course became a popular form of education, in part because technological advances in rail transportation increased the speed of mail service and drove down the cost of postage. Like the Chautauqua and the free public library, the correspondence course was seen as a tool for self-improvement and upward mobility. By 1906 the Pennsylvania-based International Correspondence School (ICS) could claim an enrollment of 902,000 students,[17] while by 1923 its enrollment had grown to 2.5 million.[18] Adjusting for U.S. population growth, the ICS's 1923 enrollment would be equivalent to a 2013 enrollment of roughly 7 million students. As the twentieth century unfolded, radio (broadcast and two-way), the telephone, and television were all employed to provide distance education. In the United States, educators began experimenting with radio-based "schools of the air" in the 1920s, and even though the last survivor of the type continued to broadcast into the mid-1990s, the format is widely regarded as a failure.[19] Radio-based education had more success in rural Australia, where it was first employed in the early 1950s and continues to the present, though the medium has shifted from radio to the Internet. The first educational television broadcast in the United States originated from the University of Iowa in 1934,[20] and in the decades that followed a number of other U.S. institutions of higher education experimented with teaching via television. A landmark event in U.S. educational television was the establishment of the Public Broadcasting System during the latter half of the 1960s. One limiting factor of early attempts at teaching with television was that all communication was one-directional, flowing from an active teacher to largely passive learners. Improvements in satellite technology in the final decades of the twentieth century led to television-based education in which communication could flow back and forth between remotely located teachers and students as well as among students who, though enrolled in the same class, might be widely dispersed. Because satellite time is not cheap, the heaviest users of this type of educational technology were large corporations, the military, and public-education systems with obligations to serve students located in remote, sparsely populated areas as is the case in parts of Australia, Canada, and Alaska.

The digital computer began to emerge as a tool for education as early as the late 1950s, and its adoption as a tool for distance education was not far behind. One of the most successful and long-lasting computer-aided instruction systems was PLATO (Programmed Logic for Automatic Teaching Operations), which began in 1961 as a single-station computer learning system but by the 1980s had grown into a mass-marketed commercial product that allowed students at multiple locations to work through on-screen learning modules while receiving pre-programmed feedback from remote computers.[21] The evolution of ARPANet into the Internet threw open the door for innovative uses of digital computers in distance education. One of the earliest of these was MUD, which stood for "multi-user dungeon" in its original RPG (role-playing game) version but was retroconned to stand for "multi-user domain" (sometimes "dimension") when used for educational purposes. The most popular form of educational MUD was MOO (MUD Object Oriented), an online, text-based virtual-reality system that enabled multiple learners and teachers to simultaneously gather and interact in virtual rooms. Diversity University, the first educational MOO, was created in 1993 and served as a virtual space for everything from informal discussions to full-fledged online courses. For example, in spring 1994 two instructors of first-year college writing classes located in, respectively, Pennsylvania and Wyoming used the Diversity University MOO to join their two writing classes into a single "Internet discourse community" in which students of varied cultural and historical backgrounds could communicate and learn from each other as they engaged in the writing process.[22]

The combined history of distance education and computer-aided learning has shaped online education, but the real Gutenberg moment did not occur until the advent of the Web. At least for the developed world, the pervasiveness and accessibility of the Web has made it possible to take online education precisely to where learners are—at home, at work, or on a commuter train—without the need to build expensive, often proprietary, infrastructure as was the case with such older educational technologies as PLATO and satellite-based television systems. At the same time the flexibility of the Web as a platform for a growing variety of educational technologies means that almost any teaching or learning activity—synchronous or asynchronous—can be conducted over the Web. Clearly, the Web was the spark that set off the twenty-first-century explosion of online education.

THE FORMS OF ONLINE EDUCATION

Just as early printed books took on the form of the then-familiar manuscript book, some forms of online education are almost indistinguishable from traditional in-person education. Such an example is found in the type of online course that consists of little more than a video camera pointed at a teacher employing the same lecture format used in an in-person classroom. When such courses are presented live via the Web they may offer the possibility of real-time interaction with remote students, though of course there is no real-time interaction once the lectures have been saved for viewing on a repository such as YouTube Edu, iTunes U, or an institutional repository. The length and scope of such courses are usually based on the traditional academic term (semester or quarter), a practice that ignores one of the recognized virtues of online education: that online learning can, as appropriate, take place across a time span either longer or shorter than an academic term and have a scope that is either larger or smaller than what is possible within the framework of traditional academic credit units. Whether an online course takes on a form that is highly traditional or more innovative, it may nonetheless employ one or more traditional educational tools, such as homework assignments, readings (possibly from a print-format textbook), tests, the assigning of major projects or papers, and traditional schemes for grading and awarding academic credit.

Employing a different approach are those hybrid courses (also known as "blended courses") in which students engage in a mix of both in-person and online learning. The degree to which a course may mix the online (synchronous or asynchronous) with the in-person varies widely by subject matter, course level, instructor, and intended learning outcomes. Closest to the in-person educational format is the hybrid flipped course in which students may view online video segments (lectures, demonstrations, dramatized scenarios, performances, documentaries, etc.) or engage in other online learning activities prior to meeting in person with their fellow students and teacher to engage in discussion, solve homework problems, or otherwise take part in one or more in-person active-learning techniques. More extreme are those hybrid courses in which the bulk of instruction and learning takes place online with minimal in-person contact, perhaps as little as an initial orientation. An example of the latter type of hybrid course occurs when a campus uses online instruction to conduct a traditional large lecture-hall class without the need for a lecture hall.

Moving into more innovative educational spaces are entirely asynchronous online courses that dispense with, or diminish the importance of, the lecture while otherwise employing a traditional mix of readings and assignments coupled with the possibility of student-to-teacher and student-to-student interaction via such means as wikis, blogs, or e-mail. Asynchronous online courses permit learners to do their course work at whatever time best fits their schedules, an attractive attribute for learners with full-time jobs as well as those who may reside many time zones away from where the course originates. Except for the possibility of student-to-student interaction (via such means as wikis and e-mail) and the replacement of postal mail service with the speed and convenience of the Web, the format of asynchronous, non-lecture-centered online courses is strikingly similar to the format of the traditional correspondence course as it has existed since the nineteenth century.

Of all forms of online education, the one that has thus far strayed the furthest from traditional in-person instruction—and has generated the most buzz from both within and outside of the education profession—is the massive open online course (MOOC). The initial popularity of the MOOC is undeniable. In fall 2011, over one hundred thousand students signed up for a MOOC offered by Professor Andrew Ng of Stanford University on the subject of machine learning.[23] This was not a onetime phenomenon. MOOCs offered by high-profile faculty affiliated with elite institutions have attracted students by the tens of thousands and are credited with setting off what some have labeled "MOOC Mania." The most ringing endorsement of the MOOC, at least thus far, was the Georgia Institute of Technology's August 2013 announcement that it would become the first elite university to offer a degree—a master's in computer science—entirely via low-cost MOOCs.[24]

The techniques employed by MOOCs have dropped a virtual wrecking ball on traditional in-person instruction, starting with the fact that the dominant business model for MOOCs allows learners to take them for free. Two emerging models for supporting free MOOCs are (1) advertising or (2) charging a fee to those students who wish to earn an official certificate for completing and passing the course. While dropout rates for MOOCs have been estimated to run as high as 90 percent, the fact that students enroll in them by the thousands means that the number who complete any given MOOC is much higher than would be possible in even the largest in-person class.[25] Requiring students to purchase textbooks—an expense beyond the means of most students living in impoverished regions of the world—is a challenge for MOOCs that rely on anything other than open-access information resources. Clearing copyrights for a MOOC can be a huge undertaking, though on the bright side this challenge has led to faculty reaching out to libraries for assistance with copyright issues and has sparked an "open resources" movement among MOOC providers.[26] Taking a different tack, Coursera is working with various publishers on a pilot program to provide free access to digital textbooks.[27] A single MOOC may employ a large variety of education tools, though often deploying them in small doses. For example, rather than using video to record and share a traditional fifty-minute lecture, MOOC video lectures tend to be much shorter, typically ten minutes or less. Because of the vast number of students enrolled in popular MOOCs, most tutoring and evaluation of student work is performed by student peers rather than the instructor. In a variation on the peer theme, in March 2013 Harvard University sent e-mails inviting thousands of alumni who had taken the in-person version of Professor Gregory Nagy's popular humanities course, "Concepts of the Ancient Greek Hero," to serve as tutors and discussion leaders for the MOOC version of the course.[28]

SQUARE HOLES, ROUND LEARNERS

For librarians, online education, regardless of which form it may take or tools it may employ, means serving learners who do not necessarily fall into familiar categories or patterns. Online learners may range in age from preschoolers to senior citizens and may be tackling subjects ranging in complexity from the ABCs to graduate-level work at a major research university. Some online students, especially those enrolled in MOOCs, will not have ready access to their instructor, so librarians may be one group to which they turn for help when they find themselves struggling with the subject matter of a course or, more prosaically, with the challenge of negotiating an unfamiliar online learning environment. Because the grading of some online courses relies on proctored exams, online learners may ask local librarians to serve as proctors.

SOME TOOLS OF ONLINE EDUCATION

Even though trying to list the rapidly evolving tools of online education is a fool's game, the following is a, to date, reasonably complete survey of the current tools and how they are being used:

TEXT

Text-based information is presented via a variety of standard formats such as HTML, .doc, .pdf, .xls, and .txt.

IMAGES

Visual information is presented via a variety of standard file formats such as HTML, .gif, .jpeg, .tiff, .png, and .pdf.

MIXED TEXT AND IMAGES

Because many formats—notably HTML and .pdf—support both text and images, the mixing of the two is common. Digital slideshows are a popular means of presenting a mix of text and images, in some cases with accompanying audio narration.

E-MAIL

E-mail remains a common means of communication between and among teachers and students in the online education environment. E-mail communication can be one-to-one or one-to-many.

CHAT

Chat permits synchronous text communication. Co-browsing features allow one chatter to do such things as lead a second party to a particularly useful website or through a set of steps necessary to carry out a particular online task.

BLOGS

An instructor may use a single-author blog to communicate with students regarding assignments, course discussions, or other matters of common interest. A multiple-author blog allows for an online, asynchronous discussion involving an entire class. A course may include multiple threaded blogs, each focusing on a sub-topic relevant to the course. Participation in a blog (or wiki, see below) is often a requirement in online courses for which grades and/or credit are awarded.

WIKIS
Similar to a blog in that it allows for an online, asynchronous discussion involving an entire class, a wiki varies from a blog in that it typically lacks an owner who controls the discussion and therefore may be less structured.

TELEPHONE
The telephone allows for audio-only communication between distant individuals or, in the case of a conference call, groups. Most smart phones allow for video as well as audio transmission, though this is normally limited to two-party calls.

WEB CONFERENCING
Web-conferencing applications allow synchronous voice and video interaction between distant parties. This can be as simple as initiating a two-way Skype call or as sophisticated as using Web-conferencing applications that simultaneously transmit real-time video and audio of multiple conference participants.

SHARED ONLINE WHITEBOARD
A shared online whiteboard allows an instructor and distant learners to interact synchronously, with multiple participants contributing text and drawn images.

VIDEO
Video can consist of live (synchronous) content or served (asynchronous) content. Video can be as simple as a webcam pointed at a classroom lecturer or as sophisticated as tightly edited content of cinematic quality.

GAMES
Web-based video games are used to help learners master everything from preschool basics to complex engineering challenges. The most so-

phisticated of these games are similar in appearance and complexity to the commercially produced games that millions play for entertainment. Examples of games currently being used for online education include *Discover Babylon*, which teaches students about archaeological field-work, and *Immune Attack*, which teaches students about cell biology.[*]

LEARNING OBJECTS

While learning objects vary widely in format and purpose, they share the characteristic of being short and focused on a specific learning outcome. An example might be a five-minute online tutorial on a subject such as "The Characteristics of a Peer Reviewed Journal Article." Learning objects tend to have an active-learning component and ideally include a built-in testing/assessment component. Learning objects also tend to be reconfigurable to allow for different learning outcomes as well as portable so they can be reused for multiple purposes or courses. Many of the tools in this list can be considered learning objects.

AVATARS

Although not yet widely used in online education, avatars take the form of a graphical human character with which (whom?) learners can interact. Powered by artificial intelligence, avatars guide learners by answering their questions or directing them to appropriate online resources.

COMMERCIAL PACKAGES

Commercially produced online learning packages may provide an entire turnkey course or only specific tools such as homework problem sets, tutorials, or examinations. Some commercial online learning packages are bundled with print and/or electronic textbooks. For example, the commercial MathXL package supplements a suite of mathematics and statistics textbooks by providing online tutorials, homework, and assessment systems.

---

[*] Catherine M. Casserly and Marshall S. Smith, "Revolutionizing Education through Innovation: Can Openness Transform Teaching and Learning?," in *Opening Up Education: The Collective Advancement of Education through Open Technology, Open Content, and Open Knowledge*, ed. Toru Iiyoshi and M. S. Vijay Kumar, 261–275 (Cambridge, MA: MIT Press, 2008), 261.

It is possible that online learners may choose to make use of whatever library they find most convenient—either physically or virtually—rather than resort to the library that is affiliated with the institution offering the course in which they are enrolled. A homeschooled Canadian teenager pursuing an online international baccalaureate degree could seek assistance at her local college library or ask a question via that library's digital chat service. A public librarian in Garden City, Kansas, may find herself assisting a local learner who is enrolled in a graduate-level MOOC offered by an Ivy League university. How to serve such learners, and quite possibly if they will be served at all, is a question more and more librarians and libraries will find themselves facing as the reach of online education extends. Online learners whom librarians serve may fall anywhere in the matrix shown in table 6.1.

Of course public librarians have always dealt with students representing a mix of (mostly local) institutions, while academic librarians have always dealt with members of the general public as well as students who attend institutions other than the one that issues the academic librarian's paycheck. The difference with online education is that such cross-institutional encounters are likely to be more frequent, to be more often virtual than in person, and to involve courses offered by institutions separated not only by miles (and

Table 6.1.

Learner affiliated with library?	Course affiliated with library?	Hypothetical example:
Yes	Yes	**Learner:** Student at North High School. **Online Course:** North High Advanced Composition. **Library of Choice:** North High Library.
Yes	No	**Learner:** Springfield Public Library cardholder. **Online Course:** River City Community College "Introduction to Cognitive Psychology." **Library of Choice:** Springfield Public Library.
No	Yes	**Learner:** Student at Yakutsk Polytechnic University. **Online Course:** Normal State University "Python Programming MOOC." **Library of Choice:** Normal State Library.
No	No	**Learner:** Student enrolled at River City Community College. **Online Course:** Normal State University "Python Programming MOOC." **Library of Choice:** Springfield Public Library.

plenty of them), but also by borders, languages, laws, and markedly different educational cultures. It is hard enough when a high-school teacher on the other side of town gives an eccentric assignment that requires students to use information resources the local public library may not possess. How much more difficult does this become when the assignment is given by a teacher who is two thousand miles away and with whom the student has never so much as exchanged an e-mail, much less met in person? Complicating this is the troublesome issue of what proprietary online information resources are available to remote learners. Publishers will certainly argue that academic site licenses are not intended to include learners whose only connection to an institution is enrollment in a free MOOC. And librarians who have experience with cooperative digital chat-reference services already know how tricky—though manageable—a challenge it can be to determine exactly what proprietary online resources may or may not be accessible to a customer affiliated with a distant and (to the librarian) unfamiliar institution.

Obstacles aside, most librarians feel an obligation to provide service to anyone who asks for it. Such an attitude is certainly behind the spirit of the Association of College & Research Libraries' "Standards for Distance Learning Library Services," which opens with the following declaration:

> Every student, faculty member, administrator, staff member, or any other member of an institution of higher education, is entitled to the library services and resources of that institution, including direct communication with the appropriate library personnel, regardless of where enrolled or where located in affiliation with the institution. Academic libraries must, therefore, meet the information and research needs of all these constituents, wherever they may be. This principle of access entitlement, as applied to individuals at a distance, is the undergirding and uncompromising conviction of the *Standards for Distance Learning Library Services*.[29]

Of course the above statement of principle refers to learners explicitly affiliated with the library's parent institution. Is it reasonable, however, to provide such a level of service to every unaffiliated online learner who happens to crawl across the library's digital threshold? While limiting or denying service to any category of information seeker seems punitive, isn't it the obligation of the institution that is providing the online learning opportunity to also provide library services and information resources? Consider a

worst-case scenario: should a budget-strapped public or academic library expend resources supporting a learner enrolled in a for-profit online university
that pads its bottom line by forgoing the expense of providing library services
to its own students?

THREATS AND OPPORTUNITIES FOR LIBRARIES

If (and I mean that sincerely) online education proves to be the juggernaut
that many believe it will be, does this represent a threat or an opportunity for
libraries? That this question is far from answered is evident from the title of
one of the first major conferences on the subject of libraries and MOOCs, the
OCLC/University of Pennsylvania Libraries–sponsored "MOOCs and Libraries: Massive Opportunity or Overwhelming Challenge?"[30]

In some corners, online education is seen as a looming threat to education as we know it. The darkest scenario is a future in which all education
takes place online; the teaching profession is reduced to a relative handful of
part-timers who earn, at best, Mumbai-tech-support salaries for their work;
and schools, colleges, and universities are converted into shopping malls,
low-income housing, or minimum-security prisons. Should education be
forced down a path resembling the plot of a Philip K. Dick novel, libraries
will almost certainly go down with it. Of course that is the extreme scenario.
For one thing, there are any number of skills that will likely never be mastered
entirely online, such as flying an airplane, conducting a psychological evaluation, or hitting a curveball. Also, online education could grow to become far
more dominant than it now is without ever monopolizing the educational
landscape to the point that all other forms of education disappear. Perhaps
(and this is really the most likely scenario) online education simply evolves
to become an indispensable educational tool while leaving the existing educational infrastructure more or less intact.

Barring an unlikely educational-apocalypse scenario, online education
presents libraries with far more opportunities than threats. Most obviously,
online education requires access to digital information resources of the sort
that libraries have been successfully managing for a couple of decades now.
As online education grows in importance, libraries should find themselves
ideally positioned for managing (i.e., acquiring, organizing, and facilitating
access to) the digital information resources that will be required by millions

of online learners; to take advantage of their position, though, libraries will need to rethink their strategies for serving online learners.

SERVING OUR OWN OR SERVING THEM ALL?

As more educational institutions offer online courses, school and academic libraries need to think about how they will serve their traditional customers who are enrolled in or teaching online courses. While there may be a temptation to take the approach of waiting for the learners and faculty involved with online education to reach out to the library, the dangers of such an approach are that the students and faculty will end up poorly served or the library will simply be left behind as a non-player in the online education arena.

Providing a library Web presence (portal or page) aimed at online learners "creates a personalized space for discovery, access, and help while letting students know the library understands their distance situation."[31] While creating such a space is likely to be helpful to some online learners, it remains a passive approach in that learners must somehow discover the space on their own or be directed to it before they can take advantage of it. When online courses are centered around a course-management system (CMS), a more direct approach is to integrate available library services (e.g., chat reference, online guides, term-paper consultation services) and relevant information resources (e.g., databases, e-book collections, open-access repositories) directly into the CMS presence or each online course. Making direct links from CMS course pages to librarian-developed learning objects could prove especially beneficial to online learners and, in the case of reusable learning objects, a real time-saver for librarians. Learning objects may be as simple as online subject guides and pathfinders or as complicated as full-fledged tutorials and educational gaming packages. No less an authority than Clifford Lynch writes that "formal and informal guides to the literature in various subjects, bibliographies, pathfinders, and other tools may also take on expanded importance in an open education environment."[32] As learning objects become more complex, the resources required to create and maintain them scale beyond what is available to individual librarians and, possibly, entire library organizations. A survey published in 2011 reports that, of the librarians who used software to create learning objects, 68 percent learned how to use the software on their own, while 25 percent of respondents reported "little or no training in online learning pedagogy."[33] If librarians are going to be players in online learning, they need training so that they can better understand and effectively respond to the needs of online learners. Regardless of any strategies librarians may develop for leveraging the power of a CMS, one persistent challenge is that editorial access to the CMS presence for any given course is typically controlled by the course instructor, an individual who may require persuading before granting editorial access to librarians or, in the worst case, may be totally unwilling to grant such access.

Requiring even more cooperation from instructors of online courses, but potentially productive of excellent learning outcomes, is the practice of embedding librarians in online courses. In a typical embedded-librarian scenario, a librarian works with an instructor to establish a formal relationship with the learners enrolled in a specific online course. This might include having the librarian formally introduced to the class (via the course syllabus and other means), establishing recommended methods of communication between class members and the librarian (e-mail, wiki, digital-chat office hours), and the librarian providing instruction and personal assistance through a variety of asynchronous and synchronous means (assignments, learning objects, video clips, and live appearances via videoconferencing). In the words of Starr Hoffman, "embedding a librarian in an online course offers a more interactive, direct substitute for the hands-on, customized library instruction provided in many face-to-face courses."[34] By the same token, embedding a librarian in an online course involves a logistical and instructional workload equal to, and possibly exceeding, that of face-to-face courses and also requires a set of skills not all librarians possess. In the event of a transformational shift in the direction of online education, "Will some librarians," as Sarah Pritchard has asked, "work only with remote users and course-embedded digital materials, never interacting with on-site users, independent researchers, or demands for resources outside a given syllabus?"[35]

Even more fundamentally disruptive to the way libraries have operated in the past is the possibility that online education could decouple learning from the concept of the alma mater. Traditionally, a student is enrolled in one school and one school only; in fact, to change schools due to dissatisfaction with your current school (or vice versa), relocation, or matriculation to a higher-level institution is considered a major turning point in life, the dramatic fuel of countless coming-of-age books and films. If online courses come to dominate the educational landscape, getting an education from a single institution could become as unusual as buying all your clothing from a single store or listening exclusively to the music of a just one musician; instead, future online learners might pick and choose courses offered by a variety of educational institutions based on the learner's educational goals, abilities, and interests. Imagine a future in which almost everyone is engaged (to greater or lesser extents) in lifelong online learning, in which everyone is taking online courses but nobody has a strong, traditional sense of affiliation with any one school (or library). How are libraries supposed to take care of their own when there is no "their own" to take care of?

The ideal solution would be for every institution or organization that offers online learning to take responsibility for meeting the information needs of its own learners on a course-by-course basis. At least some providers of online education will assume this responsibility, and it is possible that meeting the information needs of its affiliated online learners will be one criterion that separates the best providers of online education from the herd. Even so, some providers of online education will not live up to their information obligations, and even for those that do, some learners will inevitably slip through the cracks, turning elsewhere and anywhere for assistance with their information needs.

Under such a scenario, the idealistic, and possibly ideal, solution would be for libraries to treat everyone in the online world as their customer, to call upon the library world's tradition of collaboration—a tradition that has produced benefits like interlibrary loans, shared catalogs, and collaborative digital chat-reference services—to serve all comers regardless of their affiliation, or affiliations. While it may seem daunting, if not actually insane, for libraries to adopt a strategy in which anyone and everyone in the entire online world becomes their (potential) customer, that is exactly where the disruption brought about by online education may lead. However, if every library were to decide that everyone is its customer, and if libraries agreed to work cooperatively not only with each other, but also with information-related businesses and non-profits, the prospect of serving everyone becomes less daunting. Sure, the trip hazard of access to proprietary information resources will remain a challenge, though a ray of hope lies in the notion that the demands of online education may result in the triumph of the open-access movement, at least as far as scholarly publication is concerned. While some librarians may fear being overwhelmed by millions of online gypsy learners, the entire online world cannot, and will never, descend en masse on any one library. As shared library services such as OCLC's 24/7 digital-reference collaborative have already shown, the strategy of banding together to serve any and all online customers is manageable. On top of this, the reliance of MOOCs on peer-to-peer interaction means that, for better or worse, those enrolled in MOOCs are likely to turn to their fellow learners for assistance before they go looking for help from librarians. For library organizations, the most difficult part of an all-comers strategy might be convincing non-library administrators and boards that—in the online realm—a strategy of collaboration among libraries brings more value to the local customer base than does a strategy based on exclusion. While public library A cannot say for certain that its affiliated cardholders will end up getting online service from public library B or academic library Z, the fact that such assistance is available is a plus for library A and everyone it wishes to serve.

It is also reassuring to remember that, when dealing with online learners, service is more likely to be provided via persistent online learning objects than via labor-intensive interactions that follow the traditional reference-interview pattern. Looking beyond the increased-workload-dread horizon, online education opens up some exciting possibilities for libraries. If librarians were to develop pedagogically sound learning objects with broad appeal to online learners, the potential information-literacy impact of these learning objects could dwarf any instructional impacts librarians have achieved in the past. And what of the opportunities offered by library-created MOOCs? It is easy to imagine academic libraries developing popular MOOCs on such topics as "Researching and Writing an Academic Paper," "Managing Your Research Data," or "Intellectual Property and the Academic Researcher." Beyond hypothetical what-ifs, library MOOCs are already happening. For one notable early example, in March of 2013 the Wake Forest University Library offered "ZSRx: The Cure for the Common Web," a four-week MOOC designed to "foster Web literacy in parents & alumni."[36] And even though MOOCs are typically thought of as a product of academia, public libraries developing MOOCs on such non-academic topics as "Researching Your Family History" or "Investing for Retirement" would be fulfilling their traditional role of providing educational programs for the community. While creating a semester-length academic MOOC is a huge project that can easily require six months to prepare the course content and shoot and edit video clips,[37] library-related MOOCs can be far shorter in length and therefore require far less time and work to develop. In addition, the workload for any one library organization can be lightened when multiple libraries collaborate to co-produce a library-oriented MOOC.

On the other hand, if libraries choose to stay out of the business of MOOCs, others are willing to step in. In March 2014, Google launched a free MOOC called "Making Sense of Data." If this initiative proves successful, Google will certainly launch more MOOCs on topics that could, and maybe should, be taught by librarians.

CONCLUSION

Finding an appropriate role for libraries in online education may feel, to many librarians, like running alongside an accelerating train. By the time you decide where to put your resources and how many resources you will need, the online education train has moved another quarter mile down the track. Will librarians who jump on board early find that, instead of a bullet train, they have jumped on a bandwagon taking them nowhere? That they've jumped into the wrong car? That their efforts have made no impact on the passengers? Indeed, how are librarians supposed to know whether or not they have made an impact when the very thought of trying to make an assessment of so large and shifting a target as online education is thoroughly daunting. The words of educational technologist Owen McGrath truly apply to the current online education environment:

> As if all the data-gathering issues were not enough, evaluation of technology innovation in higher education has always faced two other lethal foes: span and scope. Unlike areas of educational research where longitudinal studies are feasible, technology-related evaluation efforts often suffer from acutely small time spans within which to deliver results that will be deemed relevant. Fast development cycles and short adoption curves make a mockery of many well-intentioned technology investigations.[38]

It may be that libraries that are early adopters of an online-education mission will need to work more on faith than on proven outcomes. Among early adopters there will likely be many missteps and a few outright failures. The only consolation will be that the lessons learned from these early missteps and failures will help the library profession find better paths. While not every library can be an early adopter, none can afford to be a never adopter. The economic, political, technological, and social forces at work all point in the direction of online education. The fundamental question is not if, but to what extent, online education will be integrated in the overall educational infrastructure. The urgent question is how soon this integration will happen. In *The Printing Revolution in Early Modern Europe*, Elizabeth L. Eisenstein provides the following illustration of how quickly printing technology made an impact on European culture:

> A man born in 1453, the year of the fall of Constantinople, could look back from the fiftieth year on a lifetime in which about eight million books had been printed, more perhaps than all the scribes of Europe had produced since Constantine founded his city in A.D. 330.[39]

Given the fast pace of change in the twenty-first century, it is quite conceivable that a woman born in 1991, the year the Web went public, could, at age 50, find herself living in a world in which more people get their education online than from in-person instruction. Regardless of what may be lost or gained in such a shift in the educational paradigm, libraries cannot afford to let themselves be left waiting at the station.

NOTES

1. Stephan Füssel, *Gutenberg and the Impact of Printing* (Aldershot, Hampshire: Ashgate, 2005), 19.

2. Elizabeth L. Eisenstein, *The Printing Revolution in Early Modern Europe* (Cambridge: Cambridge University Press, 1993), 22.

3. John E. Chubb and Terry M. Moe, "Chubb and Moe: Higher Education's Online Revolution; the Substitution of Technology (Which Is Cheap) for Labor (Which Is Expensive) Can Vastly Increase Access to an Elite-Caliber Education," *Wall Street Journal* (online), May 30, 2012, http://online.wsj.com/article/SB10001424052702304 019404577416631206583286.html (accessed September 26, 2013).

4. Lewis M. Andrews, "The Hidden Revolution in Online Learning: The Economics of Digital Learning Will Undermine the Liberal Biases Built into the Current

Education System," *Wall Street Journal* (online), December 26, 2012, http://online.wsj.com/article/SB10001424127887323353204578127142174902184.html (accessed September 26, 2013).

5. Catherine M. Casserly and Marshall S. Smith, "Revolutionizing Education through Innovation: Can Openness Transform Teaching and Learning?," in *Opening Up Education: The Collective Advancement of Education through Open Technology, Open Content, and Open Knowledge*, ed. Toru Iiyoshi and M. S. Vijay Kumar, 261–275 (Cambridge, MA: MIT Press, 2008), 261.

6. Steve Kolowich, "Why Professors at San Jose State Won't Use a Harvard Professor's MOOC," *Chronicle of Higher Education*, May 2, 2013, sec. Technology, http://chronicle.com/article/Why-Professors-at-San-Jose/138941 (accessed September 26, 2013).

7. Marc Perry, "A Star MOOC Professor Defects—at Least for Now," *Chronicle of Higher Education*, September 16, 2013, sec. Technology, http://chronicle.com/article/A-MOOC-Star-Defects-at-Least/141331 (accessed September 13, 2013).

8. "Florida Virtual School," Florida Department of Education, http://flvs.net/Pages/default.aspx (Accessed August 16, 2013).

9. Ray Uzwyshyn, Aida Marissa Smith, Priscilla Coulter, Christy Stevens, and Susan Hyland, "A Virtual, Globally Dispersed Twenty-First Century Academic Library System," *Reference Librarian* 54, no. 3 (July 2013): 227.

10. "ASU Online," Arizona State University, http://asuonline.asu.edu (accessed August 16, 2013).

11. Leslee B. Shell, Jennifer Duvernay, Ann Dutton Ewbank, Phil Konomos, Allison Leaming, and Ginny Sylvester, "A Comprehensive Plan for Library Support of Online and Extended Education," *Journal of Library Administration* 50, no. 7 (October 2010): 953.

12. Anthony G. Picciano, Jeff Seaman, Peter Shea, and Karen Swan, "Examining the Extent and Nature of Online Learning in American K–12 Education: The Research Initiatives of the Alfred P. Sloan Foundation," *Internet & Higher Education* 15, no. 2 (March 2012): 128.

13. Swapna Kumar and Mary E. Edwards, "Information Literacy Skills and Embedded Librarianship in an Online Graduate Programme," *Journal of Information Literacy* 7, no. 1 (June 2013): 3.

14. Rachel Cannady, Britt Fagerheim, Beth Filar Williams, and Heidi Steiner, "Diving into Distance Learning Librarianship," *College & Research Libraries News* 74, no. 5 (May 2013): 254.

15. Bruce Kingma and Kathleen Schisa, "WISE Economics: ROI of Quality and Consortiums," *Journal of Education for Library & Information Science* 51, no. 1 (Winter 2010): 45.

16. Michael Stephens, "Best of Both Worlds," *Library Journal* 138, no. 9 (May 15, 2013), http://lj.libraryjournal.com/2013/05/opinion/michael-stephens/best-of-both-worlds-office-hours (accessed September 24, 2013).

17. J. J. Clark, "The Correspondence School—Its Relation to Technical Education and Some of Its Results," *Science* 24, no. 611 (September 14, 1906): 328.

18. Denise M. Casey, "A Journey to Legitimacy: The Historical Development of Distance Education through Technology," *Techtrends* 52, no. 2 (2008): 46.

19. William Bianchi, "Education by Radio: America's Schools of the Air," *Techtrends* 53, no. 2 (March/April, 2008): 36.

20. Casey, "A Journey to Legitimacy," 46.

21. "Scientification of Education," in *Reader's Guide to the History of Science* (London: Routledge, 2000), http://www.credoreference.com/entry/routhistscience/scientification_of_education (accessed September 26, 2013).

22. Leslie D. Harris and Cynthia A. Wambeam, "The Internet-Based Composition Classroom: A Study in Pedagogy," *Computers and Composition* 13, no. 3 (1996): 353–371.

23. Teresa Johnston, "Stanford for All," *Stanford Magazine*, (September/October 2012), http://alumni.stanford.edu/get/page/magazine/article/?article_id=55991 (accessed August 15, 2013).

24. Tamar Lewin, "Virtual U.: Master's Degree Is New Frontier of Study Online," *New York Times*, August 19, 2013, sec. Education, http://www.nytimes.com/2013/08/18/education/masters-degree-is-new-frontier-of-study-online.html?pagewanted=all&_r=0 (accessed September 26, 2013).

25. Meredith Schwartz, "Massive Open Opportunity," *Library Journal* 138, no. 9 (May 15, 2013), http://lj.libraryjournal.com/2013/05/library-services/massive-open-opportunity-supporting-moocs (accessed September 26, 2013).

26. Stephen E. Arnold, "GADZOOKS, It's MOOCs," *Online Searcher* 37, no. 1 (January 2013): 15.

27. Iz Conroy, "Coursera Announces Pilot Program with Publishers to Supplement Online Courses with High Quality Content," *Wall Street Journal* (online), May 8, 2013, http://online.wsj.com/article/PR-CO-20130508-910631.html (accessed September 26, 2013).

28. Richard Pérez-Peña, "Harvard Asks Graduates to Donate Time to Free Online Humanities Class," *New York Times*, March 25, 2013, sec. Education, http://www.nytimes.com/2013/03/26/education/harvard-asks-alumni-to-donate-time-to-free-online-course.html (accessed September 26, 2013).

29. Association of College & Research Libraries, "Standards for Distance Learning Library Services," American Library Association, http://www.ala.org/acrl/standards/guidelinesdistancelearning (accessed August 2, 2013).

30. OCLC and University of Pennsylvania Libraries, "MOOCs and Libraries: Massive Opportunity or Overwhelming Challenge?," March 18, 2013, http://www.oclc.org/research/events/2013/03-18.html (accessed September 16, 2013).

31. Rachel Cannady, Britt Fagerheim, Beth Filar Williams, and Heidi Steiner, "Diving into Distance Learning Librarianship," *College & Research Libraries News* 74, no. 5 (May 2013): 254–261.

32. Clifford Lynch, "Digital Libraries, Learning Communities, and Open Education," in *Opening Up Education: The Collective Advancement of Education through Open Technology, Open Content, and Open Knowledge*, ed. Toru Iiyoshi and M. S. Vijay Kumar, 105–118 (Cambridge, MA: MIT Press, 2008), 111.

33. Lori S. Mestre, Lisa Baures, Mona Niedbala, Corinne Bishop, Sarah Cantrell, Alice Perez, and Kate Silfen, "Learning Objects as Tools for Teaching Information Literacy Online: A Survey of Librarian Usage," *College & Research Libraries* 72, no. 3 (May 2011): 250.

34. Starr Hoffman, "Embedded Academic Librarian Experiences in Online Courses: Roles, Faculty Collaboration, and Opinion," *Library Management* 32, no. 6 (September 2011): 445.

35. Sarah M. Pritchard, "MOOCs: An Opportunity for Innovation and Research," *Portal: Libraries & the Academy* 13, no. 2 (April 2013): 128.

36. Kyle Denlinger, "ZSRx: A (Mini) MOOC for Web Literacy," Coalition for Networked Information, San Antonio, Texas, April 4–5, 2013, 13, http://www.cni.org/wp-content/uploads/2013/04/cni_zsrx_denlinger.pdf (accessed March 1, 2013).

37. Mariellen Calter, "MOOCs and the Library: Engaging with Evolving Pedagogy," IFLA World Library and Information Congress, Singapore, August 17–23, 2013, 6, http://library.ifla.org/id/eprint/160 (accessed September 15, 2013).

38. Owen McGrath, "Open Educational Technology: Tempered Aspirations," in *Opening Up Education: The Collective Advancement of Education through Open Technology, Open Content, and Open Knowledge,* ed. Toru Iiyoshi and M. S. Vijay Kumar, 13–26 (Cambridge, MA: MIT Press, 2008), 19.

39. Elizabeth L. Eisenstein, *The Printing Revolution in Early Modern Europe* (Cambridge: Cambridge University Press, 1993), 15.

7

Designing Websites

Trust and Flow

As a librarian at New Mexico State University in the early 1990s, I numbered myself among the denizens of Gopherspace. A predecessor to the Web, the Gopher was a TCP/IP protocol that employed a hypertext menu design and offered limited searching capabilities. You could use the Gopher to do things like connect to distant computers (including OPACs), read plain-text files, and download documents and images encoded in such now archaic formats as BinHex and Uuencoding. From the vantage point of the twenty-first century the Gopher seems primitive, but back in the days of thirteen-inch CRT monitors and 400 MB hard drives, it was the slickest thing around.

Then one day a guy from the library IT department called me over to his computer to show me "something cool." He had obtained a piece of software called Cello, and what I saw on his monitor was, for sure, something cool. Way, way cooler than the Gopher. I speculate that this, my introduction to the World Wide Web, took place sometime in late 1993 or early 1994, as Cello was first released in June 1993. Whatever the exact date, I knew I wanted in on this new thing right away.

I located (via Gopher) a guide to writing HTML and printed it out in glorious dot matrix. Without benefit of any kind of HTML-editing software (much less a WYSIWYG editor), a group of us set out to create a library website at a time when not all that many libraries had such a thing. We wrote HTML code directly on a UNIX server called "Toonces," a pop-culture reference to a recurring *Saturday Night Live* skit about a cat who could drive (if not particularly well) a car. And so we designed (if not particularly well) a first-generation library website. I know our results would look primitive today, though I am fairly certain that, to our credit, our design did not include any animated .gifs.

Though I cannot claim that I was peeking over Tim Berners-Lee's shoulder on the day he launched the World Wide Web, I have been doing web pages longer than most people (including a multitude of "newbies" whose website design skills leave mine in the dust). Over the course of my career I have helped launch two library websites where none existed before—the first, circa 1994, for the New Mexico State University Library; the second, in 2003, for the fledgling University of California–Merced Library. I have also participated in more library website redesign projects than I can, or care to, remember. I have fussed over colors, fonts, and layouts (knowing full well that none of these were going to display consistently from one machine to the next). I have engaged in long discussions about navigability, usability, scrolling behavior, clicking behavior, mouse overs, pop-up boxes, and whether or not a particular design feature was intuitive. At times I have believed I could change the library world if only I could hit on the perfect website design.

After having done all that work, having visited hundreds of library websites, and having cast my eyes upon thousands of library web pages, my takeaway is rather humbling. They're all the same. Take the more or less status quo library home page:

1. A tasteful logo graphic.
2. Assorted photographs.
3. A box to search the library catalog (and maybe other stuff).
4. Contact us.
5. Hours.
6. News and events.
7. FAQs.
8. My Account.

Library websites are so much the same that the best thing the profession could do would be to make them even more alike than they already are. How much easier would it be for users if, say, every single library *always* presented its hours link as a blue clock on the upper left-hand side of its home page? If every library catalog search box not only looked and worked and displayed identically, but was also consistently found centered immediately below the home-page logo? If every library could agree on consistent wording to label our goods and services—for example, to always use the word *borrowing* instead of the word *circulation*? Or *circulation* instead of *borrowing*? The exact details would not matter if only our practices were rigidly consistent. Instead of needing to learn a new script for every library website, users could learn one script and apply it universally just as they did in the days when learning to use one library card catalog meant that you could use any library card catalog.

Drivers approaching an intersection know what to do when they see the sign in figure 7.1 attached to a pole by the side of the road even when the wording has been removed. Imagine the chaos if, in the interest of establishing its unique brand, every local highway department produced stop signs

FIGURE 7.1

WEBSITES BY THE NUMBERS

Even if a library website is filled with useful content and stands as an exemplar of good design, it all means nothing if the site is not actually used by those the library intends to serve. In a survey published in 2006, only 2 percent of college students reported using their campus's library website as the starting point when searching for information on a particular topic. This compares to 89 percent of college students who reported using a Web search engine as the starting point when searching for information on a particular topic.* Similarly, a 2012 report from the EDUCAUSE Center for Applied Research reports that only 5 percent of the undergraduates surveyed identified their college or university website as "the one website or online resource you couldn't live without." In comparison, when asked the same question, 33 percent of undergraduates identified Google and 16 percent identified Blackboard (an online course-management system) as their essential website.†

Wherever these statistics happen to fall on the scale that runs from "Truly Alarming" to "Suspicions Confirmed," they do point up the importance of collecting accurate website-use statistics and asking tough, sometimes disquieting, questions about what those statistics mean:

- Of the total number of visits the library website gets in a given day, month, or year, is it possible to identify which are actually human beings and which are machine-generated (i.e., bots)? Is it possible to identify which visits represent repeat visitors? Or from what domains the visits originate?
- Does the ebb and flow of visits conform to usage patterns of the physical library, or are they seemingly unrelated?
- Is the total number of visits, whatever it may be, indicative of success or of failure?
- How many visits are to pages other than the home page?
- Do the pages the library considers the most important get the most visits?
- How much time does library staff spend working on pages that receive few visits?

- Do changes to the library website make any difference in how much or what ways the website is being used?

If it seems that total website usage is low, the library can make attempts to increase usage through publicity campaigns. The downside to this approach is that, according to the WolframAlpha website, as of March 2014 there are approximately 625.3 million websites competing for visitors. This does not mean a library should not try to promote use of its website, only that it had better try very hard and demonstrate a lot of perseverance if it wishes to succeed.

If, on the other hand, the problem is not total number of visitors but that certain pages within the website are getting fewer visitors than the library thinks they should, it is possible to revise those pages to be more attractive and useful and, more importantly, to feature them more prominently. The main restriction on making a page more prominent within a website is that this will likely happen only at the expense of making some other page less prominent.

However website visitor numbers stack up, the most important point is that those responsible for the site must be willing to learn from the numbers and make changes not merely in how the site is organized and presented, but also in how the library staff conceives of the ways the library is used and valued (or not) by the community it serves (or not).

---

* Cathy De Rosa, Joanne Cantrell, Janet Hawk, and Alane Wilson, *College Students' Perceptions of Libraries and Information Resources* (Dublin, OH: OCLC Online Computer Library Center, 2006), http://www.oclc.org/reports/perceptionscollege.en.html (accessed May 15, 2013).

† Eden Dahlstrom, *ECAR Study of Undergraduate Students and Information Technology, 2012* (Louisville, CO: EDUCAUSE Center for Applied Research, 2012), http://www.educause.edu/ecar (accessed May 20, 2013).

using distinctive shapes, colors, fonts, and wording.* As crazy as that sounds, it is not far different from what libraries do with their websites.

More important than asking why all library websites look essentially the same from a distance yet vary in details from up close is to ask why no library,

---

* This was exactly the case in the early years of the automobile. The forced standardization of road signs brought about a major improvement in automotive safety.

after twenty years of tinkering with the Web, has been able to come up with the killer library website app, the one design that so excels in ease of use and visual appeal that every other library immediately rushes to adopt it? Some library websites are arguably more usable or more attractive than others, but can any be crowned as hands-down masterpieces? No. Has any library, in spite of all the thousands of hours put in by smart librarians and skilled Web developers, created an absolutely foolproof, can't-miss website? Not even close.

LIBRARY WEBSITES: CONSTRAINTS ON SUCCESS

How come library websites are not more successful than they are?

Lack of Focus

Library websites lack focus because they are, perhaps necessarily, obligated to serve too many purposes. Some of the more common library website obligations include the following:

- search engine
- information-literacy tutorial
- guide to one or more physical locations
- source of information about the library organization
- conduit for fund-raising and/or community support

Compare the Google home page to any library home page you like. Over the years the Google home page has remained resolutely minimalist and entirely focused on one function—Google as Internet search engine. While you can dig down through the Google website to find things like corporate information, privacy policies, and so on, you do this via entirely unobtrusive links found at the top and bottom of the home page. A few of the things you will never see on the Google home page include:

- photographs of Google headquarters, Sergey Brin, or, for that matter, anything else
- newsy items trumpeting the achievements of Google, its employees, or its customers
- paid advertisements

- Google's mission statement
- a lack of white space

Google famously plays graphic games with its logo to mark holidays and important events, but nothing interferes with or overshadows Google's primary search-engine function. This steadfast focus has certainly contributed to Google's success.

Taking a highly focused approach may be easier for a business than for a library. While the Ford Motor Company might easily declare that the primary function of its website is to sell new Fords, would it be as easy for a library to declare that the primary function of its website is, say, searching the OPAC and that everything else—hours, location, database searching, special collections, contact information, library events, and fund-raising—be relegated to secondary status? Probably not. On the other hand, could libraries benefit from home-page designs that focus on just a few core functions? Probably so.

Information Is More Complex than Shopping

Speaking of Ford Motor Company, most consumers would agree that buying a new vehicle is a complex purchasing decision. Even so, a U.S. consumer in the market for a new passenger vehicle in 2012 could choose from only about 300 models representing about 45 different makes—typical numbers for any given model year in recent times. Of course once a consumer focuses in on a general type of passenger vehicle—sedan, hybrid, sports car, SUV, pickup truck, van, etc.—and settles on a price range, the number of model choices drops off dramatically. Even if you throw in the need to pick options like color, engine size, and various amenities, the number of choices facing a new-car buyer is insignificant compared to, say, the number of choices facing a health-care consumer winnowing through the most recent five years of popular and scientific information on the subject of gastric bypass surgery. Or an engineer researching the efficiency of solar panels. Or a literature student looking for critical interpretations of *Adventures of Huckleberry Finn*.

A relatively small number of choices is why a website that sets out to help a consumer navigate the entire universe of new cars faces a much easier task than a library website that sets out to help customers navigate the entire universe of information. Designing a website to effectively guide an inexperienced library customer through the simplest information need—finding a known item—is difficult; helping that same customer satisfy a complicated information need—such as identifying appropriate books and journal articles on a specific academic topic or pulling together credible sources to inform a major health-care decision—is many times more difficult. How does choosing among forty-five vehicle makes compare to nearly twenty-five thousand peer-reviewed journals?[1] How does choosing among three hundred vehicle models compare to the 50 million journal articles estimated to have been published since 1665?[2] And let's not forget to add books and non-scholarly sources to that pile of information possibilities. While information on every available model of new car, as well as many additional models of used cars, can be contained in a single commercial website such as Cars.com, the information that libraries strive to make available is dispersed across thousands of individual libraries, siloed in hundreds of unconnected databases, and spread among millions of websites. When it comes to directing library customers through anything like a comprehensive search for information, there are simply too many choices, too many silos, and too many potential distractions waiting to undermine the best efforts of library website designers.

In 1990 Edward R. Tufte wrote, "Clutter and confusion are failures of design, not attributes of information."[3] I agree with that statement so much that I have it framed and hanging on my office wall; however, I also reluctantly believe there is a tipping point past which the sheer volume of information overwhelms even the best design. The volume of information in which libraries deal is far beyond that tipping point.

Anti-stickiness

Just about every commercial website uses sticky content—chat rooms, games, online forums, news, customer reviews, entertainment, exclusives, discount offers, contests, prizes—to keep visitors on their sites as long as possible and to get them to return as often as possible. The business thinking is that the more time visitors spend on a website, as well as the more often they come back, the more likely they are to buy something or click on a paid advertisement. One notable example of a sticky website is that of the Disney Channel. Aimed at children and designed to build and maintain interest in Disney Channel programming, the website is loaded with slick, constantly updated games, videos, music, quizzes, image galleries, and other features focused on keeping young visitors entertained and coming back to see what is new.

(There is always something new, every day.) The website of the Disney Channel's closest competitor, Nickelodeon, employs almost identical sticky tactics.

Usability experts Jakob Neilsen and Marie Tahir have observed that external links make a website like "a house in which every single window is also
a door."[4] While sticky websites rigorously avoid external links, libraries see
providing their customers with the maximum number of window/door com-
binations as an ethical obligation. The goal of connecting library customers
with information demands routinely sending them off to remote databases or
websites from which they may never return. One of the biggest challenges for
information-literacy tools like interactive, multipart research-process tutorials is that once learners go off to try whatever it is they just learned, the chance
that they will return to finish the tutorial is slim.

Customer Investment

Customer reviews and crowd-sourcing can be powerful forces for enhancing a website. One of the advantages of using Amazon.com to identify
potentially useful books is the customer reviews.[†] For example, as of March
2013 Clayton Christensen's *The Innovative University: Changing the DNA of
Higher Education from the Inside Out* (publication date July 26, 2011) had
received fifty customer reviews on Amazon.com. By comparison, by March
2013 there were zero customer reviews of *The Innovative University* posted
in OCLC's WorldCat, a database that serves multiple libraries and, of course,
allows customers to post reviews. While it has become routine for libraries
to allow customers to publicly post comments either on library web pages or
through the library OPAC, the number of comments is often disappointingly
small. Why? This is in part due to the fact that no library attracts the large
critical mass of customers necessary to generate more than occasional postings. In 2012 Amazon racked up 164 million unique customers.[5] If every single person in the New York Combined Statistical Area were a card-carrying
customer of the New York Public Library, the NYPL would still trail Amazon
by 142 million customers. And how do the customer bases of the biggest
academic libraries compare to that of Amazon? The math is not even worth
doing. Customer bases aside, another reason that library websites do not rack

---

[†] Although some of these reviews are bogus, written by self-promoting authors and their allies, it
is often easy to tell these from less biased reviews; even so, biased reviews can be decent sources of
information about the content and nature of a book.

up huge numbers of customer postings is that people are far more inclined to comment about something they buy as opposed to something they borrow or get at no cost (e.g., online access to a periodical article). If someone buys a car with great gas mileage or superior performance, they may well brag about it; if they borrow the same car, the impetus to sound off is not as strong because the customer investment, of money and ego, is lacking.

Libraries Lack the Resources to Create Blockbuster Websites

The above-mentioned Disney Channel and Nickelodeon websites, with their slick features and constantly updated content, are just two examples of commercial websites that demand small armies of programmers, designers, and content creators to flourish. For other examples of lavish commercial websites, take a look at the promotional website—or websites[‡]—of any major film that is currently showing, or about to open, in theaters. Even though such websites usually have limited shelf lives—from a few months before a film's premiere through the marketing blitz for the DVD—the expense that goes into creating Hollywood's highly polished promotional websites would bust the budget of any library. Some of the features found on the most elaborate movie websites are over the top in their technological sophistication. The website for the forgettable stalker film *Obsessed* included a practical-joke feature that allowed visitors to generate personalized stalker-made videos—just upload a photo of an unsuspecting friend and let the software do the rest. The website for *The Simpsons Movie* (which, atypically for the genre, remained online for more than six years following the film's premier) offered visitors the opportunity to create Simpsons avatars, play games, and take tours of Springfield.

The entertainment industry aside, the website budgets for big companies like Apple, Wal-Mart, Staples, YouTube, and Bank of America are so vast that even the most generously funded library websites are doomed to look second-rate in comparison. And the impact of generous website budgets goes far beyond looks and hooks, as big companies can afford to invest in user studies of which library website designers can only dream. For exhibits A and B, consider

---

[‡] Major films often have multiple promotional websites. For example, the science-fiction film *Cloverfield* featured twelve promotional websites. The comedy film *Tropic Thunder* featured, in addition to its main website, fictional biographical websites for each of the film's three main characters as well as a website for a faux mockumentary about the making of the film within the film.

just two of the many highly specialized website usability studies undertaken by Google researchers: "An Eye Tracking Study of How Font Size and Type Influence Online Reading"[6] and "Discriminating the Relevance of Web Search Results with Measures of Pupil Size."[7] The latter study involved twenty-two human subjects. The average library is lucky if it can muster the resources to get twenty-two customers to fill out a self-satisfaction questionnaire.

A BETTER LIBRARY WEBSITE?

Given a perfect library, customers could connect with the information they need so effortlessly, so transparently, so intuitively that there would be no need for a library website. Or an OPAC. Or reference services. Or instruction. We are a long way from the perfect library, which, to find the silver lining, is probably good news for those in the library profession. But given both the distance separating real libraries from perfection as well as the constraints limiting the effectiveness of library websites, how might a library go about building a better website, one that would most effectively meet the needs of its customers?

The last thing the world needs is a set of detailed commandments on how to design a library website. Andrew Pace, the erstwhile head of systems at the North Carolina State University (Raleigh) Library, is credited with having said, "Making minor changes to library catalog systems is like putting lipstick on a pig." That goes double for library websites. If building the ideal library website were merely a matter of tweaking website design, somebody would have figured it out by now. This is not to say that it is a waste of time to study usability, to test website prototypes with real customers, or to practice iterative website design. Those are all good and necessary things. In the end, however, no amount of commendable design diligence is going to result in a transcendent library website. Instead of fixating on website design, libraries might do better to consider the importance of trust and flow, two concepts that have been studied a great deal by scholars of e-commerce yet little, if at all, by library scholars.

TRUST

Libraries in the physical world have built-in attributes that establish their status as trusted institutions. Library buildings are often examples of impressive architecture, a means of establishing trust—and trust's first cousins, power and authority—that has been employed from before the time of the pyramids through the age of the skyscraper. Most libraries also have the trust-building advantage of having been in business for decades if not centuries, something that is not all that common in the online world. Another way that physical libraries establish trust is through their association with cities, counties, states, schools, colleges, and universities. If students feel loyalty to Southwest Missouri State University, then they are predisposed to trust a library operating under its auspices. If residents of Springfield, Georgia, have a sense of civic pride, they are predisposed to trust the Springfield Library. Perhaps most importantly, the people who work in libraries can become trusted figures to those who regularly visit libraries. If, through face-to-face interactions, library customers come to feel that a library's employees demonstrate competence, benevolence, and integrity, those good feelings are likely to increase their trust in the library organization as a whole.

While literature and popular culture may too often teach people to fear the stereotypically stern, occasionally hostile librarian, the library itself is, with some exceptions, depicted as a trusted place of self-discovery and learning for everyone, from Roald Dahl's tiny Matilda Wormwood, who checks out little-red-wagonloads of thick tomes from her local public library, to Stephen King's adult Andy Dufresne, who turns Shawshank Prison's decrepit library into a bright spot in both his own life and the lives of his fellow inmates. In fictional dystopian futures, the library is rarely a collaborator in the plot to repress freedom; instead, it is the censoring or shutting down of the trusted library that becomes a symbol of repression. This idea is starkly dramatized in the *Twilight Zone* episode "The Obsolete Man" in which the character of Romney Wordsworth (Burgess Meredith)§ faces execution for the crime of being a librarian—a capital offense in a totalitarian state that has outlawed books and literacy.

When the trusted library moves from the physical to the online world, however, it loses some of its trust-building attributes. While it helps greatly that a physical library retains its name in the online world, other cues that build trust tend to get lost. It takes considerable resources to build an ar-

---

§ Library trivia: Burgess Meredith also stars in one of the most famous of all *Twilight Zone* episodes, "Time Enough at Last," in which he plays the role of Henry Bemis, a man who loves books and libraries but is denied sufficient time for reading in a world that is more concerned with dollars and cents than with the life of the mind.

chitecturally impressive library building; it takes next to nothing to build a superficially impressive-looking website. Phishing flourishes on the Web because an e-mail sent from a dingy one-room apartment in Vladivostok can be made to look exactly like one sent from the shining headquarters of a Fortune 500 financial institution. Why anyone should trust a website that belongs, or claims to belong, to a library more than a website that belongs, or claims to belong, to a store, company, blogger, or movie studio becomes a valid question in the uncertain sameness of the online world. To overcome this uncertainty, library websites must establish trust.

Trust, a more complicated concept than it might seem at first glance, is an area of scholarly research within the fields of psychology, sociology, philosophy, and economics, each field producing extensive literatures on the subject. Within the sub-field of e-commerce, the first empirical studies on the impact of trust appeared in 2002. In the decade following those initial studies, scholars published over 1,200 papers on trust and e-commerce with no sign that scholarly interest in this topic is abating. E-commerce firms are, for obvious reasons, keenly interested in establishing trust with their customers.

At its most basic level, trust requires a trustor (for example, a library customer) who cedes some greater or less degree of control to a trustee (for example, a library). The trustor is made vulnerable by what has been described as "the prevailing asymmetry in information" that exists between trustor and trustee in the online environment.[8] In simpler terms, when two parties in a transaction have unequal amounts of information, the party with less information is at a disadvantage. This is especially true online, an environment in which many tangible information cues are absent. For example, while shopping for shoes online you may be able to read descriptions and look at photos but are denied the tactile information that comes with actually trying on a pair of shoes and taking a few steps to see how they feel. Library customers operating in the online environment consistently find themselves on the minus side of the information equation. Concepts that are comfortably familiar to those who work within a library organization—everything from what information resources are available online to how those information resources may be accessed from remote locations to library policies governing the use of online information resources—are often question marks to library customers.

To understand how library customers feel as a result of the information imbalance, think of an outdoor activity in which you have never participated—perhaps kayaking, mountain climbing, sailing, or skydiving. To start participating in such an activity you might hire a guide to show you the ropes. In order for your learning outcome to be successful, you (as trustor) need to trust that the guide (as trustee)

- has a high degree of competence in the activity you are undertaking,
- will be able to bring you to a level of competence that allows you to success-fully participate in the activity, and
- will look out for your interests and not subject you to any undue risk.

Even if you thoroughly enjoy trying new outdoor activities, and even if you have a high level of trust in both your guide and all the relevant support structures (the manufacturing standards that ensure a climbing rope is strong enough to support your weight, the reserve parachute you can deploy if the main chute fails, or the Coast Guard that will turn out to rescue you if the sailboat capsizes), you necessarily must pass through a somewhat uncertain, possibly uncomfortable, maybe even traumatizing learning period during which your lack of information makes you dependent on your guide and his or her superior store of information. The asymmetry in information forces you to trust, and even though the greeting-card ideal of trust places it right up there with concepts like love, friendship, and faith, the truth is that trust inevitably involves risk.

Trust and Risk

When a novice mountain climber trusts a guide, the risk is obvious: an incompetent or reckless climbing guide can get a client killed at thirty-two feet per second squared. While at first glance it may seem that there is little or no risk involved in trusting a library website, this is not the case. The risks that users of library websites undertake fall, in fact, into the same general risk categories that users of e-commerce websites undertake, namely that

- using a website might take more time, effort, or money than it is worth;
- the website might misuse personal information; or
- the product purchased from the website might not deliver as expected.[9]

Risk 1: Time, Effort, and Money

The fact that library websites do not always fulfill customers' information needs proves that using a library website involves the risk of wasted time and effort. In contrast, one of the main attractions of using a Web search engine is that typing a few words into Google or Bing risks minimal time and effort while, unlike a library website, always producing results that give at least the appearance of success. Though it is possible to argue that the amount of time and effort risked when using a library website is not that great, the definition of *not that great* depends entirely on the customer and the circumstances. To a retiree dabbling in family genealogy, an unproductive hour on a library website is perhaps no big deal; to a student with a paper due the following morning, a wasted hour is a calamity (self-inflicted though it may be).

As compared to e-commerce customers, library customers are less likely to engage in direct monetary transactions via a website, though it is increasingly common for library customers to have the option of paying fees and fines online. It is quite likely, however, for library customers to trust a library website to lead them to reliable information on such financial matters as major purchases, estate planning, and investment strategies. In these situations the risk of financial loss is real even though it is not as direct as the risk that comes with typing one's credit-card number into a website form.

Risk 2: Personal Information

An early, non-empirical article on online trust reports that, of the 45 million Americans over the age of sixteen who had (as of 1997) used the Web at least one time, only 10 percent had ever made an online purchase, in large part because "they do not trust those who are collecting the data."[10] While online purchasing has become far more widespread than it was even a decade ago, online customers still have trust issues in that they (1) do not have control over any entity (be it business or library) that asks for their personal information and (2) cannot control downstream (mis)use of their personal information once they have divulged it. Libraries must build trust with online customers by following such essential data-security practices as using secure online forms, not retaining circulation information any longer than absolutely necessary, and keeping databases of user information safe from online intruders. For libraries that deal in credit-card transactions, the use of proven, highly secure third-party e-commerce software solutions is essential.

The last thing any library needs is to end up on the wrong end of a news story about hackers gaining access to a database containing its customers' personal or financial information. Wisely, most libraries have strong, publicly accessible privacy policies.** While privacy policies are good practice on purely ethical grounds, research in the field of e-commerce finds that website privacy policies do, in fact, build trust and increase customers' willingness to divulge personal information.[11]

Risk 3: Failure to Deliver

In the world of e-commerce, the risks associated with failure to deliver are rather clear-cut: the customer pays for something that is not delivered or the thing paid for and delivered turns out to be not as advertised, defective, or late in arriving. In the library world, failure to deliver is more nuanced. Library customers may see the following as examples of failures to deliver:

- a library not owning or subscribing to an information resource the customer wishes to use
- an information resource being unavailable (because it is lost, checked out, temporarily off-line, contained in a database that the customer cannot access, or part of a non-circulating collection that the customer cannot readily visit)
- an information resource being unavailable in the customer's preferred format (print instead of online, or vice versa)
- a delay in obtaining an information resource (waiting for a book to arrive via interlibrary loan, being put on a waiting list to check out the latest best seller or to obtain a high-use item held in a reserve collection)

Carrying matters to extremes, frustrated library customers may see the non-existence of specific information—What do you mean you don't have data on the number of left-handed Druids in first-century Wales?—as a failure to deliver. Disappointed students may hold the library at fault for failing to deliver the information they needed to earn higher grades than the ones they received. It does not matter that such failures to deliver may be due to the

---

** The American Library Association offers a "Privacy Tool Kit" to help libraries follow best practices in establishing their privacy policies. See http://www.ala.org/offices/oif/iftoolkits/toolkitsprivacy/privacypolicy/privacypolicy.

customer's own actions or to circumstances far beyond the library's control; they nonetheless reduce customer trust.

Building Online Trust: The Components of Trust

In 2002, McKnight et al. identified three key components for building online trust: competence,[††] benevolence, and integrity.[12]

- Competence: carrying out basic operations well. Timeliness, accuracy, and reliability are all hallmarks of a competent organization.
- Benevolence: acting in ways that meet customers' interests rather than putting the interests of the organization first or, in the worst case, intentionally acting in ways that are harmful to customers' interests.
- Integrity: acting honestly.

The literature on the impact of trust on e-commerce consistently reinforces, and in some cases expands on, the three above components. For example, Turel et al. include justice (fair treatment) as an important component of online trust, especially when it comes to encouraging repeated use of an e-commerce service. Elements of justice include treating all customers equally (distributive justice), employing fair decision-making processes concerning outcomes (procedural justice), and treating customers respectfully (interpersonal justice).[13] While most people who work in libraries are quick to defend their libraries as just organizations, the fact is that libraries often fail to practice distributive justice by, for example, treating cardholders differently from non-cardholders or granting some categories of users greater privileges than other categories (e.g., faculty versus students, adults versus children). Even if there are good reasons for not treating every customer the same, the result can still feel like injustice to those who are granted fewer or lesser privileges.

Physical World Trust

Given that libraries are, with rare exceptions, physical as well as online entities, a reasonable question to ask is whether or not the practices of a library operating in the physical world help to build trust in the online world. If library customers perceive a physical library as competent, benevolent, honest,

---

[††] Some researchers prefer the word *ability* over *competence*. The underlying concept, however, remains unchanged.

and just, it seems logical that the trust this engenders should spill over into the online environment. In the world of e-commerce, it certainly appears that consumer trust in such well-established, well-known brick-and-mortar businesses as Sears, Wal-Mart, and Home Depot has contributed to the success of their e-commerce arms. On the other hand, the success of the born-digital Amazon.com has surpassed that of the e-commerce arm of Barnes & Noble, a firm whose brick-and-mortar retail presence dates from the time of the First World War. Stefan Tams contends that trust does not carry over from the physical to the virtual world, that

> Web site trust is not directly associated with a vendor itself, but with its impersonal structures that have been put into place to enable consumers to anticipate successful transactions with the store. This type of trust-building mechanism establishes vendor trust indirectly through the features of the store's Web site.[14]

At the same time, however, Tams does concede that reputation, "the extent to which consumers believe that a vendor is honest and concerned about them," attaches to the business itself and so carries over from the physical to the virtual world.[15] So it seems that running a competent, benevolent, honest, and just library in the physical world, besides being a desirable end in and of itself, certainly does nothing to hinder customer trust in the library's online presence and may even help to enhance it.

Guarantees

For e-commerce sites, guarantees are a key tool for building customer trust. For libraries, on the other hand, guarantees are a problem. Since using a library rarely involves an exchange of money, libraries cannot offer money-back guarantees. When it comes to physical objects, typically books, it is difficult for libraries to guarantee that a particular item will be available at a specific date and time, especially when a library must depend on customers to return items on time or on other libraries to promptly deliver items through interlibrary loan. In a world in which rapid, if not instantaneous, delivery has become the norm, customers have a difficult time understanding why a library cannot guarantee precisely when a book will arrive and feel frustrated by library hedge phrases like, "Usually within five days or less," or, "Possibly as soon as tomorrow . . . *if* the person who has it checked out responds to the recall notice." And, no, unlike almost everything else in a consumer-driven society, willingness to pay extra will not make the process move along any faster. Along similar lines, libraries cannot guarantee that using a particular database or reading a certain book chapter will result in a higher grade, a better job, a happier life, or a healthier body. In the area of library services, reference librarians do not make guarantees that their advice is 100 percent accurate and complete; even worse from the customer's perspective, reference librarians recite what are, in effect, anti-guarantees when they remind customers that they are not attorneys or doctors and so cannot speak to the validity or interpretation of any legal or medical information.

Website Design and Content

After opening this chapter by downplaying the importance of website design, it is now time to back off at least a little bit. A number of researchers in the field of e-commerce find that websites that appear normal—that conform to the popular ideas of what an e-commerce website should look like—are more likely to be trusted that those that push the design envelope. As one researcher puts it, "If a vendor's Web site appears normal (i.e., appropriate for doing business) . . . then a consumer perceives situational normality. A well-designed Web site that reflects competence, integrity, and reliability would enhance this aspect of system trust."[16] For libraries, this means that a website design that appears slipshod or that deviates from the library norm is likely to inspire distrust.

Another key element of trusted e-commerce websites is the presence of useful information about products or services.[17] Because online customers cannot touch before they buy, information becomes a substitute (if an imperfect substitute) for the tactility of the physical world. For library websites, such informational content as images of book covers, reviews, testimonials, abstracts, and clearly written descriptions and instructions all help to build trust.

Functionality

Website functionality is an online manifestation of organizational competence. Websites that rarely if ever go down and that provide customers with consistently reliable forms, search engines, and remote connection tools (VPNs, proxy servers) are powerful trust builders. On the other hand, unreliable websites that are plagued with broken links, images that don't load, site slowness, outdated or incorrect information, misspellings, and similar errors serve to undermine trust.

The Value of Trust

To state the obvious, the reason that e-commerce firms care about website trust is that research has established a direct relationship between website trust and profits. Libraries are not interested in profits, but, like e-commerce firms, libraries should be interested in developing website trust as a way of promoting their status as preferred providers of information and related services. Everything a library can do to enhance website trust will result in more customers choosing the library website over the multitude of options available to information seekers in the online world.

FLOW

In 1975, psychologist Mihaly Csikszentmihalyi (pronounced "CHICK-sent-me-high-ee") published *Beyond Boredom and Anxiety: Experiencing Flow in Work and Play*, the book in which he first described the concept of flow.[18] Csikszentmihalyi followed up his initial work by publishing two additional books[‡‡] and numerous articles on the topic of flow. In a nutshell, flow is a state of happiness that comes with being entirely focused and energized in the interest of learning or performance. In a 1996 interview, Csikszentmihalyi described flow as

> being completely involved in an activity for its own sake. The ego falls away. Time flies. Every action, movement, and thought follows inevitably from the previous one, like playing jazz. Your whole being is involved, and you're using your skills to the utmost.[19]

Impossible to experience in the vacuum of passivity, flow can occur only as the result of an activity that is immersive and challenging, such as playing sports, reading, writing, painting, solving puzzles, and so on. Examples of flow from the sporting world include those times when a baseball batter

---

‡‡ Csikszentmihalyi, Mihaly, and Isabella Selega Csikszentmihalyi. *Optimal Experience: Psychological Studies of Flow in Consciousness*. Cambridge: Cambridge University Press, 1988. Csikszentmihalyi, Mihaly. *Flow: The Psychology of Optimal Experience*. New York: Harper & Row, 1990.

is so "in the zone" that pitches seem to slow down or when a long-distance runner experiences a feeling of reenergization after breaking through "the wall." In the creative arts, examples of flow range from Fyodor Dostoyevsky writing *The Gambler* in twenty-six days while simultaneously writing *Crime and Punishment* to the Grateful Dead freely improvising during one of their trademark marathon concert jams. A computer-based example of flow occurs when video gamers get so wrapped up in a virtual experience that they tune out the physical world for hours, even days, at a time, ignoring food, family, and hygiene (or so the gamer stereotype would have us believe).

According to Csikszentmihalyi's theory, for flow to occur an activity must

- have a clear structure that allows for progress and goals,
- provide clear and instantaneous feedback that allows one to adjust performance to maintain a state of flow, and
- achieve a balance between the degree of difficulty and the ability of the participant.[20]

Video games provide an excellent example of how the three conditions necessary for flow can be met in the online environment. A successful video game

- is structured around clear markers of progress and goals, typically taking the form of increasingly challenging levels through which players progress as they head toward the ultimate goal of reaching the top level and mastering the game;
- provides clear and instantaneous feedback in multiple ways: instantaneous on-screen responses to the gamer's commands; the ability (in multiplayer games) to communicate in real time with other players; running tallies of points scored, tokens or weapons collected, tasks completed, and levels mastered; and (most dramatically) instant feedback the moment a player's avatar has been blasted, devoured, crushed, shot, or otherwise wiped off the face of the screen; and
- balances degree of difficulty with the player's skill level. Creating a mindlessly easy, and therefore boring, game is simple. Creating a game that

cannot be won, such as one with an undefeatable boss,[§§] is equally simple. Creating a game that is challenging but not impossible, a game in which the final condition for flow is met, is the goal of every serious video-game developer.

In 1996 Hoffman and Novak published the first scholarly article linking the concept of flow to computer-mediated environments—specifically e-commerce websites, which at the time tended to be more informational than retail in nature. The authors defined flow as

> the state occurring during network navigation, which is (1) characterized by a seamless sequence of responses facilitated by machine interactivity, (2) intrinsically enjoyable, (3) accompanied by a loss of self-consciousness, and (4) self-reinforcing.[21]

Hoffman and Novak further describe the flow experience as one "which formalizes and extends a sense of playfulness" to the point that nothing outside the immediate experience matters. The authors also identify two categories of online consumer behaviors—goal directed and experiential—and propose that flow is more likely to occur with someone who is behaving experientially (e.g., browsing or surfing) than with someone who is goal directed. In a later study, however, Novak, Hoffman, and Duhachek found that those who tend to use the Web for experiential purposes are actually less likely to experience flow than are those who use it for goal-directed purposes.[22]

In a computer-mediated environment, flow has been shown to enhance learning, communication, exploratory behavior, elaborate processing of information, and acceptance and use of information technology.[23] Significantly, flow has been found to enhance online customers' perceived sense of control,[24] a state of mind that increases customer satisfaction with self-service technologies (of which websites are a notable example).[25] In addition, research into flow has shown that participation in "an engaging, enjoyable online experience" enhances customer attitudes toward both the website and its parent organization.[26] A 2012 study of travel agencies (a type of business

---

[§§] In video gaming, a boss is a computer-generated opponent who must be defeated, usually at the climax of the game. A boss is the most difficult opponent to defeat within a given game, typically due to some combination of factors such as size, strength, speed, fighting skill, or invulnerability to certain weapons. A fight with such a character is called a "boss fight" or "boss battle."

whose services bear more than passing resemblance to those of libraries) concluded that the "playfulness" of a website increased flow and that customers who experienced playfulness and flow on a travel agency website were more likely to do business with that agency even if the service quality of its physical store was not equal to that of other travel agencies.[27]

By the end of the first decade following Hoffman and Novak's seminal 1996 article, scholars had published over fifty empirical articles linking flow to positive outcomes for e-commerce websites,[28] with research in this area continuing through to the present day. Studies of the role of flow in computer-mediated environments have issued from the fields of psychology, consumer behavior, communications, human-computer interaction, and management information systems. On the other hand, a search of the library literature in 2014 showed zero articles on the role of flow. If librarians have paid no attention to flow, they are hardly any better at paying attention to the closely related concepts of fun and pleasure. Other than a few attempts to "make learning fun" on library websites aimed at children, library website designers seem oblivious to the fact that researchers in the field of e-commerce have reached near consensus on the importance of website pleasure, publishing such boldly unequivocal statements as "the more fun, interesting, and relevant a company's Web site is, the more effective it will become."[29]

Designing with Flow in Mind

Of course there is no magic formula for compelling flow to occur. However, approaching website design with an awareness of the three above-mentioned conditions necessary for flow to occur—(1) clear progress and goals, (2) instantaneous feedback, and (3) balance between difficulty and ability—is a good starting point.

While providing clear progress and goals for an entire library website may not be achievable, it could certainly be done with elements of a website, such as an online tutorial or a process-focused task such as, for example, walking a customer through the submission of an interlibrary loan request. One land mine for website designers and content creators who wish to clarify progress and goals is that the provision of excessive or irrelevant information works against the generation of flow.[30] In general, library websites tend to err on the side of providing far too much information rather than excessive terseness.

When it comes to providing instantaneous feedback, increasing website interactivity is one highly practical tactic, as it has been shown that website customers who perceive higher levels of interactivity are more likely to experience flow.[31] A classic example of a feature that works against interactivity is an online form that provides no feedback when the submit button is clicked, leaving the customer wondering if the form was actually submitted or not. Avoiding such interactivity dead spots while providing ample opportunities for interactivity should be high on the list of any website developer's priorities.

Finally, the notion of presenting customers with a challenge is perhaps the most counter-intuitive of the conditions for enhancing flow, as most website designers work hard at reducing or eliminating challenges rather than creating them. While presenting an appropriately balanced challenge is difficult (some might argue impossible) when serving customers of varying abilities, doing so is necessary in order to focus customer attention and keep customers interested in the website.[32] The development of game-like features is one possible avenue for integrating challenges into a library website.

As a complex, fleeting, and entirely holistic phenomenon, flow is difficult to measure and impossible to guarantee. However, like a lot of things that are difficult to measure, flow is more meaningful than most things that are easy to measure. Could anyone argue that getting one thousand home-page hits from customers who took one look and clicked off is, by any measure, more significant than having ten customers experience a state of flow while on the library website? Even if a library's website team would have a hard time coming up with data to prove to a skeptical administrator or an external accreditation team that customers regularly experience flow while using the library website, this does not mean that flow, playfulness, enjoyment, or fun should be ignored when designing a library website.

CONCLUSION

Libraries have spent years working to improve the design of their websites. While there have been design improvements, judging from the current state of the art it seems unlikely that there will ever be a world-changing design breakthrough leading to the absolutely foolproof, can't-miss library website. Concurrent with the evolution of the library website, e-commerce was exploding into a multi-billion-dollar-per-year phenomenon. The profits of e-commerce have funded (1) highly sophisticated websites with which comparatively modestly funded library websites cannot compete and (2) an extensive body of scholarly research into the effectiveness of e-commerce websites. It behooves the library profession to become more familiar with the scholarly research surrounding e-commerce websites, as many of the findings have practical implications for library website design. Specifically, the library profession should familiarize itself with the roles of both trust and flow in website effectiveness.

NOTES

1. Bo-christer Björk, Annikki Roos, and Mari Lauri, "Global Annual Volume of Peer Reviewed Scholarly Articles and the Share Available Via Different Open Access Options," Toronto, Canada, Conference on Electronic Publishing, June 25–27, 2008, http://citeseerx.ist.psu.edu/viewdoc/summary?doi=10.1.1.162.991 (accessed May 20, 2013).

2. Arif E. Jinha, "Article 50 Million: An Estimate of the Number of Scholarly Articles in Existence," *Learned Publications* 23, no. 3 (July 2010): 258–263.

3. Edward R. Tufte, *Envisioning Information* (Cheshire, CT: Graphics Press, 1990), 51.

4. Jakob Nielsen and Marie Tahir, *Homepage Usability: 50 Websites Deconstructed* (Indianapolis, IN: New Riders, 2002), 3.

5. George Anders, "Jeff Bezos Gets it," *Forbes Asia* 8, no. 6 (May 2012): 34–42.

6. David Beymer, Daniel Russell, and Peter Orton, "An Eye Tracking Study of How Font Size and Type Influence Online Reading," Liverpool, UK, British HCI Group, September 1–5, 2008, doi:10.1145/1531826.1531831 (accessed May 15, 2013).

7. Flavio T. P. Oliveira, Anne Aula, and Daniel M. Russell, "Discriminating the Relevance of Web Search Results with Measures of Pupil Size," *Proceedings of the SIGCHI Conference on Human Factors in Computing Systems*, Boston, April 4–9, 2009, doi:10.1145/1518701.1519038 (accessed May 20, 2013).

8. Dennis C. Ahrholdt, "Empirical Identification of Success-Enhancing Web Site Signals in E-Tailing: An Analysis Based on Known E-Tailers and the Theory of Reasoned Action," *Journal of Marketing Theory & Practice* 19, no. 4 (Fall 2011): 441–458.

9. David Gefen, Izak Benbasat, and Paul A. Pavlou, "A Research Agenda for Trust in Online Environments," *Journal of Management Information Systems* 24, no. 4 (Spring 2008): 275–286.

10. Donna L. Hoffman, Thomas P. Novak, and Marcos Peralta, "Building Consumer Trust Online," *Communications of the ACM* 42, no. 4 (April 1999): 80–85.

11. Farhod P. Karimov, Malaika Brengman, and Leo Van Hove, "The Effect of Website Design Dimensions on Initial Trust: A Synthesis of the Empirical Literature," *Journal of Electronic Commerce Research* 12, no. 4 (2011).

12. D. H. McKnight, Vivek Choudhury, and Charles Kacmar, "Developing and Validating Trust Measures for e-Commerce: An Integrative Typology," *Information Systems Research* 13, no. 3 (September 2002): 334–359.

13. Ofir Turel, Yufei Yuan, and Catherine E. Connelly, "In Justice We Trust: Predicting User Acceptance of E-Customer Services," *Journal of Management Information Systems* 24, no. 4 (Spring 2008): 123–151.

14. Stefan Tams, "Toward Holistic Insights into Trust in Electronic Markets: Examining the Structure of the Relationship between Vendor Trust and Its Antecedents," *Information Systems & e-Business Management* 10, no. 1 (March 2012): 149–160.

15. Stefan Tams, "Toward Holistic Insights into Trust in Electronic Markets: Examining the Structure of the Relationship between Vendor Trust and Its Antecedents," *Information Systems & e-Business Management* 10, no. 1 (March 2012): 149–160.

16. Robin Pennington, H. Dixon Wilcox, and Varun Grover, "The Role of System Trust in Business-to-Consumer Transactions," *Journal of Management Information Systems* 20, no. 3 (Winter 2003): 197–226.

17. Catherine Demangeot and Amanda J. Broderick, "Consumer Perceptions of Online Shopping Environments: A Gestalt Approach," *Psychology & Marketing* 27, no. 2 (February 2010): 117–140.

18. Mihaly Csikszentmihalyi, *Beyond Boredom and Anxiety: Experiencing Flow in Work and Play* (San Francisco: Jossey-Bass, 1975).

19. John Geirland and Mihaly Csikszentmihalyi, "Go with the Flow," *Wired*, September 1996, 47–49, http://www.wired.com/wired/archive/4.09/czik_pr.html (accessed May 11, 2013).

20. Mihaly Csikszentmihalyi, "The Flow Experience and Its Significance for Human Psychology," In *Optimal Experience: Psychological Studies of Flow in Consciousness,* ed. M. Csikszentmihalyi and I. S. Csikszentmihalyi, 15–35 (Cambridge: Cambridge University Press, 1988).

21. Donna Hoffman and Thomas P. Novak, "Marketing in Hypermedia Computer-Mediated Environments: Conceptual Foundations," *Journal of Marketing* 60, no. 3 (July 1996): 50–68.

22. T. P. Novak, D. L. Hoffman, and A. Duhachek, "The Influence of Goal-Directed and Experiential Activities on Online Flow Experiences," *Journal of Consumer Psychology* 13, nos. 1–2 (2003): 3–16.

23. Christina M. Finneran and Ping Zhang, "A Person–Artefact–Task (PAT) Model of Flow Antecedents in Computer-Mediated Environments," *International Journal of Human-Computer Studies* 59, no. 4 (2003): 475–496; Guda Van Noort, Hilde A. M. Voorveld, and Eva A. Van Reijmersdal, "Interactivity in Brand Web Sites: Cognitive, Affective, and Behavioral Responses Explained by Consumers' Online Flow Experience," *Journal of Interactive Marketing* 26, no. 4 (November 2012): 223–234.

24. C. Mathwick and E. Rigdon, "Play, Flow, and the Online Search Experience," *Journal of Consumer Research* 31, no. 2 (September 2004): 324–332.

25. J. E. G. Bateson, "Self-Service Consumer: An Exploratory Study," *Journal of Retailing* 61, no. 3 (Fall 1985): 49.

26. Mathwick and Rigdon, "Play, Flow, and the Online Search Experience."

27. Chia-Lin Hsu, Kuo-Chien Chang, and Mu-Chen Chen, "The Impact of Website Quality on Customer Satisfaction and Purchase Intention: Perceived Playfulness and Perceived Flow as Mediators," *Information Systems & e-Business Management* 10, no. 4 (December 2012): 549–570.

28. Yi Maggie Guo and Marshall Scott Poole, "Antecedents of Flow in Online Shopping: A Test of Alternative Models," *Information Systems Journal* 19, no. 4 (July 2009): 369–390.

29. Maria Sicilia and Salvador Ruiz, "The Role of Flow in Web Site Effectiveness," *Journal of Interactive Advertising* 8, no. 1 (September 2007): 1–31.

30. Sicilia and Ruiz, "The Role of Flow in Web Site Effectiveness."

31. Van Noort et al., "Interactivity in Brand Web Sites."

32. Kavita Srivastava, Asmita Shukla, and Narendra K. Sharma, "Online Flow Experiences: The Role of Need for Cognition, Self-Efficacy, and Sensation Seeking Tendency," *International Journal of Business Insights & Transformation* 3, no. 2 (April 2010): 93–100.

8

Artificial Intelligence in the Library

The Time Is Some Day (Maybe)

Just as factory jobs were eliminated in the 20th century by new assembly-line robots, Brad [Rutter] and I were the first knowledge-industry workers put out of work by the new generation of "thinking" machines. "Quiz show contestant" may be the first job made redundant by Watson, but I'm sure it won't be the last.

—*Jeopardy! champion Ken Jennings on being defeated by IBM's Watson computer.*[1]

In both the world of computer science and the world of science fiction, a concept known as "the Singularity" has generated equal amounts of deep philosophical thought and unbridled angst. Simply put, the Singularity is the point at which humans will be able to create machines with greater-than-human intelligence; as these super-intelligent machines presumably go on to create ever-more-intelligent machines, the value of merely human intelligence will drop precipitously. Depending on which prognosticator you choose to believe, in the wake of the Singularity, humanity could be violently wiped out by its own machines, allowed to go slowly extinct, or permitted to exist while being kept complacent by the hobbies (e.g., Facebook) and drugs (e.g., Twitter) created by its machine masters. As a scenario for the climactic event of the human era, technology's concept of the Singularity bears considerable resemblance to Christianity's concept of the Rapture, and as with the Rapture some very dark visions of the Singularity have made their way into popular culture, two iconic examples being *The Matrix* and *Terminator* film franchises. Although the Singularity has yet to happen (here fans of *The Matrix* might ominously add *"as far as we know"*), and while it is possible it may never happen, a sobering number of scientists have speculated that if the Singularity occurs, it will be during the present century. As scientist and science-fiction author Vernor Vinge observed of the Singularity, "We will be in the Post-Human era. And for all my rampant technological optimism, sometimes I think I'd be more comfortable if I were regarding these transcendental events from one thousand years remove . . . instead of twenty."[2]

The Singularity is, of course, the ultimate outcome of the pursuit of artificial intelligence (AI). While the first written use of the phrase *artificial intelligence* was in the title of a 1955 Dartmouth summer research project led by computer scientist John McCarthy and a group of colleagues, the idea of artificial intelligence had been kicking around long before the heyday of UNIVAC and *I Love Lucy*. In the non-scientific realm the idea of artificial intelligence has been posited in works of imagination ranging from the ancient folklore tale of the Golem to Mary Shelley's 1818 novel *Frankenstein* to Karel Čapek's 1920 stage play *R.U.R.* (notable for the first use of the word *robot*). In the scientific realm, the 1950 publication of Alan Turing's "Computing Machinery and Intelligence" introduced the now-famous Turing Test.[3] According to the Turing Test, a machine can be said to possess the equivalent of human intelligence if it is capable of carrying on a conversation (conducted via text to eliminate visual and vocal tip-offs) in such a way that interrogators cannot tell with certainty whether they are communicating with a human or a machine. Though Turing expected that machines would be able to pass his test by the end of the twentieth century,[4] machine-based artificial intelligence has yet to reach this benchmark.

Even so, recent decades have seen some remarkable progress in artificial intelligence. In 1997 IBM's Deep Blue (controversially) defeated chess champion Gary Kasparov, while in 2011 IBM's Watson impressively defeated two former champions of television's long-running *Jeopardy!* quiz show. In the workaday world of applied artificial intelligence, Google's PageRank search-engine algorithm correlates remarkably well with human ideas of importance, though PageRank is far from being able to pass the Turing Test. In pursuit of even better search tools, Google, the NASA Ames Research Center, and the University Space Research Association have established the Quantum Artificial Intelligence Lab to study the most challenging problems in artificial intelligence. The field of machine learning—a branch of artificial intelligence based on the idea that computer systems can (independently or with minimal human collaboration) learn from their own analyses of large data sets—has produced many practical applications for artificial intelligence. For an example from the world of online information retrieval, LexisNexis's "Lexis Advance" technology uses machine learning to "build statistical models each time data is processed, and every time the computer gathers and processes more information, the machines learn."[5] Other common examples of applied machine learning include the following:

- home thermostats that learn to save energy by sharing data with other Web-connected thermostats
- credit-card-fraud detection systems that learn to recognize and respond to atypical spending patterns
- trainable speech-recognition technology used in everything from cell phones to computer games to aircraft control systems.

So with all these advanced practical applications, where is artificial intelligence when it comes to providing public services to library customers? A fall 2013 search of the database *Library Literature and Information Science Full Text* using the phrase "artificial intelligence" in combination with such search terms as "libraries," "public service," and "reference" resulted in less than a dozen hits relevant to using AI to provide direct assistance to library customers. The oldest relevant hit, "Artificial Intelligence: Promise, Myth and Reality," dates from 1984, and while the author, Robert Mason, warns that "in the near future hype, exaggeration, and unrealistic expectations are likely to dominate,"[6] he also expresses confidence that advances in artificial intelligence will provide "not only interactive but also 'proactive' services that search knowledgebases and provide the information even before the user is aware that it is needed."[7] Looking even further into the future, the Library and Information Technology Association (LITA) President's Program for 1992 consisted entirely of presentations by librarians, futurists, and science-fiction authors speculating on a future in which artificial intelligence is a reality, with the contents of the program being published in book form as *Thinking Robots, an Aware Internet, and Cyberpunk Librarians*.[8] Eight years after the LITA program, Maryellen Mott Allen's "The Myth of Intelligent Agents" holds that artificial intelligence is not ready for the prime-time arena of library public services, though the author nonetheless speculates that information professionals "will undoubtedly one day see the kind of intelligent-agent systems the AI community insists are in development."[9] In the 2005 article "Artificial Intelligence and Information Retrieval," author Peter Jackson is more confident about the future of artificial intelligence in libraries, though he concludes that

> the most promising way forward for AI is to design systems in which sophisticated data processing serves as an adjunct to human intelligence, rather than trying to mimic or displace such intelligence. . . . A successful AI application need not be intelligent in the traditional, science fiction sense so beloved by Hollywood.[10]

The above-mentioned fall 2013 search of *Library Literature* also retrieved two articles reporting on what proved to be short-lived attempts to integrate artificial-intelligence-based avatars into library websites.[11] All in all, hardly a resounding set of endorsements for artificial intelligence applications as tools of library public services.

But not so fast. A search of *Library Literature and Information Science Full Text* using the phrase "expert systems" retrieved scores of articles relevant to library public services. Expert systems may not be artificial intelligence in the "science fiction sense so beloved by Hollywood," but they certainly are a form of artificial intelligence—one that has been part of the library world for decades. For example, CONIT, an early expert system for searching Medline and other databases, was just one of several expert systems in use in libraries by the early 1980s.[12] By the end of the twentieth century essentially every significant bibliographic database available to libraries employed expert systems to one extent or another, as any search interface that automatically corrects spelling, accepts natural-language queries, or ranks results by relevance is, in fact, an expert system. The point is that even though the thought of "introducing" AI into libraries may arouse fears of heartless machines, reckless expenditures on pipe-dream technology, the breaking of traditions, and loss of jobs, the reality is that AI is already in the library front door and has been lounging around the reference area for going on three decades now. The question for librarians is not, "Should we use AI?" but rather, "Can we expand

THE FISKE READING MACHINE

On January 5, 1926, retired U.S. Navy Rear Admiral Bradley A. Fiske patented the Fiske Reading Machine. A lifelong inventor and holder of a number of significant patents relating to naval gunnery, Fiske is most notable for proposing the tactics and inventing the mechanics for launching anti-ship torpedoes from airplanes, a development that, literally and metaphorically, helped sink the battleship, the most powerful weapons system afloat prior to the ultimate manifestations of Fiske's original idea. In retirement Fiske created his reading machine for the joint purposes of relieving eyestrain, dramatically reducing the cost of printing, and allowing an individual to carry several volumes worth of

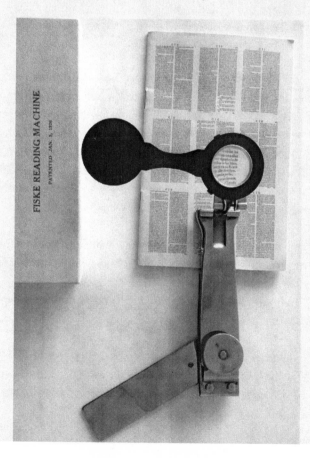

reading material in a purse or pocket. The Fiske Reading Machine is not easily described, though an article from the 1922 *New York Times* does a credible job of it:

> The machine is a tiny affair. It consists of a light frame of aluminum, which carries a strip of paper containing reading matter whose characters have been reduced by photo-engraving to a size about one-one-hundredth of the size of ordinary typewritten characters. A lens surmounts the frame, and through this the characters are magnified so as to be easily read. A roller attached to the frame is moved by the forefinger to bring the reading matter steadily in line with the eye. The whole device weighs little more than five ounces and is intended to be used with one hand. It can be carried in the coat pocket without causing a bulge. The instrument is six and a quarter inches long, one and seven-eighths inches wide and only a quarter of an inch thick.*

For nearly anyone living in the twenty-first century the comparison is obvious: the Fiske Reading Machine was a Jazz Age attempt to create a Kindle. Although Fiske's device ultimately failed to gain acceptance, it was not because Fiske's goals were unworthy of pursuit; rather, as with so many failed inventions, the Fiske Reading Machine sought to achieve goals that were beyond the capabilities of the technology of its time. The lesson here raises questions for anyone who is thinking about achieving a worthy goal via technology:

- Is my goal coupled with a technology that will never achieve that goal?
- Is my goal coupled with an emerging technology that, while not yet up to the task, has the potential to achieve the goal?
- Is my goal coupled with a technology that is currently capable of achieving that goal?

Even when the answers are not apparent, which is almost always the case, asking these questions is not a bad exercise. Of course the question that takes precedence before any of these three is more basic: "Is my goal worth pursuing in the first place?"

---

* "Admiral Fiske's New Invention," *New York Times*, March 5, 1922, 94.

our use of AI to better meet our customers' information needs?" In the words of Valeda Dent, "The challenge for those in libraries and other information service areas is to separate fact from fiction, and utilize agent technology for support and problem-solving in a way most helpful to users."[13]

INTELLIGENT AGENTS IN LIBRARIES: THE EARLY EXPERIMENTS

If libraries are already using AI technologies such as expert systems to assist their customers on the back end, the next step is for libraries to integrate intelligent agents into their websites to provide direct front-end assistance along the lines of what a living, breathing librarian might provide. To date there have not been all that many attempts to integrate intelligent agents into library websites; among these, the results are far from encouraging. Some examples follow:

Page

Launched in 2002 by Nova Southeastern University Law Library, Page was a short-lived "virtual library assistant."[14]

Ask Cosmo

Announced in 2003 by the National Library of Medicine (NLM), Ask Cosmo featured a non-animated "wise old owl" intelligent-agent avatar billed as being "familiar with hundreds of Frequently Asked Questions (FAQs). Type your question in the box and up pops an answer."[15] Ask Cosmo was retired and removed from the NLM website on January 31, 2008, due to low use and lack of product support from the vendor.*

Sarah and Suzie SitePal

Sarah and Suzie were two talking avatars that (who?) debuted on the Mount Saint Vincent University Library website in 2008. According to their developers, "The avatars are used to welcome students to the Library, to highlight Library resources and services, and to relay information about Library events."[16] By 2009 the combination of a move to a new content-management system, staff changes, and the workload of updating avatar messages resulted in the MSVU Library abandoning their experiment with intelligent agents.†

---

* Terry Ahmed, National Library of Medicine, e-mail message to the author, October 30, 2013.
† Denyse Rodrigues, Mount Saint Vincent University Library, e-mail message to the author, October 7, 2013.

Lillian

Lillian, a virtual librarian designed to answers questions about books and library holdings, was tested as a proof-of-concept on the websites of Amazon. com and OCLC. Lillian debuted in April 2006 and went out of service in December 2010.[17]

Stella

Stella is an animated intelligent-agent avatar on the website of the Hamburg State University Library (www.sub.uni-hamburg.de/en/service). Though Stella is capable of facial expressions, communication is via text rather than speech.

Pixel

A non-animated avatar, Pixel is being tested on the University of Nebraska–Lincoln Libraries website (pixel.unl.edu), designed to answer questions about the UN–Lincoln Libraries and their collections. Librarians at the University of Nebraska–Lincoln report that

> Pixel is particularly appealing to social chatters, who often prefer to chat with the bot on a "personal" level over asking library related questions. This required some modification of the categories to accommodate their need to "play" with the bot, and attempt to redirect their conversations into library related areas.[18]

Perhaps unsurprisingly, the use of profanity by social chatters is frequent enough that Pixel had to be modified to refuse to respond to profanity until the offender apologizes. Social chatting and profanity may be the result of avatars' "current pigeonhole as a novelty," and both of these off-label uses could diminish with "greater user awareness and familiarity with such systems."[19]

THE ADOPTION OF INTELLIGENT-AGENT TECHNOLOGY IN THE BUSINESS WORLD

Given the lack of breakthrough success, it is not surprising that the author of a 2011 survey of the use of intelligent agents in libraries concludes, "The application of agent technology is still at the stage of research and experimentation and is far away from being widely adopted by libraries or library related projects."[20] In spite of what little has been achieved thus far in the library

Welcome to Pixel space

Pixel is an experimental chatbot we are testing that can answer questions about the libraries and our resources. This program was developed using AIML (Artificial Intelligence Mark-up Language). You can find more information about AIML at http://www.alicebot.org/aiml.html.

Talk to Pixel like you were talking to a person who is just learning your language. Reply to questions with yes or no, or respond using the prompts Pixel supplies. The first link in a response will appear in a preview window below the response. When you click on any link it will open in a new window. We monitor the logs so when Pixel gives the wrong answer or is unable to answer a question we add information to improve her responses.

SHARE

Visit my Facebook Page at http://www.facebook.com/unlpixel

You: Do you have information on Willa Cather?

Bot: Looking for information on Willa Cather? You came to the right place, the UNL Libraries hosts the Willa Cather Archive We also have an extensive list of web accessible materials on and about Willa Cather. Try searching Encore for Cather, Willa as the search terms.

FIGURE 8.2
Screen capture of University of Nebraska–Lincoln's experimental avatar "Pixel" with question and response. Courtesy of University of Nebraska–Lincoln Libraries.

INTELLIGENT-AGENT TERMINOLOGY

The terminology associated with intelligent-agent (IA) technology can be confusing because some of the more common terms either have multiple meanings or are used somewhat interchangeably.

AGENT

While the definition of agent (which can be a machine or a human) varies, one of the most widely agreed upon definitions is that it is "an entity which functions continuously and autonomously in a particular environment, often inhabited by other agents and processes." Tellingly, in defining the term *agent*, computer scientist Brenda Laurel includes librarians among her exemplars: "In life, any person or institution who is empowered by us to take action on our behalf is an agent. Examples include secretaries, gardeners, craftspeople and laborers, teachers, librarians, and accountants."†

AVATAR
In computing, an avatar is a two- or three-dimensional representation of a character, usually a human being or an animal. One familiar form of computer avatar is found in online gaming, where avatars represent players. In the realm of online customer service, avatars act as the interface for customer-service intelligent agents. Avatars may be as simple as a non-animated static image or as complex as animated characters whose lips move in sync with the words they are speaking and whose real-time facial expressions and body movements are relevant to the message being communicated. Depending on the capabilities of the particular avatar, customers may communicate through keyboards, voice, or both; similarly, avatars may communicate with customers through text, spoken words, or both. Among avatars that speak, some employ a flat, machine-generated voice, while others employ more natural-sounding human speech. Although it is generally accepted "that human speech is more effective than either on-screen text or TTS [text to speech] voice technology," the high cost of developing avatars capable of human speech is a roadblock for small and medium-sized organizations.‡

CHATBOT
An intelligent agent designed to simulate an interaction with an actual human being. Used somewhat interchangeably with the terms *avatar* and *embodied agent*.

CONVERSATIONAL AGENT
See *Embodied Conversational Agent*.

EMBODIED AGENT

In the online environment, an embodied agent is a graphic representation that uses artificial intelligence to interact autonomously with humans. Used somewhat interchangeably with the terms *avatar* and *chatbot*. Also known as an *interface agent*.

EMBODIED CONVERSATIONAL AGENT

An embodied conversational agent is capable of carrying on a natural-language conversation by employing the verbal and non-verbal techniques used by humans. Also known as *conversational agent*.

INTERFACE AGENT

See *Embodied Agent*.

INTELLIGENT AGENT

An intelligent agent is an autonomous entity that perceives through sensors, acts on its environment, and directs its actions to achieve a rational goal. In addition, the more sophisticated intelligent agents learn or use knowledge to achieve their goals. An intelligent agent may range in complexity from a simple thermostat to a servomechanism (such as automotive cruise control) to a living human being.

PRODUCT RECOMMENDATION AGENT

A product recommendation agent (PRA) (also known as a *recommendation agent*) is a Web-based intelligent agent that helps customers make online purchasing decisions.

- Content-filtering PRAs employ data-mining algorithms to suggest products to a customer based on the preferences of previous customers. An example of a content-filtering PRA is Amazon.com's "Customers Who Bought This Item Also Bought . . ." feature.
- Attribute-based PRAs prompt customers to provide information on product attributes they desire in order to assist them in making purchasing decisions. Attribute-based PRAs are sometimes referred to as

"query-based decision aids."§ An example of a simple attribute-based PRA can be found on the Sears.com website, which allows customers to initially narrow by department ("Appliances") and then product type ("Refrigerator"). Customers can further narrow their selection by choosing a defining feature ("French Door," "Top Freezer," "Bottom Freezer," "Side by Side") followed by specific features ("Brand," "Color," "Price Range").

TEXT TO SPEECH (TTS)

Text-to-speech systems convert text to audible speech. The capability of TTS systems vary greatly, with less sophisticated systems producing the sort of artificial, inflectionless speech associated with early digital computers, while more sophisticated systems produce speech closer to natural human speech. Even the best TTS systems have difficulty accurately reproducing words that are spelled the same but pronounced differently depending on usage; for example, *I have not read the book I was supposed to read.*

---

* Yoav Shoham, "An Overview of Agent-Oriented Programming," in *Software Agents*, ed. J. M. Bradshaw, 271–290 (Menlo Park, CA; Cambridge, MA: AAAI Press; MIT Press, 1997), 271–272.

† Brenda Laurel, "Interface Agents: Metaphors with Character," in *Software Agents*, ed. J. M. Bradshaw, 71 (Menlo Park, CA; Cambridge, MA: AAAI Press; MIT Press, 1997).

‡ Lingyun Qiu and Izak Benbasat, "Evaluating Anthropomorphic Product Recommendation Agents: A Social Relationship Perspective to Designing Information Systems," *Journal of Management Information Systems* 25, no. 4 (Spring 2009): 145–181.

§ Lingyun Qiu, "Designing Social Interactions with Animated Avatars and Speech Output for Product Recommendation Agents in Electronic Commerce," Ph.D. dissertation, University of British Columbia, 2006, 22–23, http://hdl.handle.net/2429/18488 (accessed September 20, 2013).

---

world, the scholarly research on intelligent agents, along with examples of real-world business applications of IA technology, is more encouraging and worthy of serious attention.

In the mid-1990s sociologist Clifford Nass and his collaborators conducted a series of experiments that led to the development of the Computers Are Social Actors (CASA) paradigm. CASA holds that interactions between humans and computers are "fundamentally social."[21] Following multiple experiments which show that even experienced computer users treat computers like living beings, Nass et al. conclude,

> From a practical perspective, this research shows that it is not only possible to endow technologies with personalities, but under many circumstances, it may be advisable. The satisfaction derived from any computer session, for example, can be strongly affected by the interaction of the user's personality and the computer's personality.[22]

CASA has influenced research into IA technology and the development of commercial avatars whose appearance and personalities are designed to appeal to consumers. For example, researchers have found that when the ethnicity of an avatar matches that of a user, the avatar is seen as more useful and more pleasurable to interact with than when there is a mismatch of ethnicity.[23] Just as importantly, employing IA technology has been found to enhance trust,[24] a crucial factor in the success of commercial websites (see chapter 7). For both businesses and libraries, increasing pleasure and trust by allowing customers to handpick the personality, ethnicity, gender, and possibly even language of the avatar with which they interact would be a highly desirable capability in an increasingly diverse and global online world.

The benefits—current or potential—that the commercial world sees in employing intelligent-agent avatars are almost identical to those that libraries would see. First, intelligent-agent avatars allow both businesses and libraries to serve far more online customers than can be served via human employees. Yes, this represents a salary savings, but it also represents an increase in the number of individuals with which a library organization can interact and serve in meaningful ways. As one team of business researchers puts it, "avatars acting as on-screen assistants, with which the prospective customer can interact, could substitute for face to face interaction and promote user engagement."[25] It is also possible that developing a popular avatar, or set of avatars, could help build a library's image in much the same way that illustrated or animated advertising figures (Speedy Alka-Seltzer, the Pillsbury Doughboy, the GEICO Gecko, etc.) have built corporate or product images. Thus far no intelligent-agent avatar has gone viral and become an Internet meme, but there is nothing to say it cannot happen.

On the other hand, avatars are not an essential component of IA technology and may not provide the ideal interface for library customers. If intelligent-agent technologies could be seamlessly embedded into library websites without the use of an avatar, doing so would avoid costs associated with developing avatars while also avoiding a number of social and cultural pitfalls associated with avatars:

- Users may feel disappointed when they discover that the artificial intelligence behind an avatar—particularly an avatar presented in a human form—is nowhere close to passing the Turing Test.
- The novelty factor of avatars can result in them being used more as toys than as information-finding tools.
- Avatars can alienate those who—for reasons ranging from privacy concerns to religious beliefs to ingrained contrarianism—want nothing to do with the technology.

No less an authority than Don Norman, perhaps the world's leading advocate of user-centered design, writes, "It would not be wise to present an agent in human-like structures without also offering a choice to those who would rather not have them."[26] However, in the same article Norman also observes, "Agents are here to stay. Once unleashed, technologies do not disappear."[27]

Even though intelligent-agent avatar technology has certainly not disappeared in the twenty years since Don Norman declared that "agents are here to stay," this technology has yet to set the information-seeking world on fire. While no one can say when, or even if, IA avatar technology will be embraced by the online masses, the Technology Acceptance Model provides a theoretical framework for understanding what it will take for the technology to succeed. Originally formulated in the 1986 doctoral dissertation of Fred D. Davis,[28] the model was later revised and expanded by Davis and his collaborators to become the Unified Theory of Acceptance and Use of Technology (UTAUT).[29] While the scales Davis and his collaborators developed to measure acceptance and use of technology are complex, the underlying principle is easy enough to grasp. Users will adopt a technology based on (1) perceived usefulness (Does this technology help me do what I need to do?) and (2) perceived ease of use (How much effort do I need to expend to use this technology?). Any technology that is ill perceived in either its usefulness or ease of use is likely to fail; any technology that falls short on both counts is bound to fail. For a highly pertinent example, in 2004 Microsoft introduced

Clippy, a paper-clip-shaped intelligent-agent avatar that was greeted with nearly universal loathing. Although Clippy was not difficult to use, it was perceived as so useless—to the point of being counter-productive—that the few who were willing to put even modest effort into using Clippy were dwarfed by the numbers willing to go to the greater effort of turning it off. Like Clippy, the current intelligent-agent avatars have far more ground to make up on the perceived usefulness front than on the ease of use front, and until that ground is made up, the technology will not be widely accepted.

Whether or not intelligent-agent avatars are eventually accepted by the public, and whether or not libraries choose to invest in this technology, a number of businesses with strong online presences are already employing avatars. Here are just a few examples:

- Furniture giant Ikea's Anna: www.ikea.com/us/en.
- Michelin tire company's Michelin Man (aka Bibendum): www.michelin.com.
- Amtrak's Ask Julie: www.amtrak.com.
- Mobile network operator Cloud9's Cloudius: www.cloud9realtime.com/help.

In addition to companies that provide publicly available intelligent-agent avatars, a number of companies—including E*Trade, H&R Block, and AT&T BusinessDirect—employ avatars that are available only to paying customers who are logged into the website. Educational and governmental organizations are also employing avatars. For example, Stanford University's Student Services Center offers AskJane, a non-animated intelligent-agent avatar designed to answer questions on such subjects as housing, financial aid, ID cards, and the like (www.stanford.edu/group/studentservicescenter). The U.S. Army's GoArmy website features Ask Sgt. Star, a non-animated intelligent-agent avatar intended to answer the questions of potential recruits (www.goarmy.com). Site visitors communicate with Sgt. Star via text, but the avatar replies in natural-sounding human speech.

Does the fact that non-library businesses and organizations are employing intelligent-agent avatar technology mean that libraries should get on board or risk being left behind? No doubt some in the library profession will say that, regardless of what others are doing, libraries should stay away from an unproven technology that smacks of science fiction. Certainly the worst case scenarios of IA are easy enough to imagine. Would a library be held accountable if its avatar gave legal or medical advice? What if it provided a minor with the information to build a bomb or a list of ways to commit suicide? Though IA technology can be configured to avoid misuse, the risk posed is not well balanced by the less-than-amazing performance of the currently available avatars.

Even those who believe that IA avatar technology might have a place in the library must ask when, if ever, the time will be right to get on board. Complicating any decision of when to adopt avatar technology is the fact that if libraries are to use the technology, they must depend on those outside the library world to develop it. Given the present state of the technology, developing an intelligent-agent avatar in house would be a moon-shot project even for a large library consortium. Thus far most development of avatar technology has been undertaken by commercial firms focused on commercial applications. If the initial library experiments with IA technology have achieved anything, it has been to alert the companies developing this technology that libraries are a potential market. Perhaps libraries cannot yet adopt IA technology on anything more than an experimental basis, but nonetheless librarians should do more to indicate to developers that libraries are interested and looking for opportunities. Failure to stay engaged with developments in IA technology because "now is not the time" risks falling so far behind the technological curve that catching up will become impossible.

CONCLUSION

From the years 1880 to 1894, Mark Twain famously invested a sizeable fortune in the Paige Compositor, a complicated typesetting machine that attempted to emulate the delicate and precise actions of a human typesetter by using mechanical arms to pick up individual sorts (cast letters and punctuation) from their boxes in the type case, carefully compose the sorts into justified lines of text, and, once the printing job was completed, return the sorts to their proper boxes in the type case. Unfortunately for Twain's finances, the Paige Compositor, which incorporated some eighteen thousand finely machined moving parts, never managed to function for long without breaking down, and only two examples of the machine were ever built, both prototypes. The final death knell was sounded by the widespread adoption

THE IRON LIBRARIAN: A PERSONAL STORY OF AN AI EXPERIMENT

In 2009 my daughter received for Christmas a handheld electronic game called 20Q. Based on the old Twenty Questions parlor game, 20Q was first developed in 1988 as an experiment in artificial intelligence by software developer and entrepreneur Robin Burgener and is now available not only as a handheld toy, but also via a website (www.20q. net) where, thanks to machine learning, the game gets better the more it is used.* My daughter and I played with the handheld 20Q dozens of times, and I was impressed with how very difficult it was to beat a toy that many would consider to be nothing more than a stocking stuffer. Which led to a thought: If a toy costing much less than $20 has AI this good, why aren't libraries doing more with AI to improve their customers' success at information retrieval?

After pestering several library colleagues and a computer-science professor or two, I was pointed in the direction of David C. Noelle, a cognitive and computer scientist on the faculty at my institution, the University of California, Merced. I met with David and explained my idea for using artificial intelligence as well as the obstacles that typical undergraduates face when tasked with finding scholarly information for their papers and projects. First, many undergraduates take courses in fields for which the scholarly language of the field is unfamiliar. For example, an undergraduate in a psychology class might naïvely search the phrase "split personality" without understanding that psychologists do not use that phrase, instead using the more precise term "dissociative identity disorder." Second, many undergraduates do not know how scholarly information is created, formatted, distributed, or organized, nor do they know how it differs from non-scholarly information.

David was interested in this problem and, after several weeks of thinking about it, came back with an approach at which possibly no librarian would have ever arrived. Librarians, David pointed out, have historically organized information by subject because this is the most logical way to arrange large numbers of information objects (i.e., books) sitting on shelves. Call-number classification schemes are subject based just as the assignment of controlled vocabulary terms is subject based.

Subject-based organization even carries over into the online world, notably in the form of subject-specific databases. This means that if you want to search for scholarly articles on psychology topics, you have a good head start if you know that you should search the subject-specific *PsycINFO* database. Or if you are looking for scholarly literary criticism, you are well-advised to search the subject-specific *MLA International Bibliography*. As any librarian who has dabbled in teaching information literacy can attest, students do not always have a complete understanding of the concept of organizing information by subject and far too often know nothing about subject databases.

David's brilliant insight was to create an information retrieval tool that started by asking students for something they do know: the course for which they are doing research. Working from a database in which specific courses are mapped to relevant keywords and concepts, the proposed search tool could recommend appropriate subject databases, suggest more appropriate (i.e., scholarly) search terminology, and retrieve records for relevant scholarly information resources (chiefly articles and books). Because this information-retrieval tool would use machine-learning technology, the more it was used, the better it would get at interpreting queries and providing relevant results.

The approach of asking students to start by identifying the course for which they are doing research makes perfect sense; after all, "What course is this for?" is a standard reference-interview question when a librarian assists a student. Consider how a reference librarian's response to the statement, "I need information on violent behavior by the mentally ill," will vary if a student is doing research for a course in psychology versus a course in criminal justice versus a course in public health. Along the same lines, a reference librarian's response will differ for a student doing research for a freshman-level course versus a senior-level course.

Mulling over David's idea led to some blue-sky thinking about what additional features a fully developed tool, which I half-jokingly dubbed "the Iron Librarian," might offer:

- Customized versions of the Iron Librarian search box could be embedded in course-specific websites and course-management-system pages so that students would not have to identify the course for which they were doing research.
- The back end of the Iron Librarian could allow instructors or librarians to impose limits on the results for specific courses. For example, "For Biology 110-Section 02, no books or articles more than ten years old," or "For Philosophy 222-Section 01, push to the top of the results list any books or articles by the following authors . . . ."
- Offer Amazon.com-style recommendations based on previous searches: "Other students who searched for information on the **Battle of Gettysburg** also searched the *America: History and Life* database and liked the following books and articles. . . ."
- Provide unobtrusive explanations of why the Iron Librarian produced the results that it did with the intent that these explanations would serve as mini-lessons in information literacy.

The UC Merced Library contracted with cognitive scientist/programmer Derek Devnich to create a very rough working prototype of the Iron Librarian. Tested with just a few courses, the prototype worked remarkably well. Still in an extremely early stage of development and a long, long way from anything like a rollout, we are looking for opportunities to further develop, refine, and test the Iron Librarian and see how far this experiment in AI might take us.

---

* Tanis Stoliar, "20Q, Who Are You?," 2-Q.net Inc., http://www.20q.net/flat/history.html (accessed October 23, 2013).

of the linotype, a machine that completely abandoned the human method of typesetting by instead employing reservoirs of hot lead to cast and set complete lines of text. In the words of Twain's friend and co-investor, Standard Oil executive Henry Huttleston Rogers, the Paige Compositor "was too much of a human being and not enough of a machine."[30]

It is possible that trying to develop human-like intelligent-agent avatars will meet the same fate as the Paige Compositor. The more machine-like, behind-the-scenes forms of artificial intelligence, such as expert systems, may continue to run in the background while leaving the delicate and precise job of conducting anything resembling a reference interview to human librarians. On the other hand, the possibility of providing online library customers with always-available assistance at far less cost than could be done using human labor means that it would be a mistake to believe that intelligent-agent technology can simply be ignored until its performance equals or exceeds that of a human being. Somewhere between the place where intelligent-agent technology is today and the Singularity is a tipping point. If and when that point is reached, the impact on libraries will make the earlier impact of Web search engines seem featherlight in comparison.

NOTES

1. Ken Jennings, "My Puny Human Brain," *Slate*, February 16, 2011, http://www.slate.com/articles/arts/culturebox/202/my_puny_human_brain.html (accessed October 18, 2013).

2. Vernor Vinge, "The Coming Technological Singularity: How to Survive in the Post-Human Era," NASA Lewis Research Center and the Ohio Aerospace Institute, Cleveland, Ohio, March 30–31, 1993, http://www-rohan.sdsu.edu/faculty/vinge/misc/singularity.html (accessed October 10, 2013).

3. Alan Turing, "Computing Machinery and Intelligence," *Mind* 59, no. 236 (October 1950): 433–460, doi:10.1093/mind/LIX.236.433 (accessed October 17, 2013).

4. Graham Oppy and David Dowe, "The Turing Test," in *The Stanford Encyclopedia of Philosophy*, ed. Edward N. Zalta, 2011, http://plato.stanford.edu/archives/spr2011/entries/turing-test (accessed October 17, 2013).

5. Susan Brudno and Barbara Brynko, "LexisNexis: The Smart Machines," *Information Today* 30, no. 4 (April 2013): 30.

6. Robert M. Mason, "Artificial Intelligence: Promise, Myth and Reality," *Library Journal* 110, no. 7 (April 15, 1985), 56.

7. Mason, "Artificial Intelligence," 57.

8. R. Bruce Miller and Milton T. Wolf, eds., *Thinking Robots, an Aware Internet, and Cyberpunk Librarians: The 1992 LITA President's Program: Presentations by Hans Moravec, Bruce Sterling, and David Brin* (Chicago: Library and Information Technology Association, 1992).

9. Maryellen Mott Allen, "The Myth of Intelligent Agents," *Online* (Weston, CT) 24, no. 6 (November/December 2000), 51.

10. Peter Jackson, "Artificial Intelligence and Information Retrieval," *Searcher* 13, no. 1 (January 2005): 33.

11. Roy Balleste, "The Future of Artificial Intelligence in Your Virtual Libraries," *Computers in Libraries* 22, no. 9 (October 2002): 10–64; Hilary Skov-Nielsen, "New Talking Avatars on the MSVU Library Website," *Partnership: The Canadian Journal of Library and Information Practice and Research* 3, no. 2 (2008): 1–3, https://journal.lib.uoguelph.ca/index.php/perj/article/view/877/1373 (accessed October 25, 2013).

12. R. S. Marcus, "An Experimental Comparison of the Effectiveness of Computers and Humans as Search Intermediaries," *Journal of the American Society for Information Science* 34, no. 6 (November 1983): 381–404.

13. Valeda Dent, *Intelligent Agent Concepts in the Modern Library* (Rutgers, NJ: RUcore: Rutgers University Community Repository, 2007), http://rucore.libraries.rutgers.edu/rutgers-lib/23854 (accessed October 3, 2013).

14. Balleste, "The Future of Artificial Intelligence in Your Virtual Libraries," 10.

15. "A Wise Old Owl Becomes NLM's Latest Customer Service Feature," National Library of Medicine, http://www.nlm.nih.gov/news/cosmoowl.html (accessed October 24, 2013).

16. Skov-Nielsen, "New Talking Avatars," 1.

17. "Lillian," Chatbots.org, http://www.chatbots.org/chatbot/lillian1 (accessed November 4, 2013).

18. DeeAnn Allison, "Chatbots in the Library: Is It Time?" *Library Hi Tech* 30, no. 1 (2012): 95–107, http://digitalcommons.unl.edu/libraryscience/280 (accessed October 9, 2013).

19. Victoria L. Rubin, Yimin Chen, and Lynne Marie Thorimbert, "Artificially Intelligent Conversational Agents in Libraries," *Library Hi Tech* 28, no. 4 (September 30, 2010): 505.

20. Guoying Liu, *The Application of Intelligent Agents in Libraries: A Survey* (Windsor, Ontario, Canada: Leddy Library Publications, 2011), 28, http://scholar.uwindsor.ca/leddylibrarypub/4 (accessed October 3, 2013).

21. Clifford Nass, Jonathan Steuer, and Ellen R. Tauber, "Computers Are Social Actors," Association for Computing Machinery, Boston, April 24–28, 1994, doi:10.1145/191666.191703 (accessed October 8, 2013).

22. Clifford Nass, Youngme Moon, B. J. Fogg, B. Reeves, and D. C. Dryer, "Can Computer Personalities Be Human Personalities?," *International Journal of Human-Computer Studies* 43, no. 2 (1995): 235.

23. Lingyun Qiu and Izak Benbasat, "A Study of Demographic Embodiments of Product Recommendation Agents in Electronic Commerce," *International Journal of Human-Computer Studies* 68, no. 10 (October 2010): 681, doi:10.1016/j.ijhes.2010.05.005 (accessed September 30, 2013).

24. Farhod P. Karimov, Malaika Brengman, and Leo Van Hove, "The Effect of Website Design Dimensions on Initial Trust: A Synthesis of the Empirical Literature," *Journal of Electronic Commerce Research* 12, no. 4 (2011): 276.

25. Peter J. McGoldrick, Kathleen A. Keeling, and Susan F. Beatty, "A Typology of Roles for Avatars in Online Retailing," *Journal of Marketing Management* 24, no. 3 (April 2008): 433–434.

26. Donald A. Norman, "How Might People Interact with Agents," *Communications of the ACM* 37, no. 7 (July 1994): 70.

27. Norman, "How Might People Interact with Agents," 71.

28. Fred Donald Davis Jr., "A Technology Acceptance Model for Testing New End-User Information Systems: Theory and Results," Ph.D. dissertation, Massachusetts Institute of Technology, 1986, http://dspace.mit.edu/bitstream/handle/1721.1/15192/14927137.pdf?sequence=1 (accessed November 7, 2013).

29. V. Venkatesh, M. G. Morris, G. B. Davis, and F. D. Davis, "User Acceptance of Information Technology: Toward a Unified View," *MIS Quarterly* 27, no. 3 (September 2003): 425–478.

30. Judith Yaross Lee, "Anatomy of a Fascinating Failure," *American Heritage of Invention and Technology* 3 (Summer 1987): 60.

Assessment in the Online Environment

An Unmet Challenge

In October 1990 a Canadian librarian named Tom Eadie created a stir in the library world by publishing the provocatively titled "Immodest Proposals: User Instruction for Students Does Not Work; a Former User Education Librarian Challenges a Basic Belief." If the title alone does not demonstrate just how provocative Eadie's article is, consider the following quotation: "I think user education is a special service of questionable value that arose not because users asked for it, but because librarians thought it would be good for them."[1] Advocating the value of old-fashioned reference service over instruction, Eadie first condemns the lack of solid data demonstrating the effectiveness of user instruction and then points out a contradiction in the interpretation of what little instruction-related assessment data there is:

> If a user education program is implemented and reference statistics drop, then the program has achieved its goal of eliminating repetitive questions. But if reference statistics increase, then the program has had the desired effect of publicizing reference service. Not bad. A shell game with a pea under *every* shell.[2]

At the time Eadie's article appeared in *Library Journal*, I had been working as a professional librarian (with the heady title of "instruction coordinator") for about a month. As a living relic of that bygone era, I can vouch that assessing library collections and services back in the day was a simple undertaking compared to what is demanded of librarians in the twenty-first century. Circa

1990, outcomes-based assessment was only beginning to gain a foothold, so the data required to establish a library's value involved not much more than simple counting:

- number of volumes (print, of course)
- number of journal subscriptions (ditto print)
- gate count
- circulation count
- reference-desk statistics
- number of classes/students taught

Libraries got by with comparing themselves to each other (more books than our peer institutions = good) as well as to their own past performance (higher gate count and/or circulation than the previous year = good). The uncomfortably provocative Eadie aside—and unlike the skeptical grab bag of funders, politicians, administrators, and accreditation bodies populating the twenty-first-century library landscape—few inside or outside of the profession were asking libraries to demonstrate what their numbers meant in terms of actual outcomes. Libraries were not asked to prove that their well-enumerated collections and services directly improved the lives of the public they served or enhanced student learning. Because there was no such thing as the Web, there was no demand for libraries to compare themselves to their yet-to-emerge Web-based rivals. Most significant is the fact that library assessment in 1990 did not need to vex itself with the truly vexing problem of assessing how library collections and services benefited, or not, a large body of customers who rarely or never set foot inside a library building.

If a library cannot provide solid evidence showing that its services for remote customers produce desirable outcomes, then a library cannot rightfully claim that such services are worth the cost and effort they entail. No matter how strongly librarians may feel that they provide good value to remote customers, feelings are not facts. Perhaps the most pressing question for libraries in the competitive, information-rich, resource-constrained online world of the twenty-first century is how to assess in meaningful, effective ways the value of a library to its remote customers.

ADAPTING TRADITIONAL FORMS OF
ASSESSMENT TO THE ONLINE ENVIRONMENT

The most obvious answer for assessing outcomes in the online environment is to adapt for that purpose the traditional methods of assessment used in the physical library. As might be expected, this approach has its limitations.

Surveys

In a physical library building, it is of course possible to survey library visitors by means of such high-touch methods as handing out paper survey forms or having library staff interview walk-in customers. In the online environment, surveys can be administered via such means as e-mail, pop-up forms, or links to online survey pages. While obtaining good response rates to surveys in any environment has always been challenging, it is an especially daunting challenge in the online environment. A 2008 meta-analysis of published research on response rates to Web-based surveys found that "on average web surveys yield an 11% lower response rate compared to other modes."[3] Even more discouraging is the widely acknowledged fact that response rates to Web surveys have been steadily dropping due to such factors as survey fatigue and the widespread use of bogus surveys, some of which are nothing more than scams. For many, Web surveys are almost indistinguishable from banner advertisements, a format that saw its click-through rates drop from 7 percent to 0.2 percent from 1996 to 2007.[4] Besides wasting organizational time and resources, any survey that results in a low response rate is likely to provide an unbalanced picture of how remote customers use library collections and services as well as what improvements or changes customers most want to see.

Because other modes of surveying have a higher response rate than Web-based modes, surveying remote library customers by telephone or postal mail is a possibility if a library (1) has access to the postal addresses and/or telephone numbers of its remote customers and (2) using such information is not a violation of the library's privacy policy. The harsh truth is that surveying library customers via telephone is likely to generate hostility among at least some of those contacted, and, hostility aside, both telephone and postal surveys may still result in unacceptably low response rates.

Regardless of whether it employs physical or digital methods, when a library sets out to survey its customers, both the construction of the survey

PERSUASION

Completing and returning a survey is not something most people necessarily want to do, and changing that attitude may seem impossible. But if anyone can claim to be the guru of convincing people to do things they do not necessarily want to do, it has to be Robert B. Cialdini, Regent Professor Emeritus of Psychology and Marketing at Arizona State University. Cialdini has published numerous books and articles on the subject of persuading people to do everything from donating to a charity to making a purchase to completing a survey questionnaire. His best-known book, *Influence: The Psychology of Persuasion*, has sold over 2 million copies and gone through a revision and numerous reprintings since first being published in 1984.

Based on solid academic research, Cialdini's techniques for improving response rates to survey questionnaires are entirely practical. For example, Cialdini suggests including a very brief handwritten message (such as a single sentence written on a sticky note) with an otherwise machine-printed document as a means of dramatically improving response rates. In addition to *Influence: The Psychology of Persuasion*, other important works in the field include

- *Yes! 50 Scientifically Proven Ways to Be Persuasive* by Noah J. Goldstein, Steve J. Martin, and Robert B. Cialdini. New York: Free Press, 2008.
- *Influence: Science and Practice* (4th ed.) by Robert B. Cialdini. Boston: Allyn and Bacon, 2001.
- *Return on Influence: The Revolutionary Power of Klout, Social Scoring, and Influence Marketing* by Mark W. Schaefer. New York: McGraw-Hill, 2012. Focusing on influence in the online environment, *Return on Influence* is heavily influenced (ahem) by Cialdini's previous work.

and the interpretation of the results are crucial to producing valid, actionable results. Far more often than not, surveys that are constructed by in-house staff end up severely flawed. When the constructors of a survey have a stake in the outcome, bias inevitably creeps into decisions about how the questions are worded, which questions are asked, and (more subtly) which questions are not asked. One all too common example of how non-experts can go wrong when constructing a survey is the misuse of Likert scales. While the concept of the Likert scale seems obvious enough, its proper construction requires more than simply coming up with a series of statements and a corresponding set of responses ranging from "Strongly Disagree" to "Strongly Agree." First, because the numbers on a Likert scale are arbitrary, each statement must be carefully worded so that there is a symmetry to the possible responses. The central response—"Neither Agree Nor Disagree"—must accurately represent a neutral position, while the intervals between every other possible response must be equal across the board. Consistently achieving such symmetry requires knowledge, skill, and practical experience. Second, contradictory statements should be incorporated into a Likert-scale survey in order to measure each respondent's consistency. For example, a respondent who agrees with the statement, "I never use the library's print collections and rely exclusively on online information resources," should, if consistent, disagree with the statement, "The library should put the bulk of its resources into print collections rather than investing in online information resources." Third, statements should not reflect attitudes on which there is likely to be nearly universal consensus. A statement such as, "The library should strive to promote ignorance and illiteracy," should never be included in a survey that uses Likert scales because it is expected that every sincere respondent will strongly disagree. Finally, the possible responses should include a balanced range of positive and negative choices. For example, the following range:
Poor   Average   Above Average   Well Above Average   Outstanding
allows for only a single negative response.

The above examples represent just a few of the more straightforward pitfalls of constructing a survey that employs Likert scales. Some aspects of Likert scales—such as whether individual Likert items should be treated as interval-level data or as ordered-categorical data—are so nuanced that even the experts disagree. The point here is not to conduct a clinic on the Likert scale or any other survey technique; rather, it is to drive home the point that constructing surveys and analyzing the data they produce is not a job for amateurs. The very best practice in constructing surveys is to work, from the very beginning, with an impartial consultant who has training and experience in constructing social-science surveys and analyzing their results. Any amateur who designs and administers a survey and, after the fact, takes it to a statistician for analysis is likely to find that much of the data they have worked so hard to collect is either entirely worthless or fails to answer the right questions because the survey itself was improperly constructed to begin with. By the same token, attempting to analyze data without an in-depth understanding of statistics and social-science survey methodologies is a fool's errand. Another way of avoiding the pitfalls of do-it-yourself assessment tools is to administer a proven assessment instrument such as the Association of Research Libraries' LibQual+. While an organization may feel that it is saving money by developing in-house surveys, those savings will likely be negated by the lack of valid, actionable data produced.

Focus Groups

A now-ubiquitous assessment tool, the focus group found its first widespread application among marketers in the 1950s and was adopted a few decades later by social scientists. Conducting a focus group typically involves convening a panel of six to ten participants who are, ideally, representative of a target population. The members of a focus group are asked to respond to questions posed by a trained facilitator who records their responses. Like a survey, a focus group is a means of obtaining qualitative data about such things as products, services, and organizations. Also like a survey, successfully employing a focus group is more difficult than it might seem. The value of a focus group hinges on such factors as the questions asked (and not asked), the skill of the facilitator, whether or not the members of the focus group are truly representative, and how the resulting data are ultimately analyzed. Such difficulties aside, focus groups can be powerful tools for providing qualitative data, with the failed 1985 introduction of New Coke serving as a notable example of this power. Prior to changing the time-honored formula of its flagship product, the Coca-Cola Corporation spent $4 million on market research that included both surveys and focus groups. While survey data indicated that the introduction of New Coke would be well received and help to increase Coke's market share over competitor Pepsi, focus-group data

STEWARDSHIP VERSUS LEADERSHIP:
AN ASSESSMENT CONUNDRUM

We are a customer-focused organization.
We are customer driven.
We put customers first.
The customer is always right.

The world of business provides some remarkable stories of companies that are truly focused on their customers. At the Ritz-Carlton chain of luxury hotels, every employee in the company is authorized to spend over $2,000 in a single day to make a customer happy, no questions asked.* Amazon founder and CEO Jeff Bezos is known for holding meetings at which an empty chair is placed at the table to represent the customer, "the most important person in the room."† For so intense a focus on customers to have any real import, an organization needs to put more than token effort into understanding its existing and, ideally, its potential customers. Inarguably, gaining such understanding is one of the main reasons for conducting qualitative assessments of customer satisfaction and needs.

However, as important as it is to understand customers and listen to their concerns, it is nonetheless quite possible to put too much stock in customer feedback. First, responses to, and interpretations of, customer-satisfaction surveys are highly subjective. If, on average, customers give a particular library service an 8 (out of 10), what does that really mean? What does it mean if 5 percent give the service a 1, 5 percent give it a 10, and everyone else is in the middle? Second, what people say they do is rarely the same as what they actually do. Just consider the differences between the average person's actual habits of diet and exercise versus what they report when queried by their doctor. The sometimes substantial gap between an individual's self-assessment and reality is why hands-on website usability testing is superior to asking customers to answer questions about how they use a website. Third, and most significant, while customers may be able to say what they want or need today, they are (understandably) not very good at predicting what they are going to need in the future, especially when they lack expert knowledge of pending developments in technology or changes in the marketplace. This idea is expressed in a popular Internet meme that is routinely, though incorrectly, attributed to Henry Ford: "If I had asked people what they wanted, they would have asked for faster horses." Less glibly, though backed by far better research, the idea that customers cannot fully understand what they will need in the future underpins the central thesis of Clayton Christensen's influential *The Innovator's Dilemma: When New Technologies Cause Great Firms to Fail.*

Examples of how customers might lead a library in the wrong direction or hold back its progress are easy to imagine. If a public library, circa 1982, had surveyed its customers about the need to someday provide public-access computers, the overwhelming response would have been along the lines of, "Why bother?" If an academic library, circa 1997, had surveyed its customers about the desirability of transitioning (within the next five to ten years) from print to online journals, the overwhelming response would have been along the lines of, "Are you insane?" And that is not even taking into account the fact that customers can intentionally try to steer a library wrong by sabotaging its assessment efforts. Back in the days when the print journal was king of the academic library, it was understood that some faculty would manipulate the reshelving count by sending student assistants to the library to pull armfuls of the faculty member's favorite journals from the shelves and leave them on the tables. The hope was that this manipulation would insulate those favored journals from being cut in the event of a budget squeeze.

The sentence from the Tom Eadie article quoted at the start of this chapter, "I think user education is a special service of questionable value that arose not because users asked for it, but because librarians thought it would be good for them," can be read in two ways. One reading (the one that the author appears to intend) is that busybody librarians, acting *in loco parentis*, are providing a service that is unwanted by their customers, while the other reading is that librarians, acting as knowledgeable information professionals, are providing an essential service their customers do not realize they need. In the interest of providing the right services and collections, librarians must listen to their customers and work to meet their real, present-day needs. This is the essence of good stewardship. On the other hand, as knowledgeable professionals with their eyes on a rapidly changing information environment, it is incumbent on librarians to anticipate what their customers are going to need two, five, or more years in the future and to position their libraries to meet those needs, even if this comes at some cost to meeting present-day needs. This is the essence of good leadership. The conundrum is that stewardship and leadership often conflict, and knowing when to listen and when to use professional judgment is no easier than accurately predicting the future of a rapidly changing information environment.

---

* Robert Reiss, "How Ritz-Carlton Stays at the Top," *Forbes*, October 30, 2009, http://www.forbes.com/2009/10/30/simon-cooper-ritz-leadership-ceonetwork-hotels.html (accessed January 7, 2014).

† George Anders, "Jeff Bezos Gets It," *Forbes Asia* 8, no. 6 (May 2012), http://www.forbes.com/global/2012/0507/global-2000-12-amazon-jeff-bezos-gets-it.html (accessed December 15, 2013).

indicated that the strong opinions of loyal Coke drinkers would doom any attempt to change the formula of their beloved beverage. Coca-Cola chose to ignore its focus-group data, a decision that led to what is widely regarded as the greatest marketing fiasco of all time.[5]

Over the years many libraries have used focus groups to obtain feedback on their collections and services. As libraries increasingly find themselves serving geographically dispersed customers, the logistics of convening an in-person focus group can be daunting; however, using online conferencing tools to convene a virtual focus group comprised of remote users offers a practical alternative. While convening and conducting a virtual focus group is not without its challenges, virtual focus groups have been successfully used by businesses and, in 2008, by the University of Nevada–Las Vegas Library, which conducted a virtual focus group with students at a branch campus located in Singapore.[6]

Head Counts

The physical library's statistic of the head count has an online analog in the form of hits on a library's website. While both head counts and website hits are limited forms of assessment in that they do not provide any evidence as to outcomes—Did the visit to the library or website actually benefit the customer?—assessing hits is even more problematic than assessing head counts. While analytic software makes it easy to obtain raw data on the number of hits a library website receives, it is necessary to distinguish hits caused by actual human visitors from those generated by machines. Far more challenging is analyzing website hits to assess complex concepts such as website usability and customer outcomes. For both library and business websites, inferences based on aggregate data such as page hits or page-duration visits can be misleading because such data lacks context and cannot account for things like differences between visitors' purposes (simple versus complex tasks) or an individual's level of familiarity with a website (increased familiarity correlates to less time required to carry out a transaction).[7] Analysis of library website aggregate data is made even more challenging because, unlike business websites, library websites have no equivalent to such relatively clear-cut commercial metrics as sales, advertising links clicked, or the length of page-duration visits (longer visits generally correspond to more sales). Indeed, a positive business metric such as longer page-duration visits could be a negative on a library website if those longer visits represent a customer's lack of success in navigating the website and/or finding a link to needed information.

A related assessment challenge for libraries is that website hits do not account for customers who directly access library-provided information resources via bookmarks or search engines rather than via links on the library's website. It is just such situations that give rise to (possibly apocryphal) stories like that of the disgruntled faculty chemist who demands to know why his research grants are being taxed to support the campus library when, "I get all the information I need from SciFinder Scholar." The only way libraries can hope to assess their customers' unmediated use of library-provided online information resources is by obtaining usage data from vendors. While it has been a boon to assessment efforts that (1) many vendors are willing (out of self-interest) to provide usage data to their library customers and (2) COUNTER (Counting Online Usage of Networked Electronic Resources) has established standards for such data, the fact remains that obtaining, analyzing, and interpreting vendor-provided data represents a significant workload for libraries.

While traditional methods of assessment are not entirely worthless when it comes to conducting assessment on remote users, they clearly have their limits.

NON-TRADITIONAL MEANS OF ASSESSMENT

If traditional means are not ideal for assessing library outcomes for remote customers, the obvious question becomes, "What about using non-traditional means of assessment?"

Clickstream Data

Clickstream data provides, as the name implies, information about the links visitors click while using a website, though it may also include such information as what search terms visitors use. The clickstream data itself is collected via proprietary software and stored on a server where it can be first cleaned up and then analyzed to gain insight into actual (rather than self-reported) behavior of site visitors. Clickstream data can be analyzed on a highly granular level, focusing down to the navigation paths followed by individual visitors; alternatively, clickstream data can be analyzed in aggregate to identify general user tendencies or commonly experienced problems.

For over two decades commercial websites have been collecting and analyzing clickstream data to improve site performance and profitability, and as a result the business literature reflects widespread scholarly interest in the use of clickstream data. For example, Wendy W. Moe's influential article, "Buying, Searching, or Browsing: Differentiating between Online Shoppers Using In-Store Navigational Clickstream,"[8] has, from its publication in 2003 through the end of 2013, been cited 98 times according to ISI's Web of Knowledge and 303 times according to Google Scholar. Libraries, on the other hand, trail behind the business world when it comes to using, not to mention studying, clickstream data. And there are some very good reasons why libraries are behind in this area. First, acquiring the software to gather clickstream data and the tools to analyze that data is costly. Second, clickstream data is typically site specific and, as a result, might tell a library that visitor X landed on the library home page and followed path 1–2–3 to the library's link to database Y, but once visitor X clicks that database link and leaves the library website, the clickstream trail stops cold. Third—and this is big—collecting clickstream data raises significant privacy issues. For many, the idea of a library collecting data on its customers' use of a library website is no different than a government using the Web to spy on its own citizens. At the same time, most library privacy policies and librarian codes of professional ethics do not countenance the non-consensual collection of clickstream data. Libraries can avoid the privacy issue by asking customers to opt in to having their clickstream data collected, though doing so is likely to result in a high rate of opting out and may well fan the flames of paranoia among library customers.

Businesses, as might be suspected, are less constrained than libraries when it comes to the privacy issues associated with clickstream data. Clickstream data is routinely collected by websites that depend on advertising revenue, while some websites and Internet service providers go so far as to sell their clickstream data to third parties. Even so, this does not mean that businesses are completely immune from the privacy issues raised by clickstream data. In 2005, Internet service provider AOL (America Online) caused an uproar and found itself facing civil lawsuits when it naively released clickstream data that included enough personal information to identify specific individuals and link them to websites they had visited while using AOL.[9]

Data Mining

In recent years a hot-topic issue for libraries has been the challenge of curating what is familiarly known as Big Data:

> Big Data applies to information that can't be processed or analyzed using traditional processes or tools. Increasingly, organizations today are facing more and more Big Data challenges. They have access to a wealth of information, but they don't know how to get value out of it because it is sitting in its most raw form or in a semistructured or unstructured format; and as a result, they don't even know whether it's worth keeping (or even able to keep it for that matter).[10]

The focus for librarians engaged in the Big Data challenge has been on what libraries can and should do about the vast amounts of data being produced by government, business, and the academy. Yet with all the concern about other people's data, the library world has paid little to no attention to the large amounts of data produced as a by-product of library operations. Some potentially valuable library operational data, such as clickstream data, is rarely or never collected. Some, such as circulation records, is collected but intentionally purged in the interest of protecting privacy. And some, such as library website analytics, is collected in haphazard ways with no coherent plan for anything approaching systematic analysis or long-term preservation. Of course not all operational data can or should be preserved, nor does all operational data have the potential to answer important questions facing libraries. However, if libraries were able to identify the data that matters and find ways to store it, effectively mining this data could lead to answers that will ultimately allow libraries to better serve their customers.

Simply defined, data mining is the process of discovering meaningful patterns of information in very large data sets. It constitutes "a research area at the intersection of several disciplines, including statistics, databases, pattern recognition and AI, visualization, optimization, and high-performance and parallel computing."[11] The possibilities of mining data gathered from the Internet has been of interest to scholarly researchers for several decades now, with one of the earliest (1996) scholarly articles on the subject noting, "Mining information and knowledge from large databases has been recognized by many researchers as a key research topic in database systems and machine learning, and by many industrial companies as an important area with an opportunity of major revenues."[12] The first workshop on mining Web data, WEBKDD, was held in 1999,[13] and it continues to this day in the form of the Association for Computing Machinery SIGKDD Conference on Knowledge Discovery and Data Mining. Twenty-first-century retail businesses routinely use data mining for such purposes as identifying sales trends, managing customer relationships, and developing advertising campaigns. In the area of manufacturing, data mining can be used to analyze operations or predict the future availability and cost of raw materials, or in finance to develop investment strategies. Outside of business, data mining has applications in such areas as science, engineering, health care, education, and government.

So what about libraries? Painting a picture in very broad brushstrokes, what it involves for a library to get into data mining would look something like the following:

A library would need to begin by determining the high-level questions on which it wishes to focus. If, for example, a library's most pressing question is how to better serve its remote customers, then data on the reshelving rates of reference books is not going to be of enough use to justify the costs of collecting and preparing that data. Even if costs are not an issue, a huge pile of random data would be as unlikely to produce useful intelligence as would the undirected mining of such data.

Once a library decides on a focus, it must then identify the sources from which it might collect meaningful data. Some obvious sources of data include a local or consortial integrated library system (ILS), interlibrary loan data (if not already in the ILS), library website analytical data, clickstream data (if available), transactions of digital-reference sessions, qualitative data obtained from surveys or focus groups, data gathered from library social-networking tools (Facebook, Twitter, YouTube, etc.), and usage data obtained from vendors of online information resources (databases, journals, e-books, etc.).[‡] Whatever the source, the amount of data collected needs to be large enough both to avoid small-sample errors as well as to increase the likelihood that useful intelligence will result from data-mining activities. Also, the data needs to be regularly updated in order to keep pace with a dynamic information environment. Speaking of an ILS, it is worth noting that data mining is quite distinct from generating reports from an ILS or any other production system. While production systems may have report-generation capabilities, true data mining offers far more flexibility in how data can be queried and results displayed. Another important difference is that a system like an ILS is optimized for production, not data mining, so attempting to mine data within such a system while it is performing its day job of circulation, acquisitions, and the like can have consequences ranging from slowed performance to a complete crash of the system.

Once collected, data must be de-siloed by gathering it into an organized data warehouse. Before this can happen, though, the data must be processed. First of all, privacy concerns demand that the data be made anonymous before anything else can be done with it. Then the data will likely need to be reformatted so that data from different sources can be queried simultaneously. Libraries may find themselves facing black-box problems in which a proprietary system, such as an ILS, contains a great deal of useful raw data that is extremely difficult, if not impossible, to extract and render into a format that

---

[‡] A common misconception is that the term *data mining* refers to the collection of data from various sources; in fact, the process of data mining occurs only *after* the data has been collected and organized in a data warehouse.

lends itself to data mining.[14] Transaction logs, such as those pulled directly from Web servers, are extremely difficult to work with because the data they contain typically requires a great deal of cleanup to be useful. Equally difficult is harmonizing such strikingly heterogeneous data formats as raw numbers, text, images, and videos.

Before any data can go into a data warehouse it must be anonymous, clean, and formatted for data-mining operations. It is equally important that the data warehouse itself be a dedicated database with no connection to production systems.[15] Getting to the point of having a functioning data warehouse filled with viable data is neither cheap nor easy. And now the bad news: creating a functioning data warehouse is the end of neither the cost nor the work.

Effectively mining a data warehouse and presenting the results in ways that are comprehendible to human decision makers requires business-intelligence software capable of online analytical processing (OLAP). As a decision-support system, OLAP facilitates navigating a data set "through different variables, aggregation types, timeframes and other dimensions."[16] Business-intelligence software employs sophisticated statistical techniques to detect in large amounts of data meaningful, previously undetected patterns (known in the jargon of the data-mining profession as "interestingness").[17] Given a robust data warehouse with which to work, business-intelligence software can flag patterns as interesting, present data in rich graphical displays that human beings can readily understand and manipulate, and even send automatic notices when pre-set thresholds are crossed or specified conditions are met. Potentially, business-intelligence software could allow libraries to provide the kind of personalized online experience users have come to expect from commercial websites like Amazon, though customers would need to voluntarily waive certain privacy rights to take advantage of services that could, for example, analyze a customer's previous searches of a library's website and catalog in order to recommend relevant books, appropriate subject-specific databases, or more effective search strategies.

As powerful as the best business-intelligence software packages may potentially be, they have their downsides. First of all, the cost of such packages can be prohibitively expensive. One of the earliest library attempts at using business-intelligence software occurred in 1998 at the University of Waterloo when librarians there stumbled upon the fact that they could use IBM's Cognos business-intelligence software package at no cost courtesy of a campus site license.[18] More significant than the cost of the software is the amount of time and thought that must go into configuring the software so that it is, in effect, asking the right questions of the data and reporting back meaningful intelligence. As stated in a 2013 article on the topic of analyzing large data sets, "Working with any data does require an idea; a hypothesis and a view to know what kind of patterns you might be interested in."[19] There are no shortcuts when it comes to knowing what questions are worth pursuing or to developing a hypothesis that might illuminate those questions through data mining.

Another aspect of data mining that allows no shortcuts is the application of any intelligence uncovered in the data-mining process. While data mining can detect interestingness in the data, putting that data into context, deciding if it is actionable, and, if so, deciding what actions to take, remains, to date, the job of thoughtful, knowledgeable human intermediaries. Though data mining might flag as interesting the fact that use of a library's databases plunges every Monday evening from late August through mid-December, it is up to human beings to decide if that interestingness represents anything more than the fact that the library's customers are especially devoted to television broadcasts of NFL football games. Also, without knowledgeable human beings involved in interpreting the results of data mining, there is the danger of being fooled by apparently meaningful patterns in the data that are merely the result of statistical randomness:

> One can *always* find *apparent* structures in data sets. Many of these structures will not be real in the sense that they represent aspects of an underlying distribution, but will be attributable to the random aspects of the data generating process. Statisticians, to whom *inference* is a fundamental activity, are acutely aware of this and have as a central concern the question of how to distinguish between the underlying "systematic" components and the random components of data.[20]

In most cases the results of data mining do not provide final answers; instead, data mining "points the researcher toward interesting patterns to explore through other examinations of the data and discussions with users."[21] Like most analytical tools, data mining provides the most complete picture when used in conjunction with other analytical tools "such as LIBQUAL,

E-metrics, cost-benefit analyses, surveys, focus groups, or other qualitative explorations."[22]

Given the cost and complexity of data mining, it should come as no surprise that the technique has not seen a great deal of use by libraries or that the library literature on the subject is scanty. The most prolific author on the topic has been Scott Nicholson, a professor in the School of Information Studies at Syracuse University. Nicholson, who coined the term *bibliomining* to distinguish data mining for the purposes of managing a library (the kind with books) from data mining as it relates to the computer-science concept of a library (a collection of sub-programs within a software program). Cited several times in this chapter, Nicholson published at least a dozen articles on the topic of bibliomining from 2003 through 2007, at which point he stopped. When asked why he stopped his research into bibliomining, Nicholson replied,

> Many data mining and big data projects focus on a solution without figuring out what the problem is first. Many patterns in data are trivial, already known, or come from a flaw in the data warehouse, so wandering around the data set can be a frustrating task. Many data mining projects were abandoned in the last ten years after this was discovered, so I would recommend that libraries figure out the specific questions they want to answer before embarking on a big data project.[23]

Indeed, if libraries are to make use of the possibilities offered by data mining, they must enter into the process with a clear understanding of the questions they wish to answer. A data warehouse is not a magic lamp, and data mining is more complicated than giving the lamp a rub and waiting for a genie to materialize with all the answers in hand. Another major challenge is that data-mining projects are often beyond the resources of a single library, making sharing data and the analytical resources for large-scale joint projects the best approach for successful data mining, fraught with difficulties though such collaborative projects may be.[24]

CONCLUSION

One of the great frustrations of libraries, non-profits, governmental agencies, and educational institutions is that the relationship between financial support and accountability seems to have become, in recent times, an inverse one: the less support governments and other funders provide, the more accountability they demand. Under such circumstances, assessment can turn into a despised chore, one that is part unfunded mandate and part bare-knuckles survival strategy—an us-against-them game in which the goal is to prove one's organizational worth to skeptical outsiders and do so with the lowest possible expenditure of organizational time and treasure. As a library manager who really knows better, I have nonetheless caught myself lamenting, "If we didn't have to spend half our time doing assessment, we could be twice as productive." Assessment for organizational survival has become an unfortunate necessity for far too many libraries, devolving assessment from a principled investigation into how a library can more effectively and thoroughly meet the needs of its customers into a symbolic drama of appeasement staged for the hoodwinking of outsiders who happen to hold the library purse strings.

The survival situation for libraries is in some ways comparable to that of the Public Broadcasting System (PBS), a government-subsidized non-profit that has been criticized by some as unnecessary in the age of cable television. Although a perennial target of budget hawks, PBS has managed to survive by, in part, demonstrating that it is different from its commercial competition, a demonstration rather easily staged when the comparison is between such distinctly different programming offerings as PBS's *Nova* and the Learning Channel's *Here Comes Honey Boo Boo*. The difference between the value provided by libraries and that provided by Ask.com, Google, or Wikipedia is more subtle (at least to those outside the library profession) and, as a result, much more difficult to demonstrate.

As difficult as it may be, libraries need to assume the burden of conducting meaningful assessment in order to demonstrate their value. If, instead, libraries satisfy themselves with trotting out superficial raw numbers—whether those numbers are print volumes, online journal subscriptions, website hits, or reference questions answered—libraries are going to come out the worse for the comparison. Like it or not, and as unfair and superficial as such comparisons may be, even the most impressive library raw numbers look pitiful when stacked up against the raw numbers tallied by the giants of the online information world. Libraries need to do meaningful, in-depth assessment to convincingly prove that they provide a value, or values, not provided by their rivals, jaw-dropping though their rivals' raw numbers may be. And to be fair, if libraries find from their meaningful assessment that they are not actually providing values that their rivals are providing as well or better, then libraries must change their practices.

It would be a far happier ending if this chapter laid out clear-cut techniques and tools for conducting meaningful assessment—especially as it relates to remote users. The fact is that there are no easy answers. Traditional methods of assessment, though of some value, fall short. Too often, using a survey or focus group to do meaningful assessment in the far-flung and dynamic online world feels like trying to catch a 747 with a butterfly net. At the same time, the difficulties that surface when trying to deploy non-traditional, technology-rich assessment tools can be deal breakers. It would be comforting to think that new, easier-to-deploy assessment tools will become available in the near future, but there is no guarantee they will or that libraries can afford to wait even as long as the near future to deploy such tools. How libraries will conduct assessments that both demonstrate their value and allow them to remain relevant to their users remains the great challenge to be met in the online environment.

NOTES

1. Tom Eadie, "Immodest Proposals: User Instruction for Students Does Not Work; a Former User Education Librarian Challenges a Basic Belief," *Library Journal* 115 (October 15, 1990): 43.

2. Eadie, "Immodest Proposals," 43.

3. Katja Lozar Manfreda, Michael Bosnjak, Jernej Berzelak, Iris Haas, and Vasja Vehovar, "Web Surveys versus Other Survey Modes," *International Journal of Market Research* 50, no. 1 (January 2008): 97.

4. Oliver Rutz and Randolph Bucklin, "Does Banner Advertising Affect Browsing for Brands? Clickstream Choice Model Says Yes, for Some," *Quantitative Marketing & Economics* 10, no. 2 (June 2012): 232.

5. Robert M. Schindler, "The Real Lesson of New Coke: The Value of Focus Groups for Predicting the Effects of Social Influence," *Marketing Research* 4, no. 4 (December 1992): 23–24.

6. Lateka J. Grays, Darcy Del Bosque, and Kristen Costello, "Building a Better M.I.C.E. Trap: Using Virtual Focus Groups to Assess Subject Guides for Distance

Education Students," *Journal of Library Administration* 48, nos. 3–4 (2008): 431–453.

7. Randolph E. Bucklin and Catarina Sismeiro, "A Model of Web Site Browsing Behavior Estimated on Clickstream Data," *Journal of Marketing Research* 40, no. 3 (August 2003): 262–263.

8. Wendy W. Moe, "Buying, Searching, or Browsing: Differentiating between Online Shoppers Using In-Store Navigational Clickstream," *Journal of Consumer Psychology* 13, nos. 1–2 (2003): 29–39.

9. "AOL Faces Lawsuit over Compromised Search Records," *Electronic Information Report* 27, no. 35 (October 2006): 3.

10. Paul C. Zikopoulos, Chris Eaton, Dirk deRoos, Thomas Deutsch, and George Lapis, *Understanding Big Data: Analytics for Enterprise Class Hadoop and Streaming Data* (New York: McGraw-Hill, 2012), 3, http://public.dhe.ibm.com/common/ssi/ecm/en/iml14296usen/IML14296USEN.PDF (accessed January 4, 2014).

11. "Data Mining," *Encyclopedia of Computer Science* (Hoboken: Wiley, 2003), *Credo Reference*, October 23, 2006, http://www.credoreference.com/entry/encyccs/data_mining (accessed December 2, 2013).

12. Ming-Syan Chen, Jiawei Han, and Philip S. Yu, "Data Mining: An Overview from a Database Perspective," *IEEE Transactions on Knowledge and Data Engineering* 8, no. 6 (December 1996): 866–883.

13. Myra Spiliopoulou Bamshad Mobasher, Olfa Nasraoui, and Osmar Zaiane, "Guest Editorial: Special Issue on a Decade of Mining the Web," *Data Mining and Knowledge Discovery* 24, no. 3 (May 2012): 473.

14. Kevin Cullen, "Delving into Data," *Library Journal* 130, no. 13 (August 2005): 31.

15. Scott Nicholson, "The Bibliomining Process," 147.

16. Scott Nicholson, "The Basis for Bibliomining: Frameworks for Bringing Together Usage-Based Data Mining and Bibliometrics through Data Warehousing in Digital Library Services," *Information Processing & Management* 42, no. 3 (May 2006): 792.

17. Paul J. Bracke, "Web Usage Mining at an Academic Health Sciences Library: An Exploratory Study," *Journal of the Medical Library Association* 92, no. 4 (October 2004): 422.

18. Cullen, "Delving into Data," 31.

19. Patricia Charlton, Manolis Mavrikis, and Demetra Katsifli, "The Potential of Learning Analytics and Big Data," *Ariadne: A Web & Print Magazine of Internet Issues for Librarians & Information Specialists*, no. 71 (July 2013), http://www.ariadne.ac.uk/issue71/charlton-et-al (accessed November 29, 2013).

20. D. J. Hand, G. Blunt, M. G. Kelly, and N. M. Adams, "Data Mining for Fun and Profit," *Statistical Science* 15, no. 2 (May 2000): 111–112.

21. Scott Nicholson, "Digital Library Archaeology: A Conceptual Framework for Understanding Library Use through Artifact-Based Evaluation," *Library Quarterly* 75, no. 4 (October 2005): 516.

22. Nicholson, "The Basis for Bibliomining," 798.

23. Scott Nicholson, e-mail to the author, December 19, 2013.

24. Scott Nicholson, "Approaching Librarianship from the Data: Using Bibliomining for Evidence-Based Librarianship," *Library Hi Tech* 24, no. 3 (2006): 372.

Index

About the Author

Donald A. Barclay is the Interim University Librarian at the University of California, Merced, where he has worked since 2002. He previously worked at libraries in New Mexico and Texas.

CPSIA information can be obtained at www.ICGtesting.com
Printed in the USA
BVOW04s1229180714

359470BV00003B/3/P